INCONVENIENT STRANGERS

INTERSECTIONAL RHETORICS
Karma R. Chávez, Series Editor

# INCONVENIENT STRANGERS

## TRANSNATIONAL SUBJECTS AND
## THE POLITICS OF CITIZENSHIP

**SHUI-YIN SHARON YAM**

THE OHIO STATE UNIVERSITY PRESS
COLUMBUS

Copyright © 2019 by The Ohio State University.
All rights reserved.

Library of Congress Cataloging-in-Publication Data is available online at catalog.loc.gov.

Cover design by Angela Moody
Text design by Juliet Williams
Type set in Adobe Minion Pro

# CONTENTS

# ACKNOWLEDGMENTS

MY DEEPEST GRATITUDE to my mentors at the University of Wisconsin–Madison—Michael Bernard-Donals, Christa Olson, Sara McKinnon, and Morris Young—who encouraged me over the years to pursue my research interests on citizenship, national identity, and difference in the context of Hong Kong. I am especially grateful for Mike, Christa, and Morris for their unwavering academic and emotional support throughout graduate school. As an international student at a predominantly white graduate program, I was painfully self-conscious of my Cantonese accent and my place in academia. Without Mike's, Christa's, and Morris's trust in the value of my work, this book likely would not exist.

Many colleagues and friends have read portions of this book at various stages, and have given me invaluable feedback along the way: Lauren Cagle, Rubén Casas, Chris Earle, Leigh Elion, Jessica Enoch, Janice Fernheimer, Jerry Lee, Nancy Reddy, Jeff Rice, Belinda Stillion Southard, and Charlie Zhang. Special thanks to Lauren Cagle, Rubén Casas, Chris Earle, and Leigh Elion for their friendship and their shared love of dogs. I am also grateful for colleagues in cultural and transnational rhetorics—especially José Cortez, Rebecca Dingo, Arabella Lyon, LuMing Mao, and Jennifer Wingard—for their ongoing enthusiasm and support for this project. The rigor of this book owes much to these generous and insightful colleagues and mentors.

This book took shape after I moved to Lexington, Kentucky. Heartfelt thanks to my community of women academics for their companionship: Amber Bosse, Julia Bursten, Lauren Cagle, Andrea Erhardt, Janice Fernheimer, Emily Goodman, Sora Kim, Katie Morrissey, Keely O'Farrell, Jess Santollo, Emily Shortslef, Michelle Sizemore, and Karrieann Soto Vega. My life is enriched by our brunch, yoga, cocktail, and dog park dates, and by the food, clothes, and laughter we have shared. My colleagues at the Department of Writing, Rhetoric, and Digital Studies at the University of Kentucky have been very supportive of my work along the way, and I am immensely grateful for that. I would also like to thank my neighbor and mentor Matt Wilson for his professional advice ever since I arrived in Kentucky.

This book is about family, and the intimate emotional ties we establish with those who are not our biological kin. While I am across the vast Pacific Ocean from the family I was born into, I am tremendously lucky to have found one in Lexington that welcomes me with open arms. Thank you, Beth Goldstein, Raphael Finkel, Penina Goldstein, Robin Michler, Alice Goldstein, and Sid Goldstein for making Lexington feel more like home. Beth Goldstein, particularly, has fed me wonderful food, and given me so much sage advice and warmth. Thanks also to Simon Michler for playing all kinds of silly games with me—I particularly enjoy our living room jam sessions. I am grateful for my parents in Hong Kong, who, when they first sent me off to the University of Pittsburgh in 2007, likely did not expect that I would spend the next twelve years in the US. I am grateful for their ongoing support.

Back in my own home, my partner and my dog—Asher Finkel and Chips—have vastly enriched my life. While he looks like a gremlin, enjoys eating garbage, and almost never comes when called, Chips is a wonderful companion who brings a lot of joy. My life would not be half as enjoyable without the food Asher and I cook and share with one another. Thank you, Asher, for tolerating my many idiosyncrasies with gumption and a great sense of humor—thanks, in particular, for humoring me when I want to go to the grocery store four to five times a week "just to look around." You and Chips have made my life so much more fulfilling.

# INTRODUCTION

AS A CHILD who grew up in colonial Hong Kong at the cusp of political transition, I noticed and was often perplexed by the complexities of racial dynamics in my everyday life. For instance, while I was desperate to earn the approval of white children on the playground, I never understood why I felt the strong need to please them. I learned that the South Asian family who lived across the hall was different because my parents would frequently comment on the smell of their food and their apartment, and so I never questioned why they never struck up a conversation with that family the way they did with our Chinese neighbors. As I grew older, I wondered why migrant domestic workers, including the ones my own family hired over the years, were treated with much less respect than local workers; I was led to believe that such treatments were the norm, and I should not question a practice that had been so beneficial to our family. Later on, when I was a graduate student in the US, I was shocked to hear the caustic, sometimes venomous, language my friends in Hong Kong—friends who otherwise were generous and kind people—used to describe mainland Chinese families who had immigrated to the city.

This book is, first and foremost, my attempt to make sense of these complex racial, cultural, and national tensions I witnessed growing up. The dynamics and experiences I observed were by no means personal: in fact, they are constituted by Hong Kong's colonial history, its prominence in the transnational capitalist economy, and its uneasy political and cultural relationship with mainland China as a semiautonomous Special Administrative Region (SAR). While the ideology of white supremacy remains after the end of the British colonial era, unlike many former colonies, Hong Kong occupies a relative position of power in the transnational economy, and thus possesses power over poorer Southeast Asian countries and migrants from those countries who come to Hong Kong for work. In addition, while mainland China as a powerful sovereign state and a global economic powerhouse can exert control over Hong Kong, the SAR nevertheless retains a great deal of soft power transnationally because of its colonial history, and thus proximity to Western modernity. Hongkongers and mainland Chinese people, therefore, do not see eye to eye despite sharing the same ethnicity and cultural lineage. This geopolitical and historical context leads to complicated negotiations among Hongkongers and other cultural groups on who *truly* belongs to Hong Kong.

As such, Hong Kong is a unique site to examine key questions of inclusion, difference, and recognition. Through legal citizenship cases brought on by marginalized and racialized groups in the city, I seek to answer the following questions: How can marginalized subjects gain recognition as rightful members of the political sphere? What strategies can these subjects deploy in order to be recognized on their own terms, rather than in a way that subsumes difference and reinforces the oppressive logic of the existing structure? How can subjects who occupy different positionality cultivate a coalition through their commonality without relegating the interests and specific lived experiences of marginalized people?[1]

This book is motivated by all these questions, but more importantly, I seek to answer this one: What rhetorical conditions and tactics can marginalized subjects create and deploy in order to motivate those at a relative position of power to engage with them as equal interlocutors whose interests overlap with and could redefine theirs? This question arises from three heated citizenship debates in Hong Kong between the early 2000s and mid-2010s surrounding, respectively, South Asian permanent residents, Southeast Asian migrant domestic workers, and mainland Chinese immigrants. These public controversies elicited significant political and emotional responses from the government and the existing citizenry in ways that reveal how citizenship is intricately intertwined with gender, race, class, cultural differences, and geopolitical power relations. As a formal status and membership conferred by the state, citizenship also carries tremendous material and emotional implica-

---

1. For discussions of these questions, see Benhabib, *Situating the Self*; Hesford, *Spectacular Rhetorics*; Mohanty, *Feminism without Borders*; Rowe, *Power Lines*.

tions. As a result, seeking to either improve their precarious living conditions or to assert their sense of belonging to Hong Kong, these three groups have all attempted to obtain legal citizenship as a way to gain inclusion and be recognized by the state as legitimate members.

However, as many have argued, citizenship is a tool for the state and the dominant citizenry to enforce biopolitical control by selectively conferring or withholding formal recognition.[2] The struggles for recognition based on citizenship are, therefore, as Kelly Oliver points out, "caught up in the logic of colonialism and oppression that made them necessary in the first place."[3] As queer studies and anticolonial scholars Amy Brandzel and Karma Chávez argue, citizenship and the recognition it confers cannot and does not in the long run undermine the power hierarchy that devalues non-normative bodies.[4] In other words, despite the fact that formal citizenship status could enable someone to live with relative safety and security (e.g., granting protection from deportation, freedom to work), it nevertheless does not transform the existing political and discursive structure so that marginalized subjects can participate in the public sphere on their own terms; built upon logics of exclusion, it also does not promote opportunities for coalition building across difference.

Rearticulating the definition and conditions of deliberation, I argue, provides a necessary intervention to dominant citizenship discourse and how different subjects relate to each other across power difference. While, as Rob Asen points out, deliberation is commonly conceptualized as "an encounter among interlocutors who engage in a process of considering and weighing various perspectives and proposals 'for what they regard as issues of common concern," I draw on feminist scholarship to extend this definition: In addition to future-oriented discussions among different parties on their shared interests, I see deliberation also as a process in which interlocutors across difference actively reexamine and reinvent their identities, perceived interests, and relations to one another.[5] I refer to this as *transformative deliberation*. In this process, one's sense of self and worldview are always subjected to change as they engage with others through reciprocal relationships.[6] It is only then that marginalized subjects can participate in deliberation as equal interlocutors, rather than as objects or abject to the nation-state. The process of transforma-

---

2. Some examples include Bosniak, *The Citizen and the Alien*; Brandzel, *Against Citizenship*; Wingard, *Branded Bodies*.

3. For critiques of citizenship as a form of biopolitical control, see Bosniak, *The Citizen and the Alien*; Brandzel, *Against Citizenship*; Kelly Oliver, *Witnessing*.

4. Brandzel, *Against Citizenship*; Karma Chávez, *Queer Migration Politics*.

5. Asen, "Deliberation and Trust," 5.

6. My definition of transformative deliberation is informed by Adams, "At the Table with Arendt"; Lyon, *Deliberative Acts*.

tive deliberation, at its core, is affective. As Brian Massumi points out, "When you affect something, you are opening yourself up to being affected in turn, and in a slightly different way than you might have been the moment before."[7] By engaging openly with others, all interlocutors—regardless of their positionality in the broader sociopolitical context—are impacted and changed in some ways; they will have, as Massumi puts it, "stepped over a threshold" and be transformed in however minor ways that sometimes escape their conscious awareness.[8]

The stepping over of the threshold that demarcates subjects from objects *and* abjects is significant because it opens up room for coalition and the mutual recognition of shared humanity. However, it is uncomfortable for interlocutors in the dominant group to accept that their subjectivity, perceived interests, privileges, and identities are not a priori and stable. It is even more challenging for them to recognize how all these features that make up their sense of self and reality will likely shift and morph once they enter into the heterogenous deliberative space with subjects they deem inferior. There is, thus, little incentive for more dominant subjects to engage in transformative deliberation with their marginalized counterparts. To address this problem, I consider the conditions and mechanisms marginalized subjects could deploy in order to motivate dominant audiences to engage in transformative deliberation and to create room for a form of recognition that does not hinge upon formal citizenship or the erasure of difference.

I propose *deliberative empathy* as a productive emotional and political response to cultivate among dominant subjects for when they encounter marginalized Others. I define deliberative empathy as a critical empathetic response that motivates the subjects to not only deeply consider the experiences of others but also to situate those experiences within specific material, sociopolitical, and historical contexts. By understanding how others' experiences and interests are situated in a material context that overlaps with theirs, interlocutors who occupy a dominant position are prompted to engage in an internal process of deliberation to consider how they ought to reinvent their identities, self-interests, and relations to others in a way that accommodates the commonality they share with others. Their lives and subjectivities, after all, are not as separate from their marginalized counterparts as they would like to believe.

Based on such definitions of empathy and deliberation, in this book I demonstrate how storytelling serves as a rhetorical and emotional vehicle that

---

7. Massumi, *The Power at the End of the Economy*, 103.
8. Ibid.

moves subjects toward each other without the complete erasure of difference. I focus specifically on the rhetorical, affective, and ethical force of familial narratives—stories about one's lived experiences and relationships with their loved ones—in generating deliberative empathy among dominant audiences. As many have argued, the family often stands in for the nation-state, and is portrayed as a vulnerable entity in need of protection against foreign entities.[9] Because of the existing linkage between family and systematic exclusion, it is important for marginalized rhetors to reclaim and redeploy the family to counter the prevalent public feelings that subjects who are not recognizable as family members must be cast out in order to secure the future and safety of the nation-state.[10] As a readily intelligible trope and a key social unit, the family can be mobilized to invent rhetorical performances that create new forms of coalition, rather than to promote processes of alienization under the name of national security and citizenship.

While the makeup of familial units differs across contexts, the affective and social relationships they denote are present in everyone's life, thus rendering familial stories readily intelligible. Familial stories told by marginalized others are particularly valuable because they highlight one's intersubjectivity. Given that the human condition is inherently relational, Jackson argues that "subjectivity is not really a fixed attribute of persons, but the product of any purposeful and committed activity we enter into with those we love and the things we value."[11] Narratives about one's relationship with one's family members and loved ones, in other words, constitute one's subjectivity. In the face of contingencies beyond one's control, the telling of one's story in relation to those who have shaped one's life allows for a sense of agency and opens room for one to imagine one's experience as belonging to an interconnected human network that is larger than oneself and those one readily identifies with.

For familial narratives to effectively engage the dominant audience to experience deliberative empathy, the stories must be situated in specific socio-cultural and economic settings, so that the audiences never lose sight of the difference between them and the storytellers, and the ways in which their own lives are affected—albeit in different ways—by the same structural forces that impact the storytellers. By acknowledging the tension between one's uniqueness and autonomy and the shared human condition of contingency and suffering, the more privileged audience enters into an ethical relationship with the storyteller. By doing so, they prompt the audience to consider how even

---

9. Ahmed, *The Cultural Politics of Emotion*; Wingard, *Branded Bodies*.

10. For discussions on how the family is used as a moral defense against exclusion, see Ahmed, *The Cultural Politics of Emotion*; Goodman, *Infertilities*.

11. Jackson, *Politics of Storytelling*.

the most intimate emotional connections one has are produced and reproduced by institutionalized power relations and structural political and economic conditions.

The emotional charge and intersubjective nature of familial stories jolt the audience out of their accustomed political response and sedimented ways of conceptualizing the personhood (or the lack thereof) of marginalized others.[12] The dominant audience, in other words, is not actively constructing arguments to dismantle or undermine the experiences and personhood of the marginalized storytellers. Familial narratives open up space for dominant audiences to experience deliberative empathy and consider inter-ests, instead of falling into the two extreme reactions identified by Dominick LaCapra when they encounter a racialized Other: to either completely assimilate them, or to deny any relations at all between the two.[13]

By situating intimate relationships and emotions within a material, political, and institutional context, familial narratives from the margin ask us to scrutinize the power relations and ideologies that construct our affective ties. As Chandra Mohanty argues, "in fact narratives of historical experience are crucial to political thinking not because they present an unmediated version of the 'truth' but because they can destabilize received truths and locate debate in the complexities and contradictions of historical life."[14] In addition, as feminist standpoint theorists posit, by emphasizing epistemic privilege, stories told by marginalized rhetors posit a new interpretive framework that disrupts the dominant pathological model of recognition. Rather than continuing to seek a form of recognition that flows from the dominant to the marginalized, the telling of familial tales from a marginalized position makes use of difference and particularities to highlight shared concerns and inter-ests.[15]

## CONTEXT: ETHNOCRACY, RACE, AND CITIZENSHIP IN HONG KONG

Embroiled in citizenship debates between the mainstream citizenry and various racialized groups, postcolonial Hong Kong is a key site for examining

---

12. Bell, *Storytelling for Social Justice.*

13. I use *inter-est* to evoke Hannah Arendt's concept of interest that emphasizes the in-between space, and the shared material concerns that connect interlocutors. Arendt, *The Human Condition.*

14. Mohanty, *Feminism without Borders,* 96.

15. Fricker, "Epistemic Oppression and Epistemic Privilege"; Mohanty, *Feminism without Borders*; Narayan, "Working Together across Difference."

how treating deliberative empathy as a desirable rhetorical effect among dominant audiences could prompt marginalized rhetors to engage in rhetorical tactics outside of the dominant citizenship framework. This book examines three prominent citizenship controversies, focusing, respectively, on diasporic South Asian permanent residents, Southeast Asian foreign domestic workers, and mainland Chinese maternal tourists who choose to give birth in the Hong Kong SAR. While all three groups are branded as Others by Hongkongers in the local affective network and citizenship discourse, these three populations occupy very different sociopolitical and economic statuses at the transnational and state levels.

Neoliberal and neocolonial values permeate the citizenship discourse in Hong Kong. As a former colony and now a Chinese SAR with a highly restricted electoral system, the Hong Kong public does not historically place a strong emphasis on civic engagement and democratic participation.[16] Lacking a history of public engagement, mainstream Hongkongers have come to privilege private economic interests—particularly the gains of their biological families—over civic values like inclusion and equity.[17] Citizenship, therefore, is largely understood as who deserves legal recognition and therefore economic opportunities and public welfare. Given Hong Kong's colonial history and its rapid economic development in the global capitalist market, local social scientists characterize Hongkongers' identity and conception of citizenship as follows:

> [It] involves no more than looking out for oneself and one's family within the rules of the global market. . . . [It] depends on no high ideals, but involves simply dependence on family, canniness as to business, considerable hard work, trust in the rule of law, and a degree of skepticism as to what the state may tell one.[18]

Vernacular discussions surrounding citizenship are often framed in two ways: as the protection of local, Hong Kong families against economic threats, and as a mechanism to introduce new immigrants whose economic productivity and cultural capital would enhance the "quality" of the Hong Kong national family.[19] The latter is often tied to the racist notion that white Euro-American immigrants are superior, and their incorporation would therefore bring

---

16. Leung, "Politics of Incorporation and Exclusion," 89.
17. Abbas, *Hong Kong*; Leung, "Politics of Incorporation and Exclusion."
18. Mathews, Ma, and Lui, *Hong Kong, China*, 160.
19. Leung, "Politics of Incorporation and Exclusion," 87.

prestige and soft power to the nation-family.[20] That white supremacy exists in Hong Kong is unsurprising as it was a British colony for 100 years, and did not leave British rule until 1997.[21]

Hong Kong's current sociocultural and political context is shaped by what local social scientists call "the dual history of British colonialism and Chinese immigration."[22] Most current mainstream Hongkongers are descendants of mainland Chinese immigrants from Guangdong and Shanghai. The number of migrants from mainland China spiked during the Cultural Revolution in the 1960s.[23] As a result, Hong Kong is an ethnically homogenous society composed of 92 percent ethnic Han Chinese.[24] At the same time, white expatriates and South Asians who arrived during the colonial era also settled in the city. This history and demographic produce what Barry Sautman refers to as an omnipresent semi-ethnocratic structure in which "one ethnic group rules at the expense of others."[25] Within this structure, individuals who form the lower levels of the hierarchy—namely, poor mainland Chinese immigrants, South Asians, and migrant domestic workers from Southeast Asia—are rendered inferior by the government and the mainstream citizenry, and are excluded from achieving full citizenship. This social structure is maintained by systematically hindering the upward mobility of those who do not belong to the dominant ethnic group and kinship network.[26]

In the Hong Kong context, at the top of the ethnic hierarchy are mainstream Hongkongers of Chinese descent, who compose of the majority of the population, and white immigrants from Euro-American countries, who bring with them cultural and economic capital.[27] Constituting 1.1 percent of the Hong Kong population in 2016, South Asians are clumped together generically as "ethnic minorities," a term used exclusively in vernacular and official discourse to refer to marginalized brown people.[28] Despite the fact that white people are a minority in Hong Kong, they are not included in this category. Instead, whites are commonly referred to as "expatriates," a term that effectively deracializes whiteness. On the other hand, while the South Asian community in Hong Kong comprises different ethnicities and countries of origin, mainstream news media commonly refer to all of them as people of the "Indo-

20. Vickers, *In Search of an Identity.*
21. Leung, "Politics of Incorporation and Exclusion."
22. Erni and Leung, *Understanding South Asian Minorities in Hong Kong,* 3.
23. Ibid.
24. Sautman, "Hong Kong as a Semi-Ethnocracy," 104; Sautman, "The Demographics."
25. Sautman, "Hong Kong as a Semi-Ethnocracy," 104.
26. Ibid.
27. Sautman and Kneehans, "The Politics of Racial Discrimination in Hong Kong,"
28. Erni and Leung, *Understanding South Asian Minorities in Hong Kong,* 4.

Pakistani race," thus creating a racialized imaginary that compresses difference within the community. South Asians in Hong Kong are frequently reminded of their denizen status through everyday acts of racial discrimination that go largely unchecked.[29]

While South Asians are referred to as the *ethnic minorities* who nevertheless make up part of the Hong Kong national imaginary, Southeast Asians are typically not even considered as members of the Hong Kong nation-family. The Southeast Asian population in Hong Kong is composed primarily of female migrant domestic workers, and they are legally prohibited from applying for permanent residency regardless of their length of stay in the city. Because of the gendered and racialized nature of their work and their precarious immigration status in Hong Kong, Southeast Asians occupy an even lower position on the ethnocratic hierarchy than South Asian residents.

While formal citizenship claims made by South Asians and Southeast Asian domestic workers, as I demonstrate in the following chapters, often unsettle mainstream Hongkongers, the current citizenry is most disrupted by the mounting tension between them and the mainland Chinese immigrants who arrived in the 2000s. Before the return of Hong Kong's sovereignty in 1997 from Great Britain to China, the Chinese government agreed that Hong Kong would be designated as a SAR with a legal, political, and economic system—largely modeled after the British system—independent from China's control. Proclaiming the "One Country, Two Systems" principle, the late Deng Xiaoping promised the Hong Kong public that "the previous capitalist system and way of life shall remain unchanged for 50 years."[30] This political promise was extremely powerful as Hongkongers were deeply concerned about their prospects prior to 1997: The public anxiety at the time was so strong that many emigrated or acquired citizenship in other countries in order to avoid living under Chinese rule.[31] Deng's promise served to maintain a sense of stability and security in Hong Kong before the formal transition of sovereignty. Under the "One Country, Two Systems" principle, the postcolonial Hong Kong government was charged with a seemingly contradictory task: It must guarantee that the interests and lifestyles of Hongkongers stay the same as they were prior to the return of sovereignty, while simultaneously showing its allegiance to Beijing by gradually integrating Hong Kong into the Chinese nation-state.

After the return of Hong Kong's sovereignty to China in 1997, the construction of a distinct Hong Kong national identity became increasingly pressing as the mainland Chinese government encroached upon the supposedly

29. Erni and Leung, *Understanding South Asian Minorities in Hong Kong*.
30. Article 5, The Basic Law.
31. For analysis of the wave of emigration prior to 1997, see Ong, *Flexible Citizenship*.

semi-independent status of the SAR through economic, political, and ideo-logical means.[32] In addition to being the biggest contributor to Hong Kong's economy, Beijing also controls the nomination and election of the Hong Kong chief executive. In 2017, chief executive Carrie Lam was elected by a committee of 1,200 members—most were allies of the Chinese government designated to execute Beijing's instructions.[33] Appointed directly by Beijing, the chief executive of Hong Kong has always been mistrusted and seen by Hongkongers as a proxy of the Chinese government; however, despite their allegiance to Beijing, the chief executive must demonstrate—or at least main-tain the appearance—that they are committed to protecting the rights and interests of local Hongkongers. The tension between mainland China and the mainstream Hong Kong public plays out most prominently in the form of annual large-scale protests on the anniversary of Hong Kong's handover back to Beijing. During these protests, activists call for universal suffrage and the protection of the SAR's semiautonomous status from mainland China.[34]

As part of its political agenda to increase the connection between the SAR and mainland China, the Chinese government began implementing policies in 2013 to increase the number of mainland Chinese in Hong Kong.[35] By 2016, there were approximately 42.8 million annual arrivals from China, effectively altering the cultural and socioeconomic landscape of the city, where the local population is approximately seven million.[36] The influx of mainlanders into the SAR has led to an enhanced sense of anxiety among Hongkongers as the space they consider home is becoming increasingly unfamiliar. As local com-mentator Grace Choi points out:

---

32. Bradsher, "Once a Model City." In September 2014, the ongoing political conflict between prodemocracy Hongkongers and the Chinese–Hong Kong government culminated to the citywide Umbrella Movement: For eleven weeks, thousands of Hongkongers—including many white-collar professionals and university and high school students—occupied the gov-ernment headquarter and two other central areas in the city to demand of the chief executive universal suffrage and elections that were free from Beijing's interference. The three student leaders of the movement were found guilty the next year for participating in a politically moti-vated unlawful rally and were sentenced to six to eight months in prison in late 2017; Joshua Wong, the leader of the group, received a second prison sentence at the beginning of 2018 for contempt of court during the movement. The electoral system in Hong Kong, on the other hand, has remained largely unchanged.

33. Ibid.

34. Bridges et al., *One Country, Two Systems in Crisis.*

35. Ong, *Neoliberalism as Exception.*

36. Hong Kong Commerce and Economic Development Bureau, Tourism Commission, "Tourism Performance in 2017."

It is the fear of the disappearance of Hong Kong and its uniqueness, and the very real danger of the city becoming just another ordinary municipality in southern China; it is the fear of seven million against 1.3 billion people; it is the fear that Hong Kong will no longer belong to Hongkongers. It is the fear of colonization by the mainland.[37]

As a result, Hongkongers are dismayed and deeply unsettled by the increased number of mainlanders who obtain permanent residency in the SAR.

Given the vexed relationship between mainstream Hongkongers and mainland China, Chinese maternal tourists and their children who are born in Hong Kong and thus are Hong Kong permanent residents are often vilified by mainstream media and are marginalized socially.[38] This population illustrates the murkiness within Hong Kong's ethnic and cultural divide: While immigrants from mainland China are ethnically the same as mainstream Hongkongers and therefore are eligible for inclusion under a *jus sanguinis* model of citizenship, their cultural background and tie to the Beijing regime nevertheless mark them as a threatening Other.[39] Taken together, these three populations highlight how racism, ethnocentrism, neoliberalism, and the history of colonialism are so intertwined within dominant citizenship discourse that there is not much room left for marginalized subjects to argue for their inclusion through formal recognition.

## DEFINITIONS OF TERMS

Since my analysis of citizenship rhetorics in Hong Kong hinges upon intersecting ideologies and different stakeholders and identity markers, I will first explain my choice of terms. I use *mainstream Hongkongers* to describe the racially and ethnically normative subjects who see themselves, and are presumed by the state, as belonging rightfully to the SAR. This group possesses more cultural, political, and financial capital in the local context than their racialized counterparts. I choose the word *mainstream* rather than *dominant* to describe this population because their status of dominance is relative: In the context of white supremacy both during and after the British colonial era, for instance, Hongkongers who are otherwise dominant are rendered less privileged. While not politically monolithic, the mainstream Hong Kong public is

---

37. Choi, "Integration Anxiety."
38. Yam, "Affective Economies and Alienizing Discourse."
39. *Jus sanguinis* refers to the model of citizenship that is determined by the nationality of one's parents, rather than by one's place of birth.

ethnically homogenous and shares several overarching ideologies: Most subscribe to the capitalist logics that during the colonial era had led to tremendous economic growth and a significant improvement in the quality of life of Hongkongers.[40] Politically, mainstream Hongkongers are against the increased encroachment from Beijing and emulate a white Euro-American conception of modernity.[41]

In addition, I use *neoliberalism* to refer to the way citizenship is yoked to private market competition in a way that underplays the structural causes of inequity and marginalization.[42] In a neoliberal regime, one must demonstrate one's economic productivity and self-sufficiency to be deemed worthy of citizenship; the state, on the other hand, no longer provides a social safety net for those who are deemed not self-enterprising or productive enough in this economic system.[43] Along the same vein, gendered labor, such as the transnational domestic work I explore in chapter 3, that does not directly generate economic output is relegated and undervalued. Neoliberal logics also collude with racism because racialized Others are structurally barred from accessing the cultural and economic capital their white counterparts possess; they are less productive economically and are thus deemed less valuable by the nation-state. The prosperity of a neoliberal nation-state hinges upon the continual marginalization of non-normative bodies, while offering them the promise of citizenship and inclusion that is never to come.[44] To conceal the racial injustice inherent in neoliberal practices, a neoliberal discourse, as Darrell Enck-Wanzer argues, actively suppresses public discussions of race in relation to social policies.[45] The personhood of racialized subjects, therefore, is frequently undermined or left unprotected by the state and the dominant citizenry.[46]

As I will demonstrate in subsequent chapters, neoliberalism not only operates at the state and transnational levels but has become what Wendy Brown refers to as a "political rationality" that influences one's everyday life: In order to survive with little to no state protection, subjects must become market actors to compete with each other in a zero-sum game that discounts the particularities and humanity of each subject.[47] Because of such competition, a neoliberal public is not conducive to promoting coalitions across dif-

---

40. Carroll, *A Concise History of Hong Kong.*
41. Yam, "Education and Transnational Nationalism."
42. Asen, "Neoliberalism"; Dingo, *Networking Arguments.*
43. Dingo, *Networking Arguments*; Ong, *Neoliberalism as Exception.*
44. Brandzel, *Against Citizenship*; Wingard, *Branded Bodies.*
45. Enck-Wanzer, "Barack Obama."
46. Wingard, *Branded Bodies.*
47. Asen, "Neoliberalism"; Brown, *Undoing the Demos,* 47.

ference. Operating within the neoliberal framework, dominant citizenship discourse that helps construct and maintain the nation-state actively discourages coalition building, and instead promotes competition and alienization.[48] It is, therefore, necessary to examine the rhetorical resources marginalized subjects could draw on that do not rely on the political and discursive framework of citizenship.

## STRUCTURE OF THE BOOK

The remainder of the book is organized into four chapters. Chapter 1 elucidates the theoretical underpinning of deliberative empathy and introduces narrative and storytelling as a mechanism to evoke such an emotional response. Chapters 2 through 4 examine the three citizenship cases in which transnational subjects are racialized and gendered in ways that prevent them from gaining formal recognition through established familial citizenship discourse. In these case studies, I pay attention to how familial tropes and metaphors are deployed in formal citizenship discourse, while remaining attuned to the rhetorical histories of these symbols at the local, state, and transnational levels. Reading intercontextually allows me to illuminate the ways in which familial tropes in citizenship discourse travel and connect with different ideological and institutional frameworks to perpetuate the exclusion of non-normative transnational subjects.[49] To explore alternative rhetorical recourse that evokes deliberative empathy to help cultivate a space for transformative deliberation, I also examine in each chapter acts of storytelling, particularly of marginalized familial narratives. These rhetorical performances make room for ethical relationships across difference—relationships that are built upon the recognition of shared human conditions and interests, rather than on the existing citizenship taxonomy that privileges only familiar and privileged subjects that do not threaten the status of the existing citizenry.

Because Hong Kong is a semiautonomous SAR within China's sovereignty, Chinese citizenship and Hong Kong permanent residency are not synonymous: If not born in Hong Kong, a Chinese citizen could obtain Hong Kong permanent residency only after residing in the SAR for seven continuous years. At the same time, one could be a permanent resident in the SAR yet not hold Chinese citizenship. This, in fact, is common among white expatriates who are Hong Kong permanent residents and are eligible for social ben-

---

48. Ioanide, *The Emotional Politics of Racism.*
49. Hesford, *Spectacular Rhetorics.*

efits in the SAR, yet continue to retain the passport and citizenship from their home country.[50] These specific legal stipulations result in different citizenship statuses and scenarios for the three populations I examine in this book.

Chapter 2 examines the South Asian residents in Hong Kong. While this community has settled in Hong Kong since the colonial era, it remains one of the most marginalized populations in the city. While most South Asians are permanent residents of Hong Kong, many of them encounter great difficulties when attempting to naturalize as Chinese citizens in order to obtain a Hong Kong passport. To date, many South Asians continue to hold passports from their originating ancestral countries—countries some of them have never even visited. This chapter first interrogates the claims made by South Asian petitioners who repeatedly deploy the familial metaphor to argue for state recognition in the form of legal citizenship. Juxtaposing their arguments with responses from the Hong Kong government and with similar claims made by white Euro-American immigrants, I demonstrate that historically racialized subjects who lack both cultural and economic capital cannot effectively gain recognition by demonstrating their affective ties and contribution to the nation-family. Examining personal familial stories told by South Asian women to the mainstream audience outside of the citizenship framework, I argue that these narratives demonstrate the importance of managing the proximity between the dominant audience and the marginalized storytellers: To promote deliberative empathy, the narratives must maintain the tension between the simultaneous difference and commonality between the two parties.

While South Asians occupy one of the lowest echelons within Hong Kong's ethnocratic hierarchy, they nevertheless enjoy more legal protection against systematic exploitation and abuse than migrant domestic workers, who are regulated by a strict set of immigration and labor laws that categorically exclude them from attaining permanent residency in Hong Kong. Racialized, gendered, and marginalized across transnational, state, and local terrains, domestic workers perform intimate reproductive labor while residing in the homes of their local employers. Chapter 3 focuses on migrant domestic workers' quest for recognition—both within and beyond dominant citizenship discourse that privileges an ethnocentric and racist conception of the nation-family. In that chapter, I argue that while achieving permanent residency status or legal recognition would have helped protect migrant domestic workers from economic exploitation and abuse, it nevertheless will not validate their personhood outside of the labor they perform, nor will it create a space for transformative deliberation that invites the mainstream citizenry to critically

---

50. ExpatFocus, "Hong Kong—Citizenship."

revise how they relate to the workers. I then examine two texts that situate migrant domestic workers outside of the dominant citizenship discourse and the nation-family framework. Comparing the respective efficacy of these texts in evoking deliberative empathy among mainstream audiences, I argue that deliberative empathy could only be effectively evoked when the audience is attuned to the way their personal lives and the lives of others are intertwined in a shared material and sociopolitical context, producing intersecting interests that demand a more coalitional relationship between the workers and the mainstream citizenry.

Focusing on maternal tourists from mainland China and children born to Hong Kong parents in China, chapter 4 examines the political, affective, and cultural conditions that inhibit deliberative empathy. By examining local vernacular discourse and the neoliberal economic arguments made by the Hong Kong government and mainstream media against Chinese immigrant families, I demonstrate how families and kinship in the private sphere function as a metonymy for formal citizenship in the public sphere. Examining the negative reactions Hongkongers have toward rhetorical acts that humanize mainland maternal tourists, I argue that mainstream Hongkongers are unable to enact deliberative empathy toward Chinese immigrants because they stand in as proxy of the encroaching Chinese government, and because the shared lineage between Hongkongers and mainlanders threatens to undo the distinction between the two.

As I illustrate in these three cases, while mainstream Hongkongers appear to be the primary perpetrators of exclusion, they are themselves caught up in structural forces beyond their control—forces that motivate and reward behaviors and attitudes that perpetuate the marginalization of gendered and racialized bodies. It is, therefore, crucial to articulate alternative rhetorical strategies that would liberate both mainstream Hongkongers and marginalized transnational subjects from an interpretive framework that renders them perpetually insecure and precarious. The concluding chapter examines racist and ethnocentric attitudes from the perspective of subconscious habits, further explicating the importance of deliberative empathy—or attunement toward the intersection among materiality, emotions, and intersubjectivity—in addressing exclusionary attitudes and practices against non-normative subjects.

# CHAPTER 1

# Deliberative Empathy, Family, and Storytelling

DESPITE ITS inherently exclusionary nature, citizenship remains a politically and emotionally powerful heuristic on how we understand our reality, identities, and relationships with others.[1] Given the affective stronghold and significant material implications citizenship has on the lives of many, I do not argue for a wholesale dismissal of the concept. Rather, I seek to address Butler's questions regarding the enduring valence of state citizenship as recognition, particularly among marginalized subjects:

> Are there not other ways of feeling possible, intelligible, even real, apart from the sphere of state recognition? And should there not be other ways? . . . How is it that we give the power of recognition over to the state at the

---

1. I subscribe loosely to Brian Massumi's distinctions of affect and emotion—namely, I see affect as a bodily intensity and potentiality that eludes signification, while emotion is affect translated and narrativized. While in a nutshell, affect can be understood as an embodied but prelinguistic sensation and intensity and emotion as its translated discursive counterpart, it is often very difficult to disentangle them from one another. As Deborah Gould points out, "affective states, for example, often generate immediate emotional displays, creating a sense that affect and emotional expression are one and the same . . . [and] affective states can instantaneously be fixed into named emotions (although always incompletely)." To capture the intersection and connection between the embodied and the representational, I use the term *feeling* to highlight both a bodily experience and its role and meaning in the social and discursive realm. Gould, *Moving Politics*, 22; Massumi, *Parables for the Virtual*.

moment that we insist that we are unreal and illegitimate without it? Are there other resources by which we might become recognizable or mobilize to challenge the existing regimes within which the terms of recognizability take place?[2]

To do that, I examine how familial metaphors of citizenship perpetuate racialized and gendered exclusion and reify norms of recognition that depend on state legitimation. I propose that while the familial has often been used to justify and enact mechanisms of exclusion and alienization, it can also be appropriated by marginalized groups as a topos to cultivate *deliberative empathy* among mainstream audiences, which promotes coalitions across difference.[3] In particular, I call for an attunement toward the material and political consequences of state recognition for marginalized bodies, while paying attention to more ethical and critical rearticulations of recognition that is based not on the identification of sameness, but on an awareness of intersubjectivity and shared human conditions.[4]

In this chapter, I first map the ways family and kinship function as structuring metaphors and tropes in the context of citizenship—specifically, how they are used to construct and justify exclusionary mechanisms based on neoliberal and racist logics. I demonstrate how *family*, a salient cultural concept in the Chinese context that has historically been connected to the nation-state, could be effectively mobilized by marginalized Others in Hong Kong to enter public discourse in a way that calls for a critical rearticulation of recognition. While research in moral psychology research suggests that dominant communities are likely to respond with quick defensiveness, anger, and disgust toward claims and subjects they deem threatening to their in-group identity and interests, I argue that such negative and reactive emotions could be hampered when racialized rhetors mobilize the family as a site of invention rather than as a metaphor for citizenship.[5] The repurposing of the family could promote a critical empathetic response among the mainstream audiences that does not subsume difference.

I then discuss the theoretical underpinning of transformative deliberation. Following the tradition of feminist political and rhetorical theorists, I see deliberation as a performative act that is always mediated by material-

---

2. Butler, "Is Kinship Always Already Heterosexual?," 26.
3. For critiques of the familial trope, see Ahmed, *The Cultural Politics of Emotion*; Berlant, *The Queen of America*; Brandzel, *Against Citizenship*; Edelman, *No Future*.
4. For critiques of state recognition, see Amaya, *Citizenship Excess*; Brandzel, *Against Citizenship*.
5. Bloom, *Against Empathy*; Greene, *Moral Tribes*.

ity and difference between the interlocutors.[6] It is exactly through materiality that shared interests across difference arise. Because of the contingency and fluidity of one's subjectivity, one's self-interests are not fixed—rather, they are multiple and always open to change as the self comes in contact and enters into relations with others. By highlighting the dialogic and intersubjective nature of transformative deliberation, I interrogate the way this process fosters coalitional discourse and practices in a way that demands more dominant subjects to recognize the mutability of their material interests, their identities, and their sense of self in relation to others. To address how interlocutors from a dominant subject position could be motivated to engage in transformative deliberation, I consider the political and affective potential of empathy. Specifically, I elucidate how deliberative empathy, when evoked among the dominant audiences, could disrupt their established feeling templates and perceptions toward marginalized Others. Such disruptions, in turn, prompt them to reexamine how their subject positions and interests overlap with those they once deemed deviant or inferior.

Given the limitations of arguments and formal citizenship claims, narratives and acts of storytelling function as a more effective mechanism to evoke deliberative empathy among more privileged audiences who lack the impetus to engage in transformative deliberation. Engaging with recent research in cognitive science and neurobiology on the way human brains react to stories, I understand storytelling as a rhetorical act that has profound affective impact on the interlocutors' willingness and ability to connect with others across difference in ways that challenge the fixity of identity categories and the existing power hierarchy. In the last section of this chapter, I discuss how by telling stories of their personal and familial lives, particularly how their lived experiences and struggles are implicated in material conditions shared by the dominant audience, marginalized rhetors are able to evoke deliberative empathy that prompts the audiences to reexamine and redefine their relations and shared interests with each other.

## CITIZENSHIP AND FAMILIAL TROPES OF INTIMACY

Citizenship is simultaneously juridical, political, and emotional. In this book, I examine citizenship primarily as a legal status granted by the state to denote formal recognition and to validate one's self-identity and sense of belonging

---

6. For example, Adams, "At the Table with Arendt"; Lyon, *Deliberative Acts*.

to the nation-state.[7] Scholars often use *citizenship* as an umbrella term to refer to many different aspects of political and civic life: In rhetorical studies, *citizenship* is commonly used to refer to acts of civic engagement and democratic participation.[8] However, despite rhetorical studies' focus on the civic dimension of citizenship, we cannot lose sight of the fact that citizenship is not only a performance and practice, but it also confers a legal status regulated by the state—a status that carries immense material and emotional consequences for many. Claims of inclusion and legal recognition, therefore, cannot be separated from intimate narratives that inform one's subjectivity and relations with others.

Focusing on the rhetorical and political implications of treating citizenship as a legal status, I argue that we must extend the interrogation of the family-citizenship metaphoric complex to cover not only overt evocations of the nuclear reproductive family but also the deployment of other tropes of intimacy that trigger the familial interpretive framework.[9] As an ontological and structural metaphor for citizenship, the family privileges subjects and values that are familiar and beneficial to the state, while undermining the sociopolitical power of racialized Others. By identifying the intersecting concepts and ideologies that constitute the familial framework, we are better positioned to challenge dominant politics of formal recognition.

The connection between family and citizenship is an emotional, rhetorical, and ontological one that influences one's worldview and political and ethical relations to others. Familial metaphors are often used in mainstream public discourse to refer to the nation-state, with terms such as *founding fathers, homeland security,* and *motherland.* As cognitive linguist George Lakoff argues, the ways one understands familial arrangements and values informs one's opinions of the nation-state and how it should be structured.[10] As Lauren Berlant has similarly posited with the term "intimate public sphere," the political is understood via constricted "lived private worlds."[11] Citizenship, in other

---

7. I am aware that the conferral of legal citizenship status does not necessarily entail equality among citizens across racial, class, and power differences. However, as Luis F. B. Plascencia, Linda Bosniak, and Judith Butler point out, legal citizenship remains affectively and politically significant for marginalized Others. Bosniak, *The Citizen and the Alien*; Butler, "Is Kinship Always Already Heterosexual?,"; Plascencia, *Disenchanting Citizenship,* 187.

8. For how citizenship is deployed as a catch-all, see Wan, *Producing Good Citizens.* For example, Asen, "A Discourse Theory of Citizenship"; Kock and Villadsen, *Rhetorical Citizenship and Public Deliberation.*

9. For such critiques, see Berlant, *The Queen of America*; Ahmed, "A Phenomenology of Whiteness"; Wingard, *Branded Bodies.*

10. Interviewed in Shankar Vedantam, "*Our Politics, Our Parenting,*" *Hidden Brain* 44, podcast, MP3, 23:17, http://www.npr.org/podcasts/510308/hidden-brain.

11. Berlant, *The Queen of America,* 5.

words, is interpreted through intimate familial values, and that grants justification for selective inclusion and exclusion of subjects based not on democratic deliberation, but on sentiments and feelings that support the dominant national imaginary.[12]

According to Lakoff and Mark Johnson's theory of metaphors, an abstract idea is often represented and understood via a more concrete concept that functions as an ontological and structural metaphor of the former.[13] In this case, functioning as a metaphor for citizenship, the family allows for the translation of citizenship from an abstract political concept to narratives, relationships, and emotions that feel concrete, intimate, and personal. As the governing metaphor of citizenship, the familial forms the foundational interpretive framework for the citizenry even when the reproductive family is not explicitly evoked. As Lakoff and Johnson argue, the governing metaphor is so potent that it continues to influence one's judgments, feelings, and behaviors toward a concept even when the metaphor is not consciously brought to the forefront. A corporatist rhetorical framework that represents the nation as family, Mary McCoy argues, represents a nation that must be kept secure and be protected from "external invasion and internal disintegration."[14] Because political membership, legal recognition, and national identity are filtered through a familial lens, relationships among citizen-subjects and those between citizens and aliens and the nation are rendered much more intimate and visceral—there is, therefore, very little room for the articulation and acceptance of difference.

The family as a governing metaphor for citizenship is inflected by interconnected conceptions the state and dominant citizenry have toward *kinship, race and ethnicity, threats, neoliberal ideologies,* and *affective ties.* First, the family is most commonly used to describe kin ties in the private sphere that are biologically constituted; the conception of kinship is racially charged as people who share the same race are deemed as sharing an ancestry and therefore a common family.[15] Systematic exclusion of non-normative bodies in the US is done by linking legal citizenship with the reproductive family: White and heteronormative nuclear families are touted as the national ideal that defines and helps reproduce "good citizenship."[16] Meanwhile, racialized

---

12. Berlant, "The Theory of Infantile Citizenship."

13. Lakoff and Johnson, *Metaphors We Live By.*

14. McCoy, "Purifying Islam."

15. Ahmed, "A Phenomenology of Whiteness."

16. For critiques of citizenship as exclusionary mechanisms, see Brandzel, *Against Citizenship*; McKinnon, *Gendered Asylum*; Berlant, *The Queen of America*; Reddy, *Freedom with Violence*; Wingard, *Branded Bodies.*

subjects, particularly fertile women, are deemed as threats to the dominant nation-family who would usurp resources meant for deserving citizens and contaminate the nation-state through their undesirable and racially inferior offspring. Laws that prevent miscegenation and outrage against "anchor babies" and their mothers are key examples that illustrate how citizenship is regulated via a biological and racialized understanding of the family.[17] In addition, by denying racialized subjects citizenship and rendering them precarious, the nation-state can continue to exploit their labor to remain competitive in the neoliberal economy. The family-citizenship complex helps the nation-state maintain a specific national imaginary and transnational economic status by privileging a presumably shared biological and racial ancestry, together with racist ideologies.

The metaphorical connection between family and citizenship is prominently at play within mainstream public discourse in Hong Kong. For example, during his public addresses, former chief executive of the SAR C. Y. Leung repeatedly made use of the familial metaphor to discuss inclusivity and equality—a promise of citizenship that was never to come for marginalized groups: "Regardless of one's ethnic background, if one considers Hong Kong to be home, then we all are members of the same family"; other prominent politicians have similarly described Hong Kong as "a big family."[18] While political leaders like Leung never make explicit who the "family" encompasses, their repeated evocations nevertheless promote a familial interpretive framework of the nation and citizenship. Through this interpretive lens, those who have not been admitted as part of the national family have little discursive and political power. However, to be recognized as a family member, one must either belong to the dominant biological or affective kinship network or possess sufficient cultural and economic capital that makes one a valuable addition to the nation-state.

In the Chinese cultural context, family is semantically and ideologically tied to the nation-state. The Chinese term for *nation-state* (國家) translate[s] literally into *state-family*. As Chinese sociologist Xiaotong Fei points o[ut] his seminal work *From the Soil: The Foundations of Chinese Societv*

---

17. Leo Chavez examines how anti-immigration sentiments extend [to] mothers who are undocumented. Chavez, *The Latino Threat*; Chavez, [For a] critiques on public discourse against pregnant migrant women [see] *Arrival*; Wingard, *Branded Bodies*; Yam, "Affective Economies [of]

18. "Carrie Lam: Mainland Newcomers are Member[s] *Pacific Daily*, September 21, 2013. https://zh.apdnew[s] Hong Kong Connections, "Unclear Identity." Radio [L] cussions on the empty promises of citizenship, see Be[i] *Citizenship*.

nese culture, the nation-state is conceived of as an expanded network and circle of families, rippling out and overlapping with one another.[19] The boundary of each family, Fei posits, is fluid: Existing family members are able to expand and restrict their circle of concern according to the emotional ties they develop with others. Linguistically, the Chinese word for *family* (家) also posits an ambiguous and shifting parameter as it signifies not only the nuclear family unit, but could be extended to include "anyone whom you want to drag into your own circle" as an indication of intimacy.[20] The boundary of the nation is thus constituted by elastic familial ties that are defined partly through kinship and partly through emotional bonds. Inclusion into existing familial networks, therefore, is crucial for securing formal recognition from the nation-state.

Fei, however, is careful to emphasize that, despite the elasticity of familial boundaries, in Chinese social relations one's biological family across space and time is always prioritized as the center of one's circle of concern. While different familial and kinship networks may overlap with one another to constitute the nation, they nevertheless each privilege their kin and own interests. Like the Euro-American family-citizenship complex, at the heart of Fei's conception of the Chinese nation-family is still the self and subjects recognizable through their sameness to the self. The privileging of one's own family is widely observed in the Hong Kong context as well.[21] Prioritizing familial interests over individual and broader public concerns informs the ways mainland Chinese and Hongkongers understand their relationship to others in the public sphere.[22] The family in the Chinese Hong Kong context, in other words, is not only salient but is also intimately connected to an exclusionary logic that prioritizes the interests of in-group members over others.

Despite, and perhaps because of, its exclusionary nature, the family-citizenship complex remains a salient category because the recognition it grants is deeply affective. As Brandzel highlights, the longing for citizenship hinges upon "a desire for intimate recognition, a banishment of the pain and agony of nonrecognition."[23] This desire is particularly potent among those who are marginalized and racialized because to be recognized is to have one's humanity and self-worth validated.[24] Such psychic and affective needs to be recognized are conditioned, according to Axel Honneth, by primary caring relationships

19. Fei, *From the Soil.*
20. Ibid., 62.
21. Ong, *Neoliberalism as Exception.*
22. Newendorp, *Uneasy Reunions.*
    Brandzel, *Against Citizenship,* xiv.
    Fanon, *The Wretched of the Earth.*

found in the familial context; they correspond and manifest in the public sphere as demands for citizenship as formal recognition.[25] Citizenship is not just the marker of one's political membership but attends also to one's intimate sense of self and affective ties to the nation and other citizens. The yearning for citizenship, however, is according to Berlant a form of *cruel optimism*, in which the subject forms and maintains affective and political "attachment to a significantly problematic object" that threatens to destroy their life and well-being.[26]

As an attempt to cultivate and demonstrate their affective ties with the nation-state and the existing citizenry, aliens seeking formal inclusion often deploy tropes of intimacy that evoke feelings of longing, belonging, and identification. While this rhetorical strategy appears reasonable, it nevertheless, as Kelly Oliver argues, perpetuates an oppressive system in which only "those who are dominant have the power to create, confer, or withhold recognition, which operates as cultural currency."[27] Tropes of intimacy within the familial interpretive framework are counterproductive for the project of inclusion because they are associated with the protection of the national family and normative reproductive families in the private sphere; as an ontological metaphor for citizenship, the familial privileges racial likeness and the existing status quo in order to push out potential threats. As Sara Ahmed argues, "'the familial' is after all about 'the familiar' . . . [and] the domestic 'puts things' in their place."[28] Echoing Fei's analysis of the Chinese conception of family and nation, the familial framework of citizenship encourages a politics of identification: In order for one to be admitted as a member of the nation-family, one must convince the existing citizenry that they could see themselves in one. In other words, formal recognition hinges upon whether the Others render themselves intelligible and innocuous enough to be incorporated as part of the dominant national imaginary.[29]

Racialized Others face a double-edged sword when attempting to gain inclusion within the familial interpretive framework: On the one hand, they must erase their difference and deploy established tropes of intimacy to demonstrate that their affective ties to the nation-state are as strong as the kin ties shared among existing citizen-subjects; on the other hand, they must reassure the public that their inclusion will not pose threats to the existing racial hier-

---

25. Honneth, *The Struggle for Recognition*.

26. Berlant, *Cruel Optimism*, 24.

27. Oliver, *Witnessing*, 26.

28. Ahmed, "A Phenomenology of Whiteness," 155.

29. My argument here builds upon scholarship on recognition and subjectivity, particularly that of Emmanuel Levinas, *Otherwise than Being*, and Oliver, *Witnessing*.

archy.[30] The caveat, however, is that without disruptions to the hierarchy, the recognition marginalized Others receive will always be contingent upon the mainstream citizenry and the state.[31] Given this tension, I argue that in addition to studying how states and the dominant citizenry mobilize the family to justify and practice exclusion, we must also examine whether racialized Others could recuperate the trope that has systematically been used to undermine their social position.

In the Chinese sociocultural context, given the primacy of the family in securing recognition at the state level, marginalized and racialized rhetors who do not belong in any established kinship network face tremendous difficulty demonstrating why they should be granted membership in the nation-state and be seen as subjects worthy of a seat at the deliberation table in the political sphere. This is a particularly difficult challenge because civic community and engagement are not prominent concepts in Confucian teaching, which continues to inform the worldviews and practices of mainstream Chinese societies. *Great Learning,* one of the four key texts in Confucianism, posits that "in order to unify the world, one must first cultivate their own virtues, harmonize their family, and govern their state" (修身,齊家,治國,平天下).[32] Absent in this formula is a heterogeneous civic community composed of public subjects that do not belong to the same kinship network or the same nation. Given this conception of the family and nation-state, marginalized rhetors in this cultural context could make use of their personal familial stories to cultivate emotional bonds with the mainstream citizenry outside of kin ties. While these rhetors do not share kin ties with the existing citizenry and thus are not natural members of the nation-family, the circulation of their personal familial stories in public could evoke a sense of commonality and shared emotions between them and the mainstream audience. Such emotions could in turn encourage the mainstream public to expand the boundary of the family and extend ethical and political recognition to those who do not fall into the category of biological families.

---

30. For examples of the complex negotiations and compromises racialized Others must make to secure formal recognition, see Inderpal Grewal's analysis on the difficulties Sikh women face when attempting to gain refugee status in the US and Sara McKinnon's discussion on asylum seekers who are expected by the US state to conform to specific gender and cultural norms. Grewal, *Transnational America*; McKinnon, *Gendered Asylum.*

31. As Plascencia shows through his ethnographic research on Mexican migrants who later become US citizens, without a systemic disruption of the existing power structure, immigrants often feel disenchanted by the promise attached to formal citizenship because they remain unable to fully belong to the nation-family. Plascencia, *Disenchanting Citizenship.*

32. The translation here is mine. For a more in-depth discussion of this teaching, see Liu, *An Introduction to Chinese Philosophy,* 17.

## TRANSFORMATIVE DELIBERATION ACROSS DIFFERENCE

In the fields of rhetorical studies and political theory, deliberation is often conceptualized in terms of deliberative democracy and participatory citizenship: Under this conception, subjects enact citizenship by actively participating in discussions with each other to reach a collective judgment through "rational discourse and reasoned argumentation."[33] I deviate from this traditional model of deliberation for two reasons: First, it is not immediately applicable or relevant to a neocolonial Asian context like Hong Kong, in which deliberative democracy has never been institutionally and politically feasible, and thus does not actively inform the public imaginary and actions of local actors.[34] Second, while scholars in both fields have increasingly drawn attention to the importance of emotions to deliberation and democratic politics, there has been a long history and a large body of work that builds upon John Rawls and Jürgen Habermas's model of deliberation, which relies on the false dichotomy between reason and emotion, dismissing the latter as inferior and unsuitable for the public sphere.[35] Since gendered and racialized subjects have historically been deemed irrational, the privileging of reason in deliberation has been used as a mechanism of exclusion.[36] As Jay Childers points out, models of deliberation that dismiss "self-interest, emotion, and other human characteristics, which make political decision-making difficult, are both unrealistic and unhelpful."[37] As such, I adopt a networked and deeply contextual framework of deliberation that takes into account how positionality, power differences, and respective material interests influence the way interlocutors feel about and interact with one another in the public sphere.

If the goal of deliberation is to cultivate sustainable change to the relationships between the mainstream citizenry and marginalized subjects, then the two parties must be able to engage in a reciprocal relationship that recognizes and highlights the mutability of their subjectivities and shared interests. Understanding deliberation as a form of coalition practice, feminist theorist Katherine Adams argues that in order for deliberative acts to carry the transformative potential to establish coalition across difference, interlocutors must

33. Scudder, "Beyond Empathy," 525. See also Bohman, "Realizing Deliberative Democracy"; Leib, *Deliberative Democracy in America*; Kock and Villadsen, *Rhetorical Citizenship and Public Deliberation*.

34. Abbas, *Hong Kong*.

35. Scholarship that asserts the importance of affect and emotions in deliberation includes Marcus, *The Sentimental Citizen*; Nussbaum, *Upheavals of Thought*; Micciche, *Doing Emotion*.

36. Cisneros, "(Re)Bordering the Civic Imaginary"; Davis, *Breaking up (at) Totality*; Marcus, *The Sentimental Citizen*.

37. Childers, "Rhetorical Citizenship and Public Deliberation," 496.

recognize the contingent nature of their shared interests and be open to the possibility of self-reinvention.[38] Like Adams, who mobilizes Arendt's concept of inter-est, Arabella Lyon considers deliberation as "examinations of both being and situated knowledge for the many coming to action, an action potentially transformative of being and knowledge."[39] When deliberation is conceptualized as a present-oriented process of becoming, achieving consensus as a future outcome is less important than the dialogic engagement at the moment among the interlocutors that focuses on the mutual reinvention and reconstitution of the Self and the interlocutors' relationships with each other. Instead of focusing on the procedures of deliberation in order to identify a future solution to solve the problem at hand, this model of deliberative acts privileges the in-between space and the transformative processes that occur between interlocutors in which differences are neither erased nor subsumed.[40]

I refer to this kind of deliberation championed by feminist political and rhetorical theorists as *transformative deliberation* because of its focus on the ongoing intersubjective engagement among interlocutors, which prompts them to continuously reinvent their subject positions and interests. At the heart of transformative deliberation are subjects who understand that their identities, interests, and relations with others are always in flux and subject to change because of deliberation. The cultivation of intersubjective engagement counters political communities that are formed by a shared and stable identity; by emphasizing the mutability of subjectivities and interests, transformative deliberation creates room for coalition moments across difference.[41] Rather than assuming that interlocutors possess fixed and fundamentally conflicting interests with one another that motivate competition, transformative deliberation, as Adams argues, posits a more collaborative and dialogic relationship between interlocutors: While each person sees interests and the reality differently, they nevertheless are "reaching towards others and trying to become visible to them, and so avoid[ ] both the deadlock of adversarial democracy and the paralysis of collective singular subjectivity."[42] By engaging with each other dialogically in the political sphere and recognizing the fluidity of one's position and interests in relation to others', interlocutors in transformative deliberation negotiate not by remaining steadfast to their perceived interests,

---

38. Adams, "At the Table with Arendt."

39. Lyon, *Deliberative Acts*, 18.

40. For procedural deliberation, see Guinier, *Tyranny of the Majority*; Young, *Justice and the Politics of Difference*.

41. Honig, *Feminist Interpretations of Hannah Arendt*.

42. Adams, "At the Table with Arendt," 16.

but by continuously "forming, clarifying, and transforming" them.[43] Rather than focusing on the potential for a final resolution, transformative deliberation privileges mutual engagement, the openness to change, and the continual examination of mutual interests and one's relations to others.

In addition, transformative deliberation cannot take place if the interlocutors do not acknowledge their mutual existence with others and their overlapping material interests. Drawing from Arendt's concept of inter-est, Adams and Lyon respectively emphasize that intersubjective engagement in transformative deliberation is always grounded in materiality. If one's subjectivity and interests are not a priori, then they must be conceptualized in relation to one's material and sociopolitical context—a context shared by many others whose positionalities, histories, and identities are different.[44] As Adams argues, "Far from facilitating connection and spaces of contact, freedom from material context erases space and deprives actors of each other, and therefore, of themselves."[45] Similarly, Lyon draws on Arendt's concept of *interspace* to explain how materiality binds subjects of different positionalities together, while allowing them to assert their difference.[46] The shared materiality prompts interlocutors to collaboratively redefine their self- and common interests; at the same time, interlocutors are able to maintain their differences because the deliberative space is constituted exactly through plural utterances and different interpretations of the shared material context. As Arendt cogently illustrates with the metaphor of a spiritual séance, the participants are simultaneously connected and separated by the table in front of them. If the table were to suddenly vanish, the people sitting across from one another would be "no longer separated but also would be entirely unrelated by anything tangible."[47] An attunement toward sociopolitical contexts and material interests, therefore, is crucial for the process of transformative deliberation.

## POLITICS OF RECOGNITION AND IDENTIFICATION

Because histories of injustice and power difference inevitably assert their influence during processes of deliberation, interlocutors across power difference who want to engage in transformative deliberation must continue to examine the ramifications of these protracted histories in order to rearticu-

---

43. Ibid., 18.
44. Adams, "At the Table with Arendt."
45. Ibid., 16.
46. Lyon, *Deliberative Acts*.
47. Arendt and Canovan, *The Human Condition*, 53.

late coalitional relationships that take into account implications of systematic oppression and power hierarchy. As Adams and Gloria Anzaldúa acknowledge, this form of relationality is only possible if one is "open to the full play of motivation and desire, and willing to negotiate all aspects of this self across the coalition table."[48] Therefore, for interlocutors to engage in transformative deliberation across power difference, they must not only recognize the shared interests and togetherness among interlocutors within the realm of interconnected human relationships and affairs, but they must also recognize the impossibility of symmetrical reciprocity and the reversals of positions.

The kind of recognition transformative deliberation calls for is distinct from the formal recognition denoted by state citizenship or normative human rights discourse, which often perpetuates what Kelly Oliver calls "the pathology of recognition": recognition that can be conferred only by more powerful actors and functions as "the soft currency with which oppressed people are exchanged within the global economy."[49] Instead of undermining structures of oppression, the dominant model of recognition is in fact perpetuating the existing hierarchy. In normative models of recognition like formal citizenship, the marginalized are treated as objects that either deserve or do not deserve to be recognized, while those in power select the bodies to whom they would grant recognition based on their own interests.[50]

Dominant models of recognition are also limiting in promoting coalition across difference because they are often based on a Hegelian tradition that renders recognition necessarily a traumatic battle of life and death.[51] In this framework, reciprocal recognition can only be achieved when the self "supersede[s] the Other."[52] As philosopher Shannon Sullivan argues, "Hegelian recognition could be described as centripetal; its driving force is inward, producing a narcissistic focus on the self at the expense of the other."[53] For rhetorical acts that attempt to overcome the violence and tension between the Self and the Other that is inherent in Hegelian recognition, identification is often posited as the ideal outcome in encounters across difference.[54] However, identification, as many have critiqued, is similarly dangerous as it often rein-

---

48. Adams, "At the Table with Arendt," 27–28; Anzaldúa, Cantú, and Hurtado, *Borderlands / La Frontera*.

49. Oliver, *Witnessing*, 52.

50. Hesford, *Spectacular Rhetorics*; Kelly Oliver, *Witnessing*.

51. Ricoeur, *The Course of Recognition*.

52. Oliver, *Witnessing*, 28. Arabella Lyon and Wendy Hesford have both eloquently critiqued the problems with the Hegelian model of mutual recognition. Hesford, *Spectacular Rhetorics*; Lyon, *Deliberative Acts*.

53. Sullivan, *Revealing Whiteness*, 105.

54. Burke, *A Grammar of Motives*; Lyon, *Deliberative Acts*.

forces the dominant self and forecloses room for mutual transformation.[55] As Lyon argues:

> As it is monologic in privileging sameness and bonding, identification is imbued with power's innate normativity, and too often, as an abstraction, it depoliticizes the most political and contingent acts of deliberation—the many becoming action—through its failure to designate inequality, history, parochialism, struggle, and marginalization.[56]

Identification that is based solely on locating similarities and sameness is unproductive in promoting transformative deliberation across power difference because it does not take into account how encounters with difference and the process of deliberation are always already rife with the remnants and ongoing influence of oppression.

In addition, identification perpetuates instead of ameliorates a centripetal form of recognition, in which the interests and feelings of the dominant actor are prioritized.[57] By privileging an ultimate unity and an erasure of difference based primarily on the interests of the dominant interlocutors, identification shifts the attention away from the cultivation of inter-est, through which solidarities and alliances are established over time without the erasure of necessary difference.[58] Instead of treating identification as the salve to Hegelian recognition and complement to transformative deliberation, we need to identify an alternative politics of recognition, one that does not undermine the necessary heterogeneity among interlocutors. Sullivan's proposal of "centrifugal recognition" is helpful here.[59] As she defines it:

> Centrifugal recognition, in contrast [to the Hegelian model of recognition], moves the self outward. It establishes and nurtures social connections between and among people. Unlike the violent self-centeredness of centripetal recognition, centrifugal recognition stretches the self toward and into other people, nourishing human sociality rather than narcissistically starving it.[60]

---

55. For critiques of identification, see Hesford, *Spectacular Rhetorics*; Lyon, *Deliberative Acts*; Mohanty, *Feminism without Borders*; Puar, *Terrorist Assemblages*.

56. Lyon, *Deliberative Acts*, 60.

57. Critiquing identification as contributing more toward *misrecognition*, Lyon pointedly writes, "our identification is all . . . pretense, cloaking cooptation and narcissism as it ignores differences." Lyon, *Deliberative Acts*, 59.

58. For Burke, identification is a remedy for division; it is the rhetorician's job to "proclaim their unity" by cultivating identification and consubstantiation. Burke, *A Rhetoric of Motives*.

59. Sullivan, *Revealing Whiteness*, 104.

60. Sullivan, *Revealing Whiteness*, 105.

Centrifugal recognition is compatible with transformative deliberation because both nurture the process of mutual becoming, rather than the prioritizing the existing interests and perceptions of dominant subjects. A more ethical and politically productive form of recognition ought to denote new subject positions and relationships among interlocutors. This rearticulation of recognition is based on the understanding that we cannot completely do away with recognition as something bestowed by another because it remains an important element in human sociality that constructs one's personhood. At the same time, we can cultivate a form of recognition that does not rely on the erasure or dismissal of otherness, but rather actively cultivates the relationality between subjects across difference through processes of transformative deliberation.

## EMPATHY AND SOLIDARITY

Understanding deliberation as a form of dialogic and mutually transformative engagement grounded in materiality opens up the opportunity for marginalized rhetors to achieve redress, as it grants them the status as interlocutors who co-appear with others in the political sphere. This opportunity, however, could only take place if those in power are willing to join marginalized subjects at the deliberation table and acknowledge that, despite their power difference, they share common concerns and interests with their less privileged peers at the material and human levels. In addition, interlocutors who occupy a more privileged position must be willing to render themselves vulnerable in the process of becoming. While intersubjectivity is a priori, the recognition that we are all bound together in the web of human relation through shared materiality is not. Thus, for those who enjoy a relative position of power and privilege, the recognition that they share common interests with marginalized subjects and could benefit from engaging in deliberation with them is more daunting than liberating. The difficulty is compounded by the fact that marginalized bodies are often branded with negative feelings such as fear, anger, and revulsion. To undo these sticky affective markers, the mainstream citizenry must first learn to feel differently toward and about their relationships with marginalized subjects.

I propose deliberative empathy as a productive emotion and rhetorical effect that prompts dominant subjects to engage in transformative deliberation. I focus on the ethical and rhetorical efficacy of empathy in promoting transformative deliberation because while empathy is not without its critics, it helps create coalition moments by prompting dominant subjects to suspend their defensiveness and other negative learned emotional reactions toward marginalized Others.[61]

Empathy and its close cousins sympathy and compassion have been widely examined across disciplines for their potential in advancing social justice and also their propensity in perpetuating existing power hierarchies. Scholars in philosophy, American studies, critical race studies, and gender and women's studies often posit that these feelings are problematic because they carry an inherently colonizing tendency to consume or subsume the Other.[62] For example, philosopher Elizabeth Spelman critiques compassion together with pity, positing that they foreclose room for deliberation and alternatives and are akin to a "selfish and cruel wallowing in the misfortunes of others."[63] For Spelman, empathy, while not spotlighting the power difference between the spectator and the suffering subject, is similarly problematic because it implies a false sense of mutual understanding and identification on the part of the spectator.[64] Spelman is not alone in mounting such critiques of these human-izing emotions: Many critical race theorists are skeptical and pessimistic as well toward the ethical potential of both sympathy and empathy.[65]

What remains inconsistent, however, are the definitions of sympathy, empathy, and compassion across disciplines: What one scholar refers to as compassion may be empathy for another. This confusion and conflation ren-ders it difficult to have productive critiques and analysis about the poten-tial and limitations of these emotions. For example, while most agree that empathy is more politically and ethically significant than sympathy because it places less emphasis on the power differential, others have posited that sym-pathy is more capable in motivating the audience to transform their affective reactions into moral concern and a desire to help others.[66] Regarding compas-

---

61. Scholars in rhetorical studies and the social sciences have elucidated the different ways affects and emotions inform communicative acts, in ways that sometimes promote social change and solidarity, sometimes aggravate ill will across difference, and sometimes hamper the subjects' desire to engage in deliberation at all. See Engels, *The Politics of Resentment*; Gould, *Moving Politics*; Gross, *The Secret History of Emotion*; Hochschild, *Strangers in Their Own Land*; Rice, *Distant Publics*; Xu, *The Politics of Compassion*.

62. For a summary of existing critiques on sympathy, empathy, and compassion, see Kim-berly Davis, *Beyond the White Negro*.

63. Spelman, *Fruits of Sorrow*, 65.

64. Ibid.

65. For example, hooks, *Black Looks*; Rogin, *Blackface, White Noise*; Wiegman, *American Anatomies*.

66. Psychologists such as C. Daniel Batson and Paul Zak prefer empathy over sympathy; on the other hand, literary scholar Suzanne Keen deems sympathy to be more complex than empathy. She argues that only when translated into sympathy would an empathetic response motivate one to help others. Kimberly Chabot Davis presents a sound literature review on

sion, Martha Nussbaum posits that it belongs to a higher order than empathy; yet, there is another group of scholars who define and critique compassion similarly as empathy, arguing that they are both equally paternalistic as they rely on the privilege of the spectator.[67] Given these competing definitions of sympathy, empathy, and compassion that impede sustained interrogation of the social functions and implications of these emotions, research in this area would benefit significantly from an interdisciplinary approach that takes into account insights from other fields.[68]

My analysis and usage of empathy draws on studies from both the humanities and the sciences. I choose to use the term *empathy* because of its association with what psychologist C. Daniel Baston calls "perspective-taking": attempts to view and understand a situation through an alternative perspective.[69] As research in psychology and literary studies has demonstrated, empathetic attempts to take the perspectives of others need not be inherently egoistic and do not necessarily involve the subsuming of difference.[70] Rather, they could trigger what psychologists and cultural studies scholars call "self-modifying feelings," "self-scrutiny," and "self-estrangement"—affective experiences that prompt one not only to understand the perspectives and feelings of others but also to reflect on how one is positioned in the world in relation to others in a way that binds.[71] Research conducted by social psychologists further reveals that inducing empathy helps mitigate the stigma subjects hold against a marginalized group; the empathetic response also motivates research subjects to actively engage in acts that help ameliorate the suffering.[72] Defending the ethical and political potential of empathy, I argue that empathy is not an inherently colonizing and passive feeling that always recenters the dominant self and promotes complacency. Rather, given the right contexts, platforms, and expressions, it could function as a productive emotion that fosters ethical relations and solidarity across difference.

---

where scholarships diverge and converge regarding these emotional responses. Batson, *The Altruism Question*; Kimberly Davis, *Beyond the White Negro*; Keen, *Empathy and the Novel*; Zak, *The Moral Molecule*.

67. For critiques of empathy and compassion, see Berlant, *Compassion*; Delgado, *The Coming Race War*; Nussbaum, *Upheavals of Thought*.

68. Davis has also argued for a more interdisciplinary approach toward studying the political effects of these closely related emotions that are frequently conflated. Kimberly Davis, *Beyond the White Negro*.

69. Batson, *The Altruism Question*.

70. Benjamin, *The Bonds of Love*; Deigh, *The Sources of Moral Agency*.

71. Kuiken et al., "Locating Self-Modifying Feelings within Literary Reading," 269; Felski, *Uses of Literature*, 35; Silverman, *The Threshold of the Visible World*, 85.

72. Batson, Chang, Orr, and Rowland, "Empathy, Attitudes, and Action."

In cognitive psychology, empathy has been criticized for its spotlight effect: namely, that it encourages the subject to focus their affective energy and resources too narrowly at an individual and personal level, thus running the risk of overlooking the larger problems at stake.[73] Countering this claim, I argue that the spotlight effect is a useful first step in combating historical and systematic dehumanization of racialized subjects by the mainstream citizenry. It mitigates dominant discourse that alienizes members of racialized groups, and instead highlights the commonalities between them and the mainstream audience. Social psychologists have found that dominant subjects commonly engage in "out-group homogenization," a process through which members from marginalized and racialized groups are conceptualized as an aggregate with no distinctions from one another.[74] Such homogenization allows for easy dehumanization as individual lives and personhoods are erased. The spotlight effect of empathy is able to mitigate the harmful effects of such homogenization by foregrounding individual lives. In fact, research in social psychology has demonstrated that when research subjects experience empathy for a single member of a marginalized group, they tend to extend their empathy toward other members of the group and revise their existing stigma about the entire group.[75] The spotlight effect, in other words, is grounds to support rather than critique the ethical and political potential of empathy in fostering coalition across difference.

In fields such as rhetorical studies, anthropology, and literary studies, empathy—particularly in relation to narratives—has often been explored as a desirable emotional connection between the marginalized rhetor and the audience.[76] As Dennis Lynch posits, "Empathy is both an attitude and a practice: it attunes our minds to the needs of others; it permits people who are arguing to discover, not just premises, but premises that work."[77] Empathy, Lynch emphasizes, is key to rhetorical practices because it gives rhetors "the desire to inquire into how others understand what is at stake in an issue and the means to follow through on that desire."[78] Empathy reminds rhetors of the relationality among subjects and the importance of recognizing the interconnected lifeworlds of another.

73. Bloom, *Against Empathy*; Lynch, "Rhetorics of Proximity."

74. Chung and Slater, "Reducing Stigma and Out-Group Distinctions"; Park and Rothbart, "Perception of Out-Group Homogeneity."

75. Batson, Chang, Orr, and Rowland, "Empathy, Attitudes, and Action."

76. For example, Keen, *Empathy and the Novel*; Mary Beth Oliver, Dillard, Bae, and Tamul, "The Effect of Narrative News Format on Empathy for Stigmatized Groups"; Skultans, "Culture and Dialogue."

77. Lynch, "Rhetorics of Proximity," 5.

78. Ibid., 6.

There are, however, significant problems in how empathy has been mobilized rhetorically, particularly in ways that invoke identification. For instance, empathy is often seen as a desirable rhetorical outcome for personal narratives because the perceived goal of this genre is often for the audience to put themselves in the shoes of the non-normative and marginalized rhetors.[79] Given this rhetorical goal, it is in the rhetor's interest to purposefully evoke feelings of familiarity and closeness among their audiences so that they would feel emotionally connected to the rhetor's experiences and perspectives. The purpose of personal narratives, according to this view, is to foster "empathetic identification" between the audience and the rhetor, assuming that the audience could understand completely the lived experiences of the rhetor.[80] This conception of empathy, however, risks reproducing oppressive relations between dominant and marginalized subjects. Identification, as I have discussed earlier, is dangerous as it often reinforces the dominant self and forecloses room for deliberation and difference. In her critique of Burkean identification, Lyon argues:

> Despite [Burke's] emphasis on acting together within identification, which rightly emphasizes performative aspects of recognition and echoes the physical meetings of the in-between, identification works at a level of abstraction similar to the generalized other, and thus identification remains concerned with denying the presence of difference, for it potentially captures "man's very essence," ignoring the gender, culture, and all manner of contingencies.[81]

If we assume that everyone could unequivocally understand one another and be completely transparent to each other regardless of material and positional differences, plurality in public discourse would be obliterated. Empathy that is founded on identification, therefore, inevitably perpetuates the erasure of difference, while privileging a form of unity among subjects that hampers the mutual becoming in transformative deliberation.

In addition, empathetic identification is problematic because it presumes *affective* instead of *cognitive empathy,* which hinders one's ability to critically assess the situation and the distance between oneself and the object of identification. As psychologist Paul Bloom points out, while affective empathy refers to experiencing the feelings of others, particularly their pain, cognitive empathy points to the capacity to understand the source of someone's suffer-

---

79. Lynch, "Rhetorics of Proximity"; Rothfelder and Thornton, "Man Interrupted."
80. Rothfelder and Thornton, "Man Interrupted," 365.
81. Lyon, *Deliberative Acts,* 63.

ing without necessarily experiencing the pain viscerally in one's own body.[82] Bloom's definition of cognitive empathy echoes what Todd DeStigter calls *critical empathy*, or "a process of establishing informed and affective connections with other human beings, of thinking and feeling with them at some emotionally, intellectually, and socially significant level, while always remembering that such connections are complicated by sociohistorical forces that hinder the equitable, just relationships that we presumably seek."[83] Critical empathy differs from affective empathy, and thus from an individualistic notion of identification. By prompting the subject to be more attuned to the political and systematic causes of situations, critical empathy challenges interlocutors to question how existing power and ideological structures constrain the ways ethical relationships are constructed and enacted. Empathy, in other words, is not the most productive when it functions merely as an emotional spotlight that shines only on those one identifies with on an individual basis. Rather, it carries the most ethical and political potential when its affective power is enacted in conjunction with a critical, deliberative process that demands interlocutors to recognize the irreconcilable difference between them.

Critical empathy could be effectively mobilized to counter the systematic dehumanization of non-normative subjects in the nation-state and foster solidarity between them and the mainstream citizenry. Within the dominant interpretive framework of citizenship in which racialized bodies are systematically excluded, the mainstream citizenry is accustomed to hearing marginalized groups make overt claims directed to them and the state for legal and social inclusion; they are therefore likely to respond to such appeals through established templates of feelings such as disgust, resentment, or sympathy that either overtly support exclusionary mechanisms or perpetuate politics of identification that recenter the concerns of the dominant group. These feeling templates not only exclude marginalized bodies from being members of the nation-family, but their stickiness in the dominant national imaginary also prevents the citizenry from engaging in the process of transformative deliberation with marginalized interlocutors.[84] As Ioanide argues, "dominant emotional economies often function to foreclose or reduce people's willingness to challenge false beliefs because embodied experiences of fear, phobia, shame, or desire take precedence over cognition or knowledge."[85] If the mainstream citizenry cannot experience or express emotions beyond the established feeling

---

82. Bloom, *Against Empathy*.

83. DeStigter, "Public Displays of Affection," 240.

84. For more discussions on the stickiness of public emotions, see Ahmed, *The Cultural Politics of Emotion*.

85. Ioanide, *The Emotional Politics of Racism*, 12.

templates, they will not be able to openly engage in transformative delibera-tion with others to consider how their interests may overlap. As an alterna-tive emotional response, empathy has the affective power to jolt, propel, and move subjects in a way that defies complete co-optation into the preexisting ideological framework.[86] Together with its attunement toward contextuality and materiality, critical cognitive empathy, in particular, could displace exist-ing feeling templates and motivate the existing citizenry to relate to racialized Others in a way that promotes transformative deliberation.

## DELIBERATIVE EMPATHY AND COALITIONAL POTENTIAL

Given the distinctions between affective and cognitive empathy, I modify empathy with *deliberative* in this book for two key reasons: to avoid conflation with identification, and to highlight the tension dominant audiences experi-ence when they attempt to reconcile their existing impulse to exclude with the urge to reexamine their relations with and perceptions of others. To accom-modate the dissonance that stems from this affective encounter, dominant audiences must engage in a process of internal deliberation to reassess how they ought to revise their worldviews and sense of self in relation to this new way of seeing and relating to others. Deliberative empathy jolts mainstream audiences from their usual discursive, political, and emotional templates of response and invites them to participate in an alternative mode of engagement that is based on mutual transformation.

By weaving critical cognitive empathy with transformative deliberation, deliberative empathy does not reinforce a binary between pathos and logos, nor does it perpetuate a framework of recognition that hinges upon identi-fication and consensus. Deliberative empathy could be seen as a catalyst for transformative deliberation, and thus a desirable response among dominant audiences. Instead of participating in the discourse of citizenship, marginal-ized rhetors could purposefully cultivate deliberative empathy among their audiences as a way to disrupt the dominant framework of formal recogni-tion. While it may seem judicious for marginalized groups to deploy tropes intelligible within the dominant citizenship discourse to advocate for their place in the nation-family, this normative rhetorical strategy reinscribes them within the dominant interpretive framework that perpetuates existing power relations and allows the state to act as the sole arbiter of recognition and iden-tification. Deliberative empathy, on the other hand, operates outside of the dominant politics of recognition. This alternative framework allows margin-

---

86. Grossberg, "Postmodernity and Affect."

alized rhetors to articulate their personhood—after all, it is their subjectivity and the shared human conditions or inter-ests that ought to be recognized, not their sameness and intelligibility as compared to the dominant group.

Deliberative empathy combines constitutive deliberative acts with the critical cognitive model of empathy that urges interlocutors to examine and redefine their subjectivity in relation to others, and to acknowledge the overlapping interests amidst their shared material context. By prompting the recognition of intersubjectivity across power difference, deliberative empathy challenges the existing power structure that codifies identity categories in a way that deters coalition. To decenter existing models of political recognition in which power remains in the hands of the state and the mainstream citizenry, the cultivation of deliberative empathy calls for rhetorical genres and modes of engagement outside of the formal arguments common in citizenship discourse. Deliberative empathy, in other words, prompts marginalized rhetors to engage with the dominant audiences in a way that does not reify the power difference and existing relationship between them, but assumes that their subjectivities and perceptions are always open to change.

## NARRATIVES AND STORYTELLING AS POLITICAL AND ETHICAL PRAXIS

Given the limits of formal citizenship discourse in prompting dominant audiences to engage in transformative deliberation with marginalized subjects, storytelling serves as an effective rhetorical and emotional mechanism to evoke deliberative empathy, which subsequently prompts dominant audiences to reconsider the feelings they attach to marginalized subjects and the relationships and the interests they share with them. While formal citizenship discourse negates the personhood of marginalized subjects, personal and familial narratives that evoke deliberative empathy expose how despite the promise it carries, citizenship nevertheless continues to deny the humanity of non-normative subjects. If the desire for and deference to formal citizenship is, as Berlant suggests, a form of cruel optimism, then deliberative empathy evoked through narratives is an affective and discursive salve that helps "rewire the ways we think about what binds people to harmful conventions of personhood."[87]

In this book, I interrogate storytelling as a mode of engagement that activates deliberative empathy and engages the more dominant audiences to par-

---

87. Berlant, *Cruel Optimism*, 159.

ticipate in transformative deliberation.[88] Specifically, I understand storytelling as a rhetorical act that has a profound impact on the audience's willingness and ability to emotionally and politically collaborate with others across difference. For humanities scholars who are concerned with cultivating an intersubjective awareness among subjects, the open-ended, inviting, and nonpersuasive nature of stories renders them effective rhetorical vehicles to promote coalitional relationships across difference.[89] In addition, the social and affective power of stories in cultivating cognitive empathy and collaboration across difference has been well demonstrated by cognitive scientists. In fact, since the 1990s, psychologists have realized that audiences consume and respond to stories in qualitatively different ways than arguments.[90] As psychologist Betsy Levy Paluck points out, when an audience encounters a story, "their defensiveness is disabled. Their counterarguing is at rest."[91] Instead of seeking to undermine the rhetor's claim, the audience tends to actively imagine the world in which the storyteller lives, and attempts to understand the causes and feelings of the rhetor's experiences. Such acts of imagination prompt the audience to experience empathy in a way that engages their critical capacity to understand how the structural acts on the personal. There is a physiological basis to why narratives are conducive to enacting dialogic engagement across difference. Recent research in neurobiology demonstrates that character-driven stories trigger the emission of oxytocin in the audiences' bodies, a hormone coined the "moral molecule" that promotes trust and collaborative behaviors between strangers.[92] These feelings, as I have argued earlier, are key to transformative deliberation as interlocutors, particularly those who occupy a more privileged position, must be open to processes of mutual becoming as they reexamine how their interests and subjectivities intersect with others'.

I focus on the three intersecting theoretical positions on narrative performance studies scholar Kristin Langellier has identified: namely, narratives as "storytelling performance; [as] social process; and as political praxis."[93] This framework prompts us to examine the way a narrative is told and the effects it

---

88. The rhetorical function of stories and narratives has been explored by rhetoric and performance studies scholars, and by scholars in folklore studies, anthropology, philosophy, and most recently, neurobiology. See Fisher, "Narration as a Human Communication Paradigm"; Jackson, *The Politics of Storytelling*; Langellier, "Personal Narratives"; Phelan, *Narrative as Rhetoric*; Shuman, *Other People's Stories*; Stone-Mediatore, *Reading across Borders*; Zak, *The Moral Molecule*.

89. Cavarero, *Relating Narratives*; Jackson, *The Politics of Storytelling*.

90. Spiegel, "Inspired."

91. Ibid.

92. Zak, *The Moral Molecule*, 64.

93. Langellier, "Personal Narratives," 244.

has on the audience, and on the shifting social dynamics between the audience and the storyteller; it also highlights the use of narratives "to negotiate present and future events," which is a key function of deliberation across difference.[94] There is slippage between *stories* and *narratives*. While strategic communication scholars identify formal distinctions between the two, humanists like Cavarero and Jackson consider all narratives as stories, as long as they render the protagonist a subject within an interconnected web of human affairs stories in a way to mediate one's relation with others and the world.[95] I understand narratives as a rhetorical genre that allows rhetors to engage the interlocutors dialogically without an overtly persuasive agenda. On the other hand, I use *stories* and *storytelling* to denote the social and public functions, performances, and circulation of narratives, particularly in ways that invite the audiences and the rhetor to examine how their lives and interests intersect, despite differences in positionalities and lived experiences.

This recognition of simultaneous difference and commonality is at the heart of transformative deliberation, rendering stories an effective mechanism to engage interlocutors from different power positions. Narratives and acts of storytelling stem from an almost universal human desire to render events coherent so that one can grapple with the ongoing uncertainties and contingencies of life shared by all, regardless of positionality and social standing.[96] While some lives are more precaritized and therefore are subjected to more contingencies than others, no one has absolute control over their life circumstances. The telling of one's stories, therefore, provides a rhetorical platform for interlocutors to explore their relationships with one another and with the uncontrollable forces in their lives. As Fisher posits, "to consider that public social knowledge is to be found in the stories that we tell one another would enable us to observe not only our differences, but also our commonalities, and in such observation we might be able to reform the notion of the 'public.'"[97] The sharing of stories, thus, promotes among audiences the recognition that despite the social distances and differences that separate them from others, they nevertheless are all entangled in the same web of human affairs in the public sphere. Such recognition, in turn, invites audiences to engage and participate in the continual unfolding of events with the storytellers and other interlocutors.

---

94. Ibid., 261.

95. Cavarero, *Relating Narratives*; Halverson, Corman, and Goodall, *Master Narratives of Islamist Extremism*; Jackson, *The Politics of Storytelling*.

96. Cavarero, *Relating Narratives*; Gottschall, *The Storytelling Animal*; Jackson, *The Politics of Storytelling*; Ochs and Capps, *Living Narrative*.

97. Fisher, "Narration as a Human Communication Paradigm," 15.

Acts of storytelling carry both political and ethical potential because storytelling is founded upon intersubjectivity and the *inter-est* that binds people together across difference.[98] For Arendt, inter-est is a concept that denotes overlapping interests among otherwise unique and separate individuals, something "which lies between people and therefore can relate and bind them together."[99] By negotiating and narrativizing the relationship between the singular and the universal in each human experience and by cultivating the "interspace" between subjects, stories help restore ethical relationships amid systematic oppression and marginalization.[100] For Arendt, each person is simultaneously an agentic subject with the ability to construct her own reality (a "who") and an object subjugated to forces, actions, and circumstances outside of her control (a "what").[101] Always embedded within what Arendt calls "the already existing web of human relationships," stories are inherently relational and intersubjective, in which the tellers and audience share agency in co-creating recognition, relationships, and identities through narratives.[102] Extending Arendt, Jackson points out that storytelling is inherently intersubjective because it "is a modality of working with others to transform what is given, or what simply befalls us, into forms of life, experience, and meaning that are collectively viable."[103] The intersubjectivity inherent in acts of storytelling, thus, creates the possibilities for transformative deliberation.

Acts of storytelling allow marginalized rhetors to transform an unjust relationship into one that emphasizes the inter-est—overlapping concerns among distinct people that enable collaborations—in two different ways: by actively acknowledging and reinventing one's personhood and unique self, and by demanding that one ought to be recognized as a *necessary* and *concrete* Other who is distinct from other subjects.[104] First, marginalized storytellers can regain a sense of agency by collaborating with others to actively reinvent their individual and collective selves in a way that "subtly alter[s] the balance between actor and acted upon."[105]

---

98. Arendt and Canovan, *The Human Condition.*

99. Ibid., 182.

100. Arendt, *Men in Dark Times.*

101. Arendt and Canovan, *The Human Condition*, 181–88.

102. Ibid., 184. Cavarero, Lyon, and Jackson have all expounded upon the relational nature of stories as well. Cavarero, *Relating Narratives*; Lyon, *Deliberative Acts*; Jackson, *The Politics of Storytelling.*

103. Jackson, *The Politics of Storytelling*, 246.

104. Arendt and Canovan, *The Human Condition*; Lyon, *Deliberative Acts.* Cavarero and Benhabib, respectively, coin the terms "the necessary other" and "the concrete other." Benhabib, *Situating the Self*; Cavarero, *Relating Narratives.*

105. Jackson, *The Politics of Storytelling*, 4.

In confounding and oppressive conditions that render marginalized subjects powerless, storytelling helps them obtain a degree of discursive control of their lived experience and material reality. For example, despite the fact that most Southeast Asian women become migrant workers in Hong Kong because of financial hardship created by the transnational neoliberal economy, they nevertheless narrate extensively about how and why they made the decision themselves to leave home, and how their decision would benefit their family in the long run.[106] By reframing their otherwise traumatic experience this way, these workers highlight their agency and love for their family while downplaying the transnational economic conditions that are beyond their control. While the workers do not directly challenge the oppressive economic system and labor practice through their stories, they are able to rearticulate their personhood outside of the victim narrative. Indeed, as Jackson points out, storytelling gives marginalized rhetors an opportunity to "redress a bias toward autonomy when it has been lost. . . . It is not that speech is a replacement for action; rather that it is a supplement, to be exploited when action is impossible or confounded."[107] Storytelling is a rhetorical tool marginalized rhetors could deploy to both acknowledge the worthiness and uniqueness of their selfhood and to reconstruct a reality in which they retain a degree of agency amid subjugation.

In addition to granting oppressed rhetors the chance to reclaim their personhood and sense of autonomy, stories also require the audience to engage in an ethical encounter that recognizes difference. Storytelling privileges the protagonist's status as a "who"—a person with a unique self and history—over what the protagonist does or what has been done to her. Storytelling always involves the recognition that one's life is distinct and worthy of narration. The focus on the "who" satisfies what Adriana Cavarero calls "a narratable self": namely, the desire all subjects have toward receiving the recognition of another and hearing their specific life story told by another.[108] This desire is particularly fervent among marginalized subjects whose personhood is not often publicly validated.[109] The form of recognition demanded by the narratable self goes beyond the mere sanctioning for one to participate as an interlocutor—rather, by seeking to be narrated by another as a *who* instead of a *what*, the narratable self invites others to engage with them in the in-between space that is built upon both commonality and difference.

---

106. HelperChoice, *Wishing Well: Voices from Foreign Domestic Workers in Hong Kong and Beyond.*

107. Jackson, *The Politics of Storytelling*, 37.

108. Cavarero, *Relating Narratives*, 34.

109. Ibid.

The recognition that storytelling calls for, thus, is one that sees the narratable Other as both *necessary* and *concrete*, to borrow Cavarero and Seyla Benhabib's terms, respectively.[110] As Cavarero points out, a subject's life can only be properly narrated by another when the narrator and the subject are distinct from each other in a way that is "inassimiable, insubstitutable, [and] unrepeatable."[111] The distance and difference between the narratable self and the speaker enacts a Levinasian relationship in which the radical Other calls for the recognition of one's ethical responsibility to another without the process of identification. Alterity and otherness, therefore, are necessary. The Other is also concrete in the sense that she carries with her "history, identity, and affective-emotional constitution" that is specific and born in relations with others.[112] To narrate the life of a concrete other, the speaker must pay attention to the particular history, relationships, and sociopolitical contexts that constitute the experiences and personhood of the narrated subject. Such attunement to the specifics and the material, as Lyon argues, allows for more robust deliberative acts, "constituting particular scenes, lives, and laws through a finding of in-between and inter-est."[113] While ethical storytelling brings one closer to the other through the cultivation of inter-est, it does not erase difference: In fact, its ethnical promise is built exactly upon the presence of difference.

Despite the ethical promise attached to storytelling, the use of personal narratives is not without its critiques.[114] For example, folklorist Amy Shuman questions the coalitional possibilities of personal narratives because while stories travel and morph through processes of appropriation and delivery, dominant audiences still too frequently presume that they fully empathize with another's life-story based on the stories they have heard. By allowing the audience to experience pleasure that stems largely from misidentification, Shuman argues, stories could "use one person's tragedy to serve as another's inspiration and [could] preserve, rather than subvert, oppressive situations."[115] For Shuman, empathy is suspect because it allows dominant audiences to feel entitled to stories that are not theirs.[116] Critics of empathy thus argue that we

---

110. Benhabib, *Situating the Self*; Cavarero, *Relating Narratives*.

111. Cavarero, *Relating Narratives*, 90.

112. Benhabib, *Situating the Self*, 159.

113. Lyon, *Deliberative Acts*, 86.

114. For example, Lynch, "Rhetorics of Proximity"; Rothfelder and Thornton, "Man Interrupted"; Shuman, *Other People's Stories*.

115. Shuman, *Other People's Stories*, 5.

116. Shuman, *Other People's Stories*.

cannot interrogate the promises of storytelling without a rigorous critique of empathy.

The model of deliberative empathy I posited above addresses these valid concerns of co-optation and misrecognition. Unlike affective empathy, which colludes with politics of identification, deliberative empathy is not contingent upon the erasure of difference, nor does it prioritize the pleasure of the dominant audiences. As a result, while I do emphasize the ethical potential of storytelling in creating coalition moments across difference, I envision a different kind of relationship between the storyteller and the audience than ones that encourage co-optation: Instead of claiming the story as their own and using the story to justify their existing worldview, audience members who experience deliberative empathy are prompted to reconsider and revise their current perceptions given the difference they encounter. By always keeping the gap of understanding and experience in the foreground, stories could promote coalitions without recentering the pleasure and interests of the dominant audience.

The power of stories stems exactly from the simultaneous particularity and universality of human experiences, and it serves as a reminder that truth is often contingent upon one's specific subject position.[117] By sharing stories, therefore, interlocutors are necessarily demonstrating the contingency, interconnectedness, and ambiguity of diverse human experiences, while cultivating an understanding of others based on simultaneous commonality and difference rather than assimilation. The emotional, affective, ethical, and rhetorical power of stories invites dominant audiences to reexamine the "moral matrix" they are embedded within—the set of moral values revered by members of the same cultural group—without eliciting binary thinking and emotions that are damaging to coalition-building.[118] By highlighting the specificities, distinctions, and interconnectedness of different lived experiences, stories help generate deliberative empathy among the audiences.

---

117. See Arendt and Schell, *On Revolution.*
118. Haidt, *The Righteous Mind,* 125.

# CHAPTER 2

# Inconvenient Strangers

*South Asians and Gendered Familial Solidarity*

IN LATE 2012, Gill Mohindepaul Singh, a popular Indian actor in Hong Kong who grew up in the city, announced that he would be emigrating to Scotland with his family. Despite the fact that he and his wife both have permanent residency status in the SAR, his wife had recently been denied Chinese citizenship and was therefore deemed ineligible for a Hong Kong passport.[1] As a result, it became difficult for his wife to travel internationally to care for their ailing son who was seeking medical treatment abroad. Because Singh is a popular actor who had starred in many soap operas, soon after his announcement local Hongkongers took to social media to demonstrate their support for Singh and his family—many criticized the Hong Kong Immigration Department for committing the error of barring someone who—unlike the offspring of mainland Chinese maternal tourists—*truly* belonged to the SAR and deserved citizenship.[2] In mid-2013, wearing a shirt that said "I Love Hong Kong" and "I am a Hongkonger," Singh said his teary good-bye on camera before boarding the plane to join his family abroad.[3]

---

1. "I'm a Hongkonger—Q Bo Bo," *Eastweek Magazine*, last modified July 12, 2012, eastweek.my-magazine.me/main/20862.

2. "Q Bo Bo Thankful for Netizens' Support," *The Sun*, last modified July 17, 2012, sun.on .cc/cnt/entertainment/20120717/00470_052.html?pubdate=20120717.

3. "Q Bo Bo Leaves Hong Kong," last modified May 14, 2013, hk.apple.nextmedia.com/ entertainment/art/20130514/18258823.

While Singh eventually returned to Hong Kong without his family to continue his acting career, his initial departure brought mainstream public attention toward the citizenship status of South Asian residents in Hong Kong. Between 2012 and 2013, a group of vocal South Asians—among them a social worker, medical doctor, entrepreneur, and teacher—appealed directly to the Hong Kong public, seeking to be recognized as formal citizens. They claimed that their Chinese naturalization and Hong Kong SAR passport applications had been wrongfully denied by the Immigration Department.[4] While these applicants had resided in Hong Kong for most, if not all, of their lives and most speak fluent Cantonese, they were told off the record by immigration officers that they would never be granted Chinese citizenship and a Hong Kong passport because they "lack Chinese blood."[5] On the other hand, white expatriates from North American and European countries have reportedly faced no such barriers when they decide to naturalize as Chinese citizens in Hong Kong.[6] However, because the Hong Kong government does not release official statistics on naturalization cases based on race and ethnicity, the South Asian community and its advocates could only make conjectural claims that the immigration system favored white expatriates over brown petitioners. The lack of concrete statistical evidence weakened the advocates' argument that the Immigration Department operated on a racist logic.

Despite their mostly anecdotal evidence, like Singh's, these petitioners' pleas received positive attention from the mainstream public even though South Asians have historically been targets of racism at the local and state levels.[7] Following such pleas, many local news reports and documentaries represented the petitioners through a sympathetic light, critiquing what they deemed to be inherent injustice in the SAR's citizenship law. However, Hongkongers' momentary sympathy toward this racialized and historically

4. While disproportionate number of South Asians in Hong Kong are working class or poor because of systematic marginalization, this group of petitioners is composed entirely of middle-class professionals. Their social status and education background give them access to sympathetic politicians and local media; they also help destigmatize the South Asian community and garner more mainstream support.

5. Joanna Chiu, "Ethnic Minorities Make Joint Application for Chinese Citizenship," *South China Morning Post,* last modified April 30, 2013, www.scmp.com/news/hong-kong/article/1226242/ethnic-minorities-make-joint-application-chinese-citizenship; "Rooted in Hong Kong for a Hundred Years, Pakistani Man Rejected for Naturalization; Reason from Immigration Department: No Chinese close relatives." *Apple Daily,* last modified December 13, 2012, hk.apple.nextmedia.com/news/art/20121213/18099692.

6. Sijia Jiang, "More Hong Kong Expats Seeking Chinese Citizenship, Minorities Left out in the Cold," *South China Morning Post,* last modified May 30, 2014, www.scmp.com/lifestyle/article/1521247/more-expats-seek-chinese-citizenship-minorities-left-out-cold.

7. Erni and Leung, *Understanding South Asian Minorities in Hong Kong,* 56.

marginalized population quickly dissipated before it generated any sustained critiques on racism and ethnocentrism. Compared to migrant domestic workers and white expatriates, South Asians occupy a more ambiguous position in this nation-family dyad: While they are racialized and are not deemed as "valuable" as white immigrants for incorporation, they are not considered as alien as migrant domestic workers because of their long ancestral history in Hong Kong. Culturally, racially, and affectively, South Asians occupy a liminal that makes them uneasy outsiders. Their experience and efficacy in negotiating the familial-citizenship complex, therefore, illuminates the rhetorical possibilities and hindrances faced by those who are marked as strangers but nevertheless are within the nation's history and imaginary.

In order to counter the lack of formal recognition and affective ties with mainstream Hongkongers, South Asian petitioners often deploy intelligible tropes of intimacy that evoke family, belonging, and home to justify their claims for legal citizenship. Extending existing scholarship on the ways nuclear reproductive families are used by states to exert biopolitical control, my analysis examines the familial as an ontological metaphor that structures fundamental understandings of citizenship. I argue that while familial tropes of intimacy are intelligible within the mainstream public, the redeployment of such tropes does not necessarily allow racialized Others to disrupt the dominant framework of citizenship and recognition—a framework that privileges the familiar and gives dominant groups the power to decide who deserves to be seen. I, therefore, posit that the repurposing of dominant familial tropes by racialized groups nevertheless reinscribes them in an interpretive framework that equates recognition with a political and legal status bestowed by the nation-state, which subsequently forecloses the opportunity to rearticulate recognition as an ethical encounter across difference.

To illuminate how familial citizenship claims and performances are entwined with racist and neoliberal logics, I also examine instances in which similar arguments are deployed by white Euro-American immigrants who have successfully naturalized. I argue that in the context of citizenship discourse, familial tropes only work for those who are already deemed ideal citizen-subjects through their whiteness and accompanying economic and cultural capital. Racialized and marginalized subjects, on the other hand, can never quite access the promise of citizenship merely by participating in the established discursive framework. What rhetorical resources, then, could liminal subjects mobilize to assert the sense of familiarity and belonging they share with the mainstream citizenry without being subsumed by the dominant interpretive framework of citizenship and the neoliberal nation-family? This chapter answers that question by juxtaposing the rhetorical attempts South

Asian petitioners made within the dominant familial citizenship framework with a diametrically different rhetorical approach: one that decenters formal and political recognition granted by the state, and instead focuses on establishing the shared interests and difference between the South Asian community and the mainstream citizenry.

To interrogate how tropes of intimacy circulate and are interpreted and performed in mainstream citizenship discourse, I first analyze local cultural and legal artifacts related to the citizenship status of South Asians, focusing in particular on a widely broadcasted TV documentary. There, I examine the claims made by five South Asian petitioners and one white petitioner who have been repeatedly interviewed by different forms of local news media. Due to their repeated media appearances, these individuals are the de facto spokespeople on the controversies surrounding Chinese naturalization cases. The claims they make and the tropes they deploy, therefore, are seen by the audience as representative anecdotes by mainstream Hongkongers.[8]

Despite the citywide publicity they received that allowed them to reach many audiences in the mainstream public, the rhetorical efforts of these South Asian petitioners have been largely unsuccessful in challenging the dominant interpretive framework that marks them as outsiders. In the latter part of the chapter, I posit that acts of storytelling outside of dominant citizenship discourse provide more fertile ground for the rearticulation of recognition for racialized subjects. Examining a collection of personal portraits and familial stories of non-Chinese women, titled *She Says: Photographing Ethnic Minority Women of Hong Kong,* I argue that this text prompts the dominant audience to practice deliberative empathy: specifically, to recognize the interconnectedness between South Asian and mainstream Hong Kong women, who are situated within the same economic and sociopolitical power grid albeit their different positions.

Doubly marginalized by their race and gender, the selfhood and experiences of South Asian women often remain unexposed and unvalidated by the public sphere dominated by men and the mainstream citizenry. I posit that by circulating the narratives of South Asian women to the mainstream public, *She Says* is able to expose the power structures that undermine their personhood and to validate their lived experiences against the backdrop of dominant stock stories told from a position of privilege.[9] Because *She Says* comprises photographs and edited interviews executed by local Hong Kong journalists, the experiences and narratives of the women are mediated. While the retell-

---

8. Burke, *A Grammar of Motives.*
9. Martinez, "A Plea for Critical Race Theory Counterstory."

ing of marginalized narratives by members of the dominant citizenry could easily tumble into problematic appropriation that recenters those in power, I demonstrate that the mediation in *She Says* not only provides ontological affirmation to South Asian women by confirming that their stories are worth retelling but also serves as a necessary reminder to the mainstream audience that they could never completely understand or identify with the lives of these women. I argue that the mediated narratives in *She Says* enacts what Dennis Lynch calls "the rhetorics of proximity," which ensures the enactment of critical and deliberative, instead of affective, empathy among the audiences.[10] Finally, I argue that by deemphasizing formal citizenship, race, and national identity as primary categories of belonging and alliance, the stories in *She Says* foster a politics of friendship and political solidarity that "refuse alignment along the secure axes of filiation" but are based instead upon the production of a common cause and shared interests.[11] While the intersectional approach of *She Says,* like most early attempts to destabilize established identity categories, has not led to immediate social change, it nevertheless points to the political and ethical potential in cultivating coalition across difference through familial narratives from the margin.

## HISTORY AND CONTEXT: FAMILIAL TROPES IN HONG KONG CITIZENSHIP DISCOURSE

While scholars have traditionally seen citizenship as "hard on the outside, soft on the inside," as Bosniak argues, this binary is untenable as the state uses citizenship not only to regulate bodies that are outside of the national border but also to impose control over marginalized people within the nation-state.[12] Rhetorical studies, in fact, have paid a lot of attention to such "threshold citizenship matters," attending to the differentials and taxonomies of citizenship once transnational subjects cross national boundaries.[13] They have shown that citizenship rhetorics necessarily engender borders and the distinction between aliens and members of the nation-state.[14] Alienage and acts of alienization, in other words, are endemic to citizenship. For subjects, like the South Asian petitioners in Hong Kong, who occupy the threshold between citizenship and alienage, it matters materially, affectively, and socially whether they could con-

---

10. Lynch, "Rhetorics of Proximity," 11.
11. Gandhi, *Affective Communities,* 10; Visweswaran, *Un/common Cultures.*
12. Bosniak, *The Citizen and the Alien,* 4.
13. Ibid., 14; Cisneros, "Rhetorics of Citizenship."
14. Cisneros, *The Border Crossed Us.*

vince the nation-state that they indeed belong and thus deserve formal recognition. Citizenship, under the dominant neoliberal and familial framework, however, favors bodies that either share kin ties with the existing citizenry and therefore are familiar, or those who possess tremendous economic and cultural capital that would benefit the nation-family.[15]

South Asians who do not fulfill any of these unwritten criteria must therefore repurpose the established familial tropes to highlight the emotional tie and sense of belonging they have developed toward Hong Kong. Indeed, to render themselves visible, recognizable, and legitimate for legal inclusion, South Asians have relied on both emotional and economic arguments to justify their membership—such claims combine tropes of affective ties with the neoliberal logics that good citizens who deserve familial inclusion must be economically productive and independent. The efficacy of such tropes in securing formal recognition, I argue, hinges primarily upon the petitioners' race, socioeconomic status, and how they fit into the dominant national imaginary based on the familial framework. Because of the history of the South Asian community in Hong Kong, South Asian petitioners are unable to successfully secure formal recognition—or recognition of their humanity on its own terms—using solely established familial citizenship tropes.

The South Asian community first settled in Hong Kong in the 1840s during the British colonial administration. Indians and Nepalese were brought directly to Hong Kong first as members of the British military.[16] Considering local Chinese people to be inept and corrupt, the colonial government put South Asians in charge of Hong Kong's police force and prison system. In addition to those brought to Hong Kong as part of the armed forces, South Asians also settled in Hong Kong for economic reasons. To facilitate trades between the British Empire and its colonies, many Indians—and later Pakistanis—were recruited by companies and the government to work as traders and sailors to transport goods in and out of Hong Kong, then a small colonial outpost that connected Britain to the South China Sea area.[17] Associated with the colonial authority, South Asians were not welcomed by the local Hongkongers of Chinese descent. In addition, because of laws that prohibited miscegenation between South Asians and Chinese, there were few opportunities for the two groups to interact positively in everyday life.[18] During that time, wealthy South Asians were given the opportunity to relinquish their original nationality and became British citizens—a coveted symbol of recognition for political and psy-

---

15. Ahmed, "A Phenomenology of Whiteness"; Wingard, *Branded Bodies*.
16. Weiss, "South Asian Muslims in Hong Kong."
17. Erni and Leung, *Understanding South Asian Minorities in Hong Kong*.
18. Plüss, "Constructing Globalized Ethnicity."

chic reasons. The promise of incorporation given to South Asians by the British colonial government intensified the animosity between the South Asian community and mainstream Hongkongers as the colonial government granted South Asians formal recognition and power to control the more alien Chinese subjects. As a result, despite being both colonized subjects in the same locale, South Asians and Chinese Hongkongers never formed any coalition based on shared interests and struggles.

The history and experiences of the South Asian community in Hong Kong illustrate the ways in which colonial power makes use of citizenship as a bait to control its subjects: Those who are deemed more similar and more valuable to the colonizers are given formal citizenship as a reward for their continual deference. As the colonized subjects are valued only for their service and labor to the colonial power, the recognition is unsurprisingly the moment they are no longer useful to the regime. In the 1960s, Britain began to revise its nationality law to limit the numbers of citizenship granted to colonial subjects; as a result of this revision, South Asians in Hong Kong who had relinquished their original nationality for British citizenship would become stateless in 1997, when Hong Kong ceased to be a British colony.[19]

At the end of the British colonial era in 1997, a sizable population of South Asians chose to settle permanently in Hong Kong.[20] After the official return of Hong Kong's sovereignty to China, the material conditions of South Asians became more precarious as Chinese Hongkongers rose to the top of the ethnocratic system and took on positions of power formerly occupied by British officials. Except for a few extraordinarily wealthy Indian families, without the backing of the colonial government, the South Asian community in Hong Kong quickly lost whatever little cultural and economic capital it had accumulated. Emphasizing the importance of building a "Chinese society," the SAR government has since implemented strict Chinese language requirements for all state employees, while systematically barring South Asian children from

---

19. Deane, "Hong Kong Minorities."

20. There are no precise numbers on how many South Asians chose to settle in Hong Kong after 1997 because of the way census statistics were collected in 1996 and 2001. According to the 1996 census report, roughly 3,450 individuals in Hong Kong carried nationalities from South Asian countries; the census conducted in 2001, four years after the return of sovereignty, notes that there were 42,124 individuals of South Asian ethnicities in the city. The problem here is that the number from 1996 did not include all the South Asians who were residing in Hong Kong at the time because some of them held a British National (Overseas) passport and thus were counted under a separate category. Despite the lack of precision, it can still be inferred from the two numbers that a large enough population of South Asians relocated after 1997 to result in the growth in 2001. Hong Kong Census and Statistics Department, "2001 Population Census"; "1996 Population by-Census."

effectively learning Chinese in school.[21] As a result, while prior to 1997 a significant number of South Asians were gainfully employed by the colonial government, particularly law enforcement, they no longer qualified for those positions under the new language requirement policy.[22] Between 1997 and 2007, there were no new hires of ethnic minorities for government positions.[23] Many take on low-paying positions as construction workers or security guards at banks and apartment buildings.[24] Others run small businesses in Tsim Sha Tsui and Jordan—working-class areas populated by some of the first Indian settlers during the colonial era. Many of these South Asian business owners converge in a dilapidated building called Chungking Mansion, participating in what local anthropologist Gordon Mathews calls "low-end globalization" that involves "the transnational flow of people and goods involving relatively small amounts of capital and informal, sometimes semilegal or illegal, transactions commonly associated with 'the developing world.'"[25] Seeing Chungking building as "an alien island of the developing world lying in Hong Kong's heart," local Hongkongers have developed a historical distaste—and even fear—toward it, believing that it houses dangerous dark-skinned criminals and perverts.[26]

While Hongkongers are familiar with the presence of South Asians in the city and do not question the legitimacy of their residency status, they nevertheless are excluded from cultural citizenship and formal Chinese citizenship. At the local level, the needs and demands of the South Asian community are seen as separate from those of the larger Hong Kong public. For example, most community nonprofit organizations are reluctant to provide service to South Asians in their neighborhoods who are in dire need of financial, educational, and professional support.[27] At the state level, the majority of South

---

21. Lai, *Colours of Justice*, 201.

22. Before the Second World War, about 60 percent of the Hong Kong police force was staffed by Sikhs. While this number declined drastically after India gained independence from Great Britain, the Hong Kong colonial government continued to recruit police officers from India and later Pakistan until 1961. However, there are no statistics on the race and ethnicity of government employees prior to the survey conducted by the Civil Service Bureau in 2011, which shows that 0.8 percent of the 26,671 government employees "were of non-Chinese ethnicities." Within that 0.8 percent, some were white. Erni and Leung, *Understanding South Asian Minorities in Hong Kong*. Hong Kong Civil Service Bureau, "Racial Profile for the Civil Service: Surveyed for the First Time," November 2011, https://www.csb.gov.hk/hkgcsb/csn/csn82/82e/features_5.html.

23. Lai, *Colours of Justice*, 260.

24. Erni and Leung, *Understanding South Asian Minorities in Hong Kong*.

25. Mathews, *Ghetto at the Center of the World*, 20.

26. Ibid., 15.

27. Lai, *Colours of Justice*.

Asians who choose to remain in Hong Kong after 1997 hold formal citizenship of their ancestor's home country, together with a permanent residency status in the Hong Kong SAR that grants them the freedom to stay and work without restrictions.[28] These South Asians, however, are not considered legal Chinese citizens because of the Pakistani, Nepalese, or Indian passports they hold. The lack of Chinese citizenship not only confounds their self-identity and sense of belonging, but it also poses complications for South Asians who must travel often between mainland China and Hong Kong for work: Without Chinese citizenship, they cannot apply for a Hong Kong passport and mainland travel permit to and from mainland China, and must instead apply for a visa as an alien every time they cross the border. The lack of Chinese citizenship also prevents South Asians from occupying prominent positions in the government, thus perpetuating the existing ethnocratic hierarchy.[29] While the South Asian community has little economic and political recourse to gain formal citizenship, the desire for it remains in a way that echoes what Berlant calls "cruel optimism": longing for the good life promised by citizenship, when that pursuit is in fact an obstacle to their flourishing.[30]

In October 2012, Radio Television Hong Kong released a documentary titled "Unclear Identity," featuring interviews with several South Asian petitioners whose naturalization applications were repeatedly denied without any clear explanations. While all petitioners featured have previously appeared in local blog posts, newspapers, and magazines, this documentary—broadcast by the city's most popular television channel—allows them to occupy familiar spaces while speaking directly to the Hong Kong public (most in fluent Cantonese) in a more embodied manner. Interviewed either in the intimacy of their home, office, or recognizable neighborhoods in Hong Kong, the South Asian subjects are shown to inhabit the same space as the mainstream citizenry. "Unclear Identity" is a prime platform for South Asian petitioners to demonstrate their eligibility to be admitted into the dominant family vis-à-vis the nation-state.

Displaying their affective ties with Hong Kong and often evoking the family explicitly, many interviewees highlight the pain and despondence the Immigration Department caused them by rejecting their naturalization petitions outright; in these arguments, they liken the experience of legal exclusion to the feeling of being ostracized by one's kin. By evoking the tropes of home and family, South Asian petitioners construct citizenship claims that

---

28. Deane, "Hong Kong Minorities."

29. Article 61, The Basic Law.

30. Berlant, *Cruel Optimism*. Brandzel and Edelman also write about the empty promises of citizenship. Brandzel, *Against Citizenship*; Edelman, *No Future*.

fit the interpretive framework of the mainstream citizenry. However, unlike mainstream Hongkongers who mobilize the family to justify ethnocentric exclusion, the South Asian community is attempting to repurpose such tropes to rearticulate the boundary of the national family so that they will be recognized not as strangers but as members of the nation-family. While public responses to the documentary were largely positive, with many Hongkongers expressing sympathy toward the petitioners, they never gained enough traction to warrant an official response from the government. The continual public indifference toward South Asians demonstrates that this community is still not deemed worthy of familial protection.[31]

## SOUTH ASIAN CITIZENSHIP AND THE RHETORIC OF FAMILIAL EXCLUSION AND KINSHIP

In "Unclear Identity," several interviewees make deeply personal and emotional claims as they recount their failed naturalization petitions. The documentary first features Abdull Ghafar "Philip" Khan, a middle-aged businessperson of Pakistani descent who was born and raised in Hong Kong; in fact, Khan's family settled in the city a century ago. Currently holding a Pakistani passport, Khan made multiple attempts to become a naturalized Chinese citizen and to obtain a Hong Kong SAR passport. His applications have always been rejected outright. Claiming that Hong Kong is his *only* home, Khan laments, "Some may think that the Hong Kong passport is just a travel document, but it is so much more than that; it's a symbol of my identity—it's about whether we are Hongkongers."[32] Historically, legal documents like the passport have been instruments for nation-states to "sort out 'who is who.'"[33] As Kate Vieira argues, immigration documents not only denote one's legal status but also materially categorize one's social and political standing.[34] Legal documents, therefore, "provide evidence of where on this rights-and-privileges continuum immigrants lie."[35] Frustrated and furious, Khan turns to the camera and sighs, "Do you not treat me as a member of this big family? [I lost] my sense of belonging. . . . I cannot obtain this passport and this nationality—does it mean that I'm a second-class citizen? At the end, am I really a

31. Yam, "Affective Economies and Alienizing Discourse."

32. "Unclear Identity," *Hong Kong Connections*, Radio Television Hong Kong.

33. Torpey, "States and the Regulation of Migration in the Twentieth-Century North Atlantic World."

34. Vieira, "American by Paper."

35. Ibid.

Hongkonger? It seems not. You treat me as a foreigner, but I have always lived in Hong Kong."[36] While Khan physically inhabits the space of Hong Kong, the rejection he faces when applying for the SAR passport illustrates that he is written out of the nation-family and his claims of affective ties are irrelevant to the state.

In Khan's narrative, home, (re)naming, and identity are all intimately connected. Partly to highlight his sense of belonging and affective tie to Hong Kong and partly for professional reasons, Khan gave himself a Chinese name—Ho-ming Kan—that sounds no different from one a mainstream Hongkonger would have. It is not enough for Khan that he identifies Hong Kong as home and himself as a member of the family whose name blends easily with the rest of the citizenry; rather, he is seeking a reciprocity from the nation-state to affirm the affective ties he has cultivated. With his Hong Kong ID card that signifies his permanent residency status, Khan is technically recognized by the state; however, as Ahmed points out, recognition is also used to estrange someone, to mark them as outside the parameter of the nation-family.[37] The renaming of Abdull Ghafar to first Philip and later Ho-ming marks Khan's desire blend into the mainstream citizenry, so that Hong Kong would truly become a home, "a purified space of belonging . . . where the subject is so at ease that she or he does not think."[38] The Hong Kong passport, in other words, is not only a marker of whether one has earned one's place in the nation-state; it also provides feelings of familial emplacement that are often denied to racialized strangers.

Khan's demonstrations of his emotional ties to Hong Kong are trumped by the state's biological and racial conception of the family. As Khan attempted to submit his naturalization petition the second time, the immigration officer on duty refused to process it. As Khan recounts in the documentary, the officer instead sneered at him, "Don't even think about it—you won't qualify. Don't bother wasting the 1,500 HKD application fee. . . . How can you possibly possess any Chinese blood?"[39] Even though being ethnically Chinese is not a necessary legal criterion a petitioner must fulfill, the immigration officer—echoing dominant racist sentiments against brown bodies—acted as the proxy of the state to exclude Khan on the basis that he does not belong to the dominant biological kinship network. By enacting a *jus sanguinis* model of citizenship law, the officer renders Khan both legally and rhetorically powerless: As someone of Pakistani descent, he would never come to possess any

---

36. "Unclear Identity."
37. Ahmed, *Strange Encounters*.
38. Ibid.
39. "Unclear Identity."

"Chinese blood"; at the same time, the claims of emotional ties he makes can never function as sufficient justification to refute an understanding of family that connects biological kinship to racist ideologies.[40] The different conceptions of the family are incongruent and the rhetorical options for racialized subjects are limited.

Speaking directly to the Hong Kong public in fluent Cantonese as he roams the city streets with great familiarity, Khan prompts the audience members to make political, ethical, and emotional decisions: They could either deny his belonging to the family despite listening to his personal history and seeing the way he inhabits the space, or they could acknowledge the injustice and contradictions at play in the current legal system and advocate for him. The muted public response Khan received, however, illustrates that his emphasis on affective ties cannot overcome a dominant kin-based understanding of the family, an understanding that is simultaneously inflected with racist and ethnocentric logics.

The rhetoric of familial rejection is also employed by Shekhar Madhukar Kumta, an accomplished medical school professor who immigrated to Hong Kong twenty-three years before, whose naturalization petitions were twice rejected outright without any explanation from the government. The documentary first shows Kumta lecturing confidently at one of the most prestigious universities in Hong Kong; it then pans to the rows of awards Kumta has received over the years for his pioneering research and teaching. Dumbfounded by the rejection, Kumta says in English, "It's a very deep hurt. You are contributing to a family and the family doesn't accept you, so you'll feel really sort of hurt and disappointed."[41] Elaborating on his experience with the Immigration Department, Kumta laments, "The whole process feels very blunt and unfair. They just said no, no reason. You feel very frustrated."[42] Kumta then points to the dissonance between the recognition he has received from the government and mainstream public for his academic accomplishments and the repeated rejection he encounters as he attempts to enter the nation-family.[43] Kumta is simultaneously kept close and pushed away by the nation-state. This partial incorporation and exclusion is key for the maintenance of a coherent national identity for the mainstream citizenry as the stranger must be kept at a close proximity to demonstrate the limit of the nation-family.[44] Kumta's and Khan's familial narratives reveal the ways national identity is concretized

---

40. Ibid.
41. Ibid.
42. Ibid.
43. Ibid.
44. Ahmed, *Strange Encounters*.

by the simultaneous inclusion and exclusion of strangers like them—politically unthreatening and economically productive strangers who would allow the dominant nation-state to appear tolerant and "multicultural." While they fulfill some criteria for familial inclusion, their race makes them more suitable as neoliberal economic vehicles than as family members.

## REDEFINING KIN TIES AND NATIONAL BOUNDARIES

Of all the failed South Asian naturalization cases that have been made public, only one petitioner has successfully been naturalized in her subsequent application. This "success story," however, is not a demonstration of a more inclusive and deliberative rearticulation of citizenship; rather, it further highlights the way legal citizenship is conceptualized via kin ties in the private sphere to privilege recognizable sameness. After her naturalization requests were rejected twice by the Immigration Department on the ground that she "did not have Chinese blood" and lacked a formal nationality, Maggie Cheung—a Hong Kong adoptee of Pakistani descent—agreed to be interviewed by several major newspapers and the city's most popular TV station; two days after her interview was released citywide, the Immigration Department accepted her naturalization petition and subsequently asked the media to refrain from following up on the case.[45]

Newspaper and op-ed articles written about this case all represent Cheung as a *true* Hongkonger despite her Pakistani ethnicity: While born to Pakistani parents, Cheung was adopted legally by a local Hong Kong family when she was three months old. In a televised interview, Margaret Ng, a prominent local politician and barrister, weighs in on the legal aspect of the case and critiques the Hong Kong Immigration Department: According to Ng, Cheung should have received legal inclusion the day she was adopted by her Hong Kong parents because the law stipulates that children of all Hong Kong citizens would automatically be granted Chinese citizenship. Ng argues that the Hong Kong Immigration Department is engaging in discriminatory practices that transgress the law. Ng's argument implies that the exclusion of South Asians who are not considered offspring of local Hongkongers is acceptable as they are not part of the kinship network.[46] While Ng supports Cheung's legal inclusion

---

45. Yeung, Tuk-ming, "Pakistani Young Woman with the Heart of a Hongkonger: Repeated Failures with Citizenship Application," *Sina News Hong Kong,* last modified November 18, 2011, www.life.mingpao.com/cfm/dailynews3b.cfm?File=20121118/nalgg/gga1.txt.

46. Ng, Ngoi-yee Margaret, "Maggie's Story."

despite her race, her claim nevertheless follows the *jus sanguinis* logic of existing citizenship laws that privilege ethnocentric kin ties.

Cheung's adoptive background comes into play not only in legal discourse
but also in the ways she is represented by the mainstream Hong Kong public.
As a member of an ethnic minority, her lived experience is certainly different from that of her mainstream counterparts; nevertheless, she is immersed
in a cultural, social—and most importantly—domestic familial context that
Hongkongers recognize. Cheung, in other words, is able to cultivate what
anthropologists refer to as fictive kinship with mainstream Hongkongers:
essential and close affective bonds that are formed not primarily through
biological blood ties but via the sharing of intimate experiences, spaces, and
substance.[47] Gradually, the kinship tie is no longer fictive but becomes indistin-
guishable from one that stems from biological closeness.[48] By living under the
same roof with established members of the dominant national family, Cheung
has come to be recognized as a core member who has deep affective and kinship ties with her local family—and by proxy, with mainstream Hongkongers
at large. As a result, news reports on Cheung's case repeatedly emphasized her
"Hong Kong roots." For instance, in an op-ed celebrating Cheung's successful naturalization, Ng writes: "Legally adopted by a Hong Kong couple, she
received local education and grew up *just like other Hong Kong children.*"[49]

While these reports do give Cheung the room to discuss in her own
voice her experience with the Immigration Department, they nevertheless all
emphasize her "Hongkongness" by repeatedly drawing the readers' attention
to her adoptive background and an upbringing that mirrors the mainstream
citizenry's. What matters more here is not the citizenship claims Cheung herself makes—claims in which she evokes emotional tropes such as injury, hurt,
and the sense of belonging and familial attachment to Hong Kong—but the
feeling among Hongkongers that she also ought to be a Hongkonger because
she has already established kin ties with a local reproductive family. In this
case, the family becomes, as Wingard suggests, part of "a metonymic chain"
that connects the family in the private sphere to the community and the
nation.[50] Because of the primacy of the familial interpretive framework, racialized Others who have filial relationships with members of the mainstream
citizenry are seen as familiar and therefore unthreatening—these private rela-

---

47. Carsten, "The Substance of Kinship and the Heat of the Hearth: Feeding, Personhood,
and Relatedness among Malays in Pulau Langkawi."

48. Carsten, *After Kinship,* 140.

49. Ngoi-yee Margaret Ng, "Maggie's Story."

50. Wingard, *Branded Bodies,* 47.

tions, therefore, become persuasive arguments to justify inclusion.[51] Instead of demonstrating how the racial hierarchy could be undermined to expand the scope of the nation, Cheung's success in fact reinforces the primacy of unthreatening sameness and familiarity in citizenship practices.

Indeed, to further represent Cheung as deserving of Chinese citizenship because of her kin tie to a mainstream nuclear family, news articles supporting her—with a title like "Pakistani Girl with a Hongkonger's Heart"—often emphasize her similarities with mainstream Hongkongers.[52] Another widely circulated news report similarly emphasizes that Cheung was formally educated in Hong Kong, and since graduating from a prestigious local university, has been contributing to society as a secondary school liberal arts teacher.[53] Most reports include a portrait of Cheung standing in a classroom; behind her is a blackboard with the following words written in Chinese: "Identification: recognition, emotion, behavior."[54] These words not only signal Cheung's expertise in teaching liberal arts through her personal experience but also suggest that she is highly educated and well versed in Chinese—in other words, that she is *just like* her middle-class Hong Kong Chinese counterparts. Despite her brownness, Cheung shares many similar experiences and traits with the dominant Hong Kong public. She garners so much media attention by presenting an uncanny redefinition of who a Hongkonger is without disrupting the connections between kinship and the familial framework of citizenship.

Initially, Cheung's race poses a barrier toward legal inclusion as her incorporation would disrupt the existing racial hierarchy that systematically relegates brown bodies. However, the kin ties Cheung has with a mainstream family successfully neutralize the ideological threat her brown body presents. As Ahmed observes, like citizenship, race is understood as an extension of the familial race: The analogical relationship between race and family "produce[s] a particular version of race *and* a particular version of family, predicated on 'likeness,' where likeness becomes a matter of 'shared attributes.'"[55] Cheung's brownness does not hinder her inclusion into the nation-family because it is deemed sufficiently tamed by her adoptive background: Cheung is seen as so much like a mainstream Hongkonger that her race is nothing more than a superficial difference that could be touted as a celebration of multicultural-

---

51. Wingard, *Branded Bodies.*

52. Yeung, "Pakistani Girl with a Hongkonger's Heart."

53. Cheung, "Hong Kong-Born Adoptee Wins Fight for Chinese Nationality," *South China Morning Post,* last modified Nov 18, 2012, www.scmp.com/news/hong-kong/article/1084957/hong-kong-born-adoptee-wins-fight-chinese-nationality.

54. Ibid., Yeung, "Pakistani Girl with a Hongkonger's Heart."

55. Ahmed, "A Phenomenology of Whiteness." 154.

ism. In fact, two years prior to her unpleasant encounters with the Immigration Department, the local news media had already taken a liking to Cheung, frequently interviewing her as she was the only volunteer in the Hong Kong's Civil Aid who was not of Chinese descent.[56] In one of the news articles, the author writes that "Maggie Cheung's Cantonese is more fluent than many Hongkongers, but ironically she doesn't know the Urdu language spoken by Pakistanis."[57] These reports, similar to those in support of her naturalization, represent Cheung as an exceptional case and somewhat of a "multicultural novelty": By accepting Cheung as a citizen, the dominant Hong Kong public is able to retain its desired "cosmopolitan" and liberal image without undermining their ethnocratic conception of family and citizenship.

Cheung's case, however, is an exception because most South Asians are unable to access the kinds of privileged education and economic opportunities that Cheung had—not to mention the emotional tie she was able to establish with the Hong Kong public by belonging to the dominant kinship network through adoption. As a result, even though they evoke similar kinds of emotional and familial tropes as Cheung does, most South Asians are unable to make citizenship claims that propel the mainstream citizenry to advocate for them as if they are members of the family. Such a discrepancy demonstrates that the effects and connotations of tropes not only change as discourse travels across national borders—as transnational rhetoricians have argued—but also shift and fluctuate even when they are circulating within the same local discursive network among the same audiences.[58] The uptake of these tropes, in fact, is more contingent upon the rhetor's existing social position and whether his or her arguments could fit neatly into the dominant interpretive framework.

## LINKING THE FAMILIAL AND THE ECONOMIC: WHITENESS AS NEOLIBERAL EXCEPTION

Attempting to convince the Hong Kong public that they are deserving citizens and family members, South Asians rely on neoliberal tropes of contribution and productivity in conjunction with tropes of affective ties and emotional

56. Cheung Mung-kit, "Eight-dimensional Personalities: CAS Member of Pakistani Descent Turned Golden Master of Ceremony," *Apple Daily,* last modified December 24, 2012, http://hk.apple.nextmedia.com/news/art/20101224/14800182; "Hong Kong Civil Aid Service Welcomes Ethnic Minorities," *AM 730,* last modified December 24, 2010, http://archive.am730.com.hk/article-37983.

57. Ibid.

58. Dingo, *Networking Arguments*; Hesford, *Spectacular Rhetorics*.

intimacy. South Asian petitioners, however, are not the only group who evoke economic contribution as citizenship and familial claims; when asked to explain their swift naturalization process, some of the most prominent Euro-Americans in the SAR often emphasize their wealth and productivity. Despite the similarity between the arguments they deploy and the neoliberal worthiness and affective ties the South Asian petitioners demonstrate, white immigrants are deemed more valuable for incorporation. Influenced by Hong Kong's colonial history and the broader transnational political and cultural context that privileges whiteness, performances of neoliberal values and Hong Kong citizenship are tightly bound up with ideologies of white supremacy. As a result, the rhetorical efficacy and actual economic productivity of South Asians are never quite enough for them to be incorporated as members whose contribution would enhance the "quality" of the nation-family.

To reveal the racial bias in the naturalization process, "Unclear Identity" juxtaposes the interview with Kumta—the accomplished medical school professor—with that of Allan Zeman, a white millionaire who relinquished his Canadian citizenship five years ago.[59] Focusing first on Zeman, the documentary shows a tall, middle-aged white man sitting in the center of a tastefully decorated office with large windows talking to a group of young, professional Hong Kong women. Even prior to this documentary interview, Zeman was no stranger to the Hong Kong audience: A pioneering developer and investor in Hong Kong's tourism and entertainment industry during the colonial era, Zeman is well known for creating the city's first theme park and night-life district—both major attractions for tourists and locals alike that generate tremendous revenues for the SAR. As a result, Zeman has received many accolades from the government; it is also not uncommon to find interviews of Zeman in local newspapers and Western news media like *Forbes,* CNBC, and CNN. Unlike Kumta, whose productivity is largely within the confines of academia, Zeman offers a contribution that constitutes a significant portion of Hong Kong's economy and collective experience.

While the citizenship claims Zeman makes rely on similar tropes of intimacy and productivity that South Asian petitioners deploy, they generate different outcomes because of the way whiteness intersects with neoliberal values and citizenship. Reclining in his office chair, Zeman explains to the camera

---

59. "Unclear Identity." Not long after the documentary was aired, Fermi Wong, the founder of Unison, marched up to the Immigration Department with Margaret Ng, demanding government officials to clarify why they considered Zeman to be making "exceptional contribution" to Hong Kong but not Kumta. They also threatened to submit this case to the High Court for judicial review. Months later, Kumta received an approval of his naturalization petition in the mail. Lai, *Colour of Justice,* 322–23.

why he decided to naturalize: "I've been living in HK for 43 years. I belong and Hong Kong is my home. My family grew up here; my children grew up here all their life. They have only been to Canada three to four times in their life. And so Hong Kong has always been our home. I never thought of anywhere else as being my home."[60] In the documentary, Khan and Jenny Andrews—a third-generation young woman of Indian descent who was born and raised in Hong Kong—both make a very similar claim. In fact, Khan and Andrews mount a much more persuasive argument than Zeman about their sense of belonging: While Zeman speaks in English during the entire interview, both Khan and Andrews speak in fluent Cantonese as both have spent their entire life in Hong Kong, attending local schools and living in middle-class and working-class neighborhoods like the majority of Hongkongers. Khan's and Andrews's claims of home and belonging, however, are rendered irrelevant by the government. The harrowing experiences they had with immigration officials distinguish them from Zeman, a white tycoon whom the Hong Kong government deeply values and respects.

While South Asians are cultural outsiders because of systematic marginalization, Zeman and most upper-class white expatriates in Hong Kong are outside of the mainstream cultural community because they occupy the upper echelon socially, economically, and racially at both the local and transnational levels. However, instead of hindering their path toward citizenship, the outsider status of wealthy white people becomes cultural capital that highlights their superiority over mainstream Hongkongers. By incorporating figures like Zeman into the national family, the Hong Kong public and government are able to reap both cultural and economic benefits that come with whiteness. Successful white businessmen with robust economic and cultural ties with Euro-American countries help position the SAR as a significant hub within the transnational finance-scape. In his interview with prominent Western media, Zeman is portrayed as a savvy and ambitious entrepreneur who has single-handedly reinvented Hong Kong's entertainment and tourism industries.[61] *Forbes*, in fact, refers to Zeman as "Hong Kong's mouse killer" as the local theme park he founded trumped Hong Kong Disneyland in profit—by incorporating a figure like Zeman, Hong Kong is able to surpass even the US.[62]

While Zeman's transnational reputation as a successful businessperson helps attract Western investments to Hong Kong, the incorporation of white entrepreneurs like him into the nation-family is also culturally and ideologically significant. In fact, while Hong Kong's economic development

60. "Unclear Identity."
61. "CNBC Transcript"; Maggie Wong, "Lan Kwai Fong."
62. Kwok and Kwok, "Allan Zeman."

now hinges primarily on mainland China, having ties with Euro-American countries remains highly valued among local Hongkongers. Because of Hong Kong's colonial legacy and the superiority of whiteness that continues to permeate at a transnational level, Western countries symbolize modernity and a privileged cosmopolitan ideal—a national image Hongkongers crave more than ever after the return of Hong Kong's sovereignty to China.[63] The remnants of white supremacy and inferiority complex among the nonwhite colonized population surfaces: It is almost an honor to the government and mainstream public that white expatriates would want to flip the colonial script, join the family, and become one of them.[64] In other words, white people are welcome as family members not only because they are privileged transnational subjects who bring in economic profits but also because their whiteness and previous Euro-American citizenship status render them valuable to Hongkongers' construction of their ideal national and self-identity. On the other hand, historically associated with the lower class, South Asians do not bring with them the same kind of cultural capital that helps enhance the image and reputation of the nation-family.

Not only does race influence the efficacy of one's claim of familial intimacy, it also differentiates the value of one's labor. After claiming their affective tie toward Hong Kong, Zeman and most South Asian petitioners interviewed follow up by emphasizing their contribution to the family through productive labor; their productivity, however, is evaluated differently according to the dominant racial hierarchy. In "Unclear Identity," Zeman—sitting at ease in his luxurious office—references his contribution to Hong Kong to justify his swift incorporation. The documentary then shows Zeman surveying Lan Kwai Fong—the nightlife district he developed that mainly attracts wealthy local Hongkongers, white expatriates, and tourists: Zeman has remade both the actual and symbolic landscape of the city through his modern, cosmopolitan image. Shaking hands with pedestrians who clearly recognize him as a celebrity, Zeman proclaims that he started developing the entertainment industry in Hong Kong thirty years ago as a pioneer. Responding to the allegations that white people like him are given preferential treatment during the naturalization procedure, Zeman nonchalantly states, "I don't think I am privileged. I was not famous when I came here; I became famous by doing things, by helping Hong Kong to become a better place, and that's why I believe I was given the right to become a local."[65] Zeman's claim exemplifies the bootstrap argument that underplays structural inequities and privilege; it also extends a neo-

63. Vickers, *In Search of an Identity*.
64. Fanon, *Black Skin, White Masks*.
65. "Unclear Identity."

colonial racial and power dynamic between him as a privileged, upper-class white male and Hong Kong as a former colony that requires his helpful hand.

The South Asian petitioners in the interview discuss their contribution to the nation-family as well. However, unlike Zeman, who could boldly and securely claim that Hong Kong would be amiss without his labor, many South Asians recount how their productivity is either dismissed or deemed irrelevant or insufficient for their citizenship petition. Economically, South Asians are at a disadvantage because they are marginalized in Hong Kong's education system and professional workplaces. As a result, their race bars them from reaching the same socioeconomic status as a white immigrant.[66] Jenny Andrews recounts that when she applied for naturalization the second time, despite having a full-time job, she was told by the immigration officer that she did not qualify because she was not making enough money to be deemed financially self-sufficient. Jenny left without submitting her application because the officer threatened to have her physically removed from the office.[67] Jenny's earning potential is severely hindered by her race; as a result, despite being a productive citizen, her income still does not qualify her as desirable citizen-subject of the nation-family. Jenny's example demonstrates the insidious connections between race and economic mobility that preclude racialized individuals from performing neoliberal values perfectly—as a result, they are rendered less incorporable than their white counterparts.

The labor South Asians perform does not translate into significant cultural capital that would warrant their incorporation as family members. Characterizing the repeated rejections he encounters as a deep injustice, Jenny's brother, Jeffrey Andrews—Hong Kong's only brown social worker and an avid grassroots activist for minority rights—vehemently states, "I am currently contributing to the [Hong Kong] society, so why can't I obtain a passport? You ask me to pay taxes, but why can't I ask to have a passport?"[68] Similarly, showcasing the awards he had received from the university and from the Hong Kong government, Kumta says that he is baffled by the contradiction: "On the one hand, this community does value my contribution—and there's evidence of that; on the other hand, I find I was completely rejected. And I cannot understand how these two can coexist."[69] While the mainstream public and the state benefit from their economic contributions, their labor and race do not grant them the necessary cultural and economic capital to be members of the family.

---

66. Erni and Leung, *Understanding South Asian Minorities in Hong Kong*.
67. "Unclear Identity."
68. Ibid.
69. Ibid.

By juxtaposing the different contexts in which familial tropes are evoked, I have demonstrated that the citizenship is regulated and performed not only through overt evocations of the reproductive family. Rather, intersecting ideologies on affective ties, race, kinship, and neoliberalism form the familial interpretive framework through which citizenship and the nation-state are understood. This analysis of citizenship discourse among these South Asian petitioners highlights the rhetorical conundrum racialized subjects face as they deploy established tropes of intimacy to seek recognition: By participating in dominant citizenship discourse to persuade the mainstream public of their worthiness of inclusion, racialized subjects inadvertently perpetuate the power hierarchy. As demonstrated by these petitioners' cases, the familial citizenship framework flattens transnational racial and cultural relationships by scaling them down to the intimacy of familial units and values: Sameness and benefits to the local citizenry are privileged as defaults without problematizing the specific historical and social contexts that have given rise to such power relations. This limited scale forecloses the opportunity for there to be an ethical encounter across racial and class lines.

## STORYTELLING AS RHETORICAL REDRESS

Three years after the initial controversy surrounding the citizenship of South Asian residents in the SAR, Hong Kong Unison—the city's most vocal rights-based advocacy group for ethnic minorities—put together an exhibit and a series of events titled *She Says: Photographing Ethnic Minority Women of Hong Kong*. Later released as a book, this collection features individual portraits of seventeen local minority women in their own homes, each with a 300- to 500-word narrative penned by a local human rights journalist.[70]

Together with the gallery opening events, this collection invites mainstream Hongkongers to engage with the South Asian community beyond the dominant framework of citizenship and recognition. Instead, via personal narratives and portraits taken in the intimate home spaces of the women, it moves the audience into an ethical and empathetic relationship with their South Asian counterparts, seeing them first and foremost as subjects sharing similar human conditions that render them simultaneously agentic and subjugated. The women and the audience are implicated together in the Arendtian realm of political interspace—a space that, as Katherine Adams puts it, "pro-

---

70. While the majority of these women are South Asian, one white, one black, and three Southeast Asian women are also included in the collection.

vides a means of centering difference and separation without shutting out the possibility of commonality."[71] As moral psychologists have pointed out, acts of dehumanization and alienization are commonly enabled by the perception of outgroup homogeneity: the assumption that there are no individual differences among members of a racialized group outside of one's social circle.[72] As a rhetorical process, alienization often involves rendering the Other as an aggregate—a mob with little internal distinction that is overpowering and threatening and therefore must be contained.[73] In order to cultivate coalition moments, these habitual tendencies to alienize and dehumanize must be disrupted by narratives that highlight the personhood of individual subjects.

What is necessary for an ethical encounter between the dominant and marginalized subjects is the recognition of what Michael Hardt and Antonio Negri refer to as "life in common": "The multitude is neither an identity, nor uniform (like the masses), the internal differences of the multitude must discover the common that allows them to communicate and act together."[74] The common is akin to the inter-est that simultaneously separates and connects subjects through their shared material concerns. In order for *She Says* to move the mainstream audience into an interspace with the South Asian women in which transformative deliberation could take place, it must be able to effectively address the problem of outgroup homogeneity and misrecognition, while at the same time providing the space for the two groups to cultivate a common that does not obliterate difference.

## THE HUMAN LIBRARY AND THE REIFICATION OF HIERARCHY

Before the exhibit was published and released as a book, Unison hosted a series of events and guided tours that provided the opportunity for mainstream Hongkongers to engage directly with the women featured in *She Says* and other members from the local South Asian community. In addition to the two sharing seminars led by social workers and South Asian community members, Unison set up a Human Library five days after the exhibit opened. Founded in 2000 by the Human Library Organization in Denmark, Human

---

71. Adams, "At the Table with Arendt," 15.

72. Kearns, Betus, and Lemieux, "Why Do Some Terrorist Attacks Receive More Media Attention Than Others?"; Saleem, Yang, and Ramasubramanian, "Reliance on Direct and Mediated Contact."

73. Yam, "Affective Economies and Alienizing Discourse."

74. Hardt and Negri, *Multitude,* 228.

Libraries have now become a worldwide phenomenon. In these events, people from stigmatized groups are "on loan" as books to members from the mainstream citizenry. During the session, library patrons are free to ask the human books any questions, and there is no prescribed structure to the conversations. Past books include refugees, homeless people, people living with HIV/AIDS, and people with disabilities. The organization's mission is to "build a positive framework for conversations that can challenge stereotypes and prejudices through dialogue"; the Human Library is, as the organization describes, "a place where difficult questions are expected, appreciated and answered."[75] Modeled after this framework, the Human Library hosted by Unison was stocked with members of the local South Asian community, including the women featured in the exhibit; each "book" could be checked out by a maximum of five people at the same time for a half-hour conversation. While the Human Library seeks to promote equality between the mainstream patrons and the marginalized "books" by humanizing the latter, its format nevertheless reinforces the existing power dynamic rather than promoting reciprocity and mutual becoming.

At its best, the concept of the Human Library facilitates rhetorical listening as it encourages participants to "listen to discourses not *for* intent but *with* intent."[76] As Krista Ratcliffe clarifies, rhetorical listening fosters a kind of understanding that is better captured as *"standing under"*: standing under specific discourses surrounding both the self and others while acknowledging that our politics and ethics could be shifted.[77] The practice of rhetorical listening echoes the model of invitational rhetoric. Proposed by Sonja Foss and Cindy Griffin, invitational rhetoric decenters persuasion as the goal; rather, it respects the lived experiences and immanence of each interlocutor, as long as they enter into the conversation with the willingness to be vulnerable and have their perspectives enriched or altered by the encounter.[78] To practice invitational rhetoric, the interlocutors must not have the desire to appropriate or assume expertise over someone else's lived experience, nor should they attempt to dominate or denigrate the perspectives of others. Instead of persuading the audience to adopt one's specific view, invitational rhetoric privileges transformations of perspectives that stem from having a deepened understanding of how others have come to see the topic at hand.[79]

75. Human Library, "Origin."
76. Ratcliffe, *Rhetorical Listening,* 28.
77. Ibid.
78. Foss and Griffin, "Beyond Persuasion."
79. Ibid.

While it seeks to promote justice and reciprocity across difference, invitational rhetoric has been criticized by rhetoric scholars for not accounting sufficiently for existing histories and patterns of oppression.[80] Dana Cloud and Nina Lozano-Reich's critique is particularly pertinent: They argue that invitational rhetoric presupposes conditions of equality between interlocutors that are extremely rare.[81] Favoring civility under the guise of supposed equality, they posit, perpetuates respectability politics and the reinforcement of social and rhetorical decorum that is commonly used to silence marginalized people.[82] While Cloud and Lozano-Reich concur that invitational rhetoric is helpful in fostering understanding and dialogues across difference, they do not see the potential for invitational rhetoric to produce substantial social change institutionally or economically.[83]

The problems Cloud and Lozano-Reich identify apply not only to invitational rhetoric but also to the practice of the Human Library: By asking South Asians to politely and patiently explain their experiences to a mainstream audience, the event perpetuates the power difference between the marginalized "books" and the patrons, in which the latter's feelings and desires are prioritized. In their original proposal of invitational rhetoric, Foss and Griffin identify a rhetor and an audience rather than seeing the two parties as equal interlocutors; for them, the responsibility of the rhetor in invitational rhetoric is to make the audience feel safe, and to make the audience aware that they have the freedom and power to choose. The rhetor, on the other hand, is assumed to have the power to orchestrate the foundation of this rhetorical encounter.[84] In the context of the Unison Human Library, the South Asian "books" played the role of the rhetors who must answer questions using their epistemic privilege. Aiming primarily to enhance the understanding of mainstream Hongkongers and to erase the stigma attached to the South Asian community, the Human Library demanded the respondents to perform the emotional labor to be truthful, informative, and educational in a way that does not alienate their audience—audiences who were open, but nevertheless were members of the oppressing mainstream citizenry. In other words, while the Human Library created an aperture for an ethical encounter, it nevertheless was based on a model that asks the marginalized to bear the rhetorical respon-

---

80. For example, Dow, "Feminism, Difference(s), and Rhetorical Studies"; Fulkerson, "Transcending Our Conception of Argument in Light of Feminist Critiques"; Lozano-Reich and Cloud, "The Uncivil Tongue"; Pollock, Artz, Frey, Pearce, and Murphy, "Navigating between Scylla and Charybdis."
81. Lozano-Reich and Cloud, "The Uncivil Tongue."
82. Ibid.
83. Ibid.
84. Foss and Griffin, "Beyond Persuasion."

sibility of explanation. This model perpetuates the harmful assumption that any encounters between dominant and marginalized subjects must privilege the feelings of the former because only their empathy and sympathy could mobilize social change. This assumption reifies the existing power structure as it posits that the dominant audiences do not have to engage in any transformation themselves, and that the future of marginalized subjects is ultimately in the hands of those in power.

In addition, while the face-to-face encounters during the Human Library would very likely produce an empathic response from the mainstream participants, the close physical and emotional proximity between the "books" and the patrons encouraged affective, instead of deliberative, empathy; thus, the patrons were less likely to engage in processes of internal deliberation about how they are implicated structurally with marginalized lives. Unless the audiences are already familiar with how the political, economic, and historical structures have contributed to experiences and material realities of the South Asian community, without the space and time during the interactions to reflect on these connections, they are more likely to be swayed by the immediacy and potency of affective empathy that comes with sitting face-to-face with a stranger who divulges in them the details of their life simply because them have asked.

In this rhetorical situation, it is tempting for the patrons to believe that the appropriate way to act is to experience affective empathy and identification, to believe that they could simply feel their way into the experience of others, rather than to pause, temporarily turn away from the sharing face, and analyze the structural causes of their lived experiences. As Lyon and Shuman point out, the impulse to identify with another often recenters the pleasure of the dominant subject, thus reifying the existing hierarchy rather than promoting the process of transformative deliberation in which the subjectivity of the dominant subject is also in flux.[85] Similarly, as Lynch argues, the promotion of affective empathy between a dominant audience and a marginalized rhetor "is complicit in a depoliticizing culture of self-realization" as it tends to focus on the dominant subjects who register the "right" feelings during the encounter while obscuring the structural and material dimensions of social struggles.[86] For the dominant audiences, what lingered after the encounter at the Human Library, therefore, likely were not questions that invited transformative deliberation, that prompted them to consider how they should reinvent their ethical and political relationships with the South Asian community, but

---

85. Lyon, *Deliberative Acts*; Shuman, *Other People's Stories*.
86. Lynch, "Rhetorics of Proximity," 6.

instead a decontextualized and depoliticized feeling of satisfaction that they have already fulfilled their ethical responsibility through identification and sympathy.

## MEDIATED STORIES AND THE RHETORICS OF PROXIMITY

Transformative deliberation across power difference requires simultaneously a diminished affective distance between the marginalized and dominant interlocutors and a constant barrier between the two so that difference is not subsumed via identification. The Unison Human Library illustrates the difficulty in negotiating this affective tension without reproducing the existing hierarchy. Lynch's "rhetorics of proximity" provides a helpful model here. This rhetorical practice, in Lynch's word, "seduces" the audience closer to the experiences of the rhetor, while always maintaining the impossibility for identification.[87] The rhetorics of proximity move the audience close enough to the subject's experience and perspective so that they are empathically engaged to be in relations with the marginalized Other; at the same time, they put down obstacles to deter affective empathy, prompting the audience to question the extent to which they truly understand the feelings and experiences of another.[88] As Rothfelder and Thornton posit, "only by simultaneously inviting and discouraging empathy can narratives show us the singularity of different experiences and allow us to respect and appreciate these differences rather than colonize and assimilate them into our own life-worlds."[89] By deploying rhetorical strategies that draw the readers closer yet keep them at arm's length, rhetorics of proximity prompt the audience—particularly those who are more privileged than the rhetor—to recognize commonality while always acknowledging the inassimilable difference between them and the marginalized rhetor.

If the Human Library has reified the existing power relations by feeding into the patrons' misguided desire that the distance between them and the South Asian informants would evaporate after the conversation, *She Says,* the printed collection that contains all seventeen portraits and narratives, is more effective in enacting a rhetoric of proximity to promote deliberative empathy. Written in the third person with ample direct quotes from the subjects, these narratives are penned by local journalist Jennifer Ngo based on open-ended interviews she conducted with the women. These narratives cover a wide range of lived experiences, ranging from two young sisters' relationship

87. Lynch, "Rhetorics of Proximity," 11.
88. Ibid.
89. Rothfelder and Thornton, "Man Interrupted," 364.

with each other, to the professional struggles encountered by an attorney, to the grief of a mother about her dead child. Each narrative is accompanied by a portrait of the interviewee. Taken at their respective homes with no specified poses, each portrait shows the persona the subject wants to exude to the audience. While some women are wearing headscarves in their portraits, many are dressed in outfits that are no different from what mainstream Hongkongers commonly wear. I argue that the images and the narrated life stories in the collection simultaneously draw the audiences closer to the commonality they share with the represented subjects while reminding them that the women's experiences are particular to their specific bodies and material conditions, and thus the audiences could never assume complete understanding.

In the prologue, Ngo recounts her interview and writing process: "I've tried to let their stories flow—and focused on whatever they've focused on during our interviews."[90] Despite Ngo's intention to make room for the women's voice to come through in her writing, the form of mediated life stories in *She Says* raises ethical questions about the appropriation of personal narratives by organizations that claim to give voice to marginalized subjects. Examining the ethics and rhetorical functions of reported personal narratives in what she calls "political-support junk mail," Shuman mounts three main critiques of the retelling of personal narratives by a third-party organization: (1) The stories are presented to highlight how the values of the protagonist coincide with those of the organization, thus motivating the audience to donate directly to the organization; (2) the retelling of these stories prioritizes the emotions of the audience, rather than satisfying the protagonist whose experiences are told; and (3) in order to motivate the audience to act on behalf of the protagonist (usually through donations to the organization), these stories posit a clear distance between the privileged audience and the marginalized protagonists to persuade potential donors that they alone possess the agency and power to change the lives of the suffering Others.[91]

The second and third critiques, taken together, point to the failure of generating what Shuman calls "mutual recognition": the understanding that "one's own trauma is tied up with the trauma of another."[92] This distance between the audience and the represented subject is often produced by exoticizing the protagonist and the context in which the story takes place, which reinforces the perception that the audience is not implicated at all in the suffering of others. While like Lynch, Rothfelder, and Thornton, Shuman is critical of the assumption that personal narratives allow the audience to achieve mutual

---

90. Wing-see Ngo, *She Says*, 6.
91. Shuman, *Other People's Stories.*
92. Ibid., 144.

understanding with the storyteller through the experience of empathy, she frames her concern differently: In addition to cautioning against identification in which the audience assumes that the distance between them and the rhetor is dissolved through the story, Shuman also critiques the sense of separation empathy could create. As Shuman posits, "empathy depends on separation and is defined as a relationship that offers distance as a means of gaining per-spectives on lives other than our own."[93] This distance, she argues, allows the dominant audience to occupy the role of a philanthropic agent who is apart from the suffering marginalized subjects whose stories they have just heard.[94] Mediated narratives are particularly suspect here because of the distance the stories have traveled before they reach the audience, thus heightening the chance of uncritical appropriation.

The model of deliberative empathy, together with the rhetorics of proxim-ity, provide a useful intervention to address Shuman's concern. As Rothfelder and Thornton point out, proximity is "a rhetorical effect managed through the interplay of distance and closeness."[95] Instead of dismissing empathy whole-sale because it fails to engage the audience at the "correct" distance, we could understand proximity as a matter of degree that can be negotiated through rhetorical acts. Deliberative empathy is complementary with the rhetoric of proximity as it cautions against the subsuming of difference through identifi-cation, while inviting the dominant audiences to turn the critical gaze upon their own selves and their relations with others. Deliberative empathy, in other words, is founded upon the simultaneous closeness and separation between dominant and marginalized subjects. Mobilizing the frameworks of proximity and deliberative empathy, I demonstrate in my analysis of She Says that while Shuman is rightfully concerned about the ethical implications of the appro-priation of personal narratives by advocacy groups, mediated personal narra-tives are not inherently problematic and unproductive in promoting coalition, nor is empathy always suspect. She Says is able to circumvent many potential pitfalls by presenting the stories in an open-ended and deeply contextualized manner that does not demand a specific interpretation or emotional reaction from the audience.

Rather, targeting mainstream Hongkongers as the main audience, She Says jolts them out of their emotional and political response template by rep-resenting South Asians as unexceptional rather than exotic, sharing similar desires, familial relationships, feelings, and struggles as the audience selves. Absent in these narratives are any demands for the and

93. Ibid., 148.
94. Ibid.
95. Rothfelder and Thornton, "Man Interrupted," 365.

liberators of the women portrayed in the book. While retold and mediated by Unison, some of these narratives challenge the liberal ideological script the organization subscribes to (i.e., the desire to represent the women as empowered neoliberal subjects who nevertheless are oppressed by systemic sexism and racism), and instead draw attention to the women's lived experiences that are not often tellable in a public context (e.g., the ongoing grief for one's dead son; the visceral details of an unexpected childbirth). By allowing the mainstream audiences a glimpse into the women's deeply personal familial lives while disrupting their expectations about what stories are tellable and untellable, these narratives trouble the emotional distance between the audience and the represented subjects, thus enacting a rhetoric of proximity that circumvents both identification and complete separation.

In her critique of political junk mail, Shuman argues that mediated personal stories cater more to the emotions of dominant audiences than the marginalized subjects whose experiences are appropriated because if these stories fail to evoke the right degree of sympathy or affective empathy from the targeted audiences, the advocacy groups would not receive the donations they are aiming for.[96] While Shuman is right in alerting us of the ethical stake in the retelling of life stories from the margin, I argue that the narration of one's story by another could provide ontological validation to marginalized subjects, thus affirming the personhood and the values of their experiences in the public political sphere.

As Arendt posits, while the protagonist of a story is actively revealing herself in a plural political space through her actions, the significance and implications of her deeds nevertheless continue to elude her; a spectator and narrator, on the other hand, could see the meaning and give shape to the story that defines the selfhood of the protagonist in a political space.[97] The value of having one's story narrated by another is, therefore, twofold: first, the narration provides "ontological affirmation" to the represented subject by bringing her selfhood into a political space of relations, thus validating that her life story is worthy on its own term, and second, it enacts reciprocity in the process of the telling and retelling of one's story.[98] As Cavarero describes, "I tell you my story in order to make you tell it to me."[99] The act of reciprocal narration cultivates a politics of friendship between the narrator and the narrated subject that helps create coalition moments between the two. The retelling of someone else's personal stories need not privilege the rhetorical effects

---

96. Shuman, *Other People's Stories.*
97. Arendt and Canovan, *The Human Condition.*
98. Cavarero, *Relating Narratives,* 56.
99. Ibid., 62.

the narration would have on a more dominant audience; rather, it can be an inherently valuable process for the marginalized subjects who tell their stories so that they could be narrated and have their humanity recognized by another.

The simultaneous hypervisibility and invisibility of South Asian women in Hong Kong makes the narration of their life stories by another all the more pressing and significant. While their brownness renders them a distinct, alien Other who does not fit into the nation-family's racial and cultural milieu, the presence of South Asians in the city is widely seen by mainstream Hongkongers as normal, unremarkable, and therefore also dismissible. In addition, because of their gender, the subjectivity of South Asian women is often subsumed into the domestic duties they perform as mothers, wives, and caretakers. They, like Cavarero posits, lack the "public scene of reciprocal and interactive exhibition" in which their selfhood is validated and they are seen on their own terms.[100] The narration of the women's life and familial stories by a Hong Kong journalist, therefore, functions as an affirmation of their unique existence and as a sign of reciprocity between the two parties—by telling their stories to the journalist, the women entrust the journalist to tell the stories not only to a wider mainstream audience but also back to themselves to satisfy the desire to have their selfhood recognized by another.

## CONSTRUCTING SUBJECTIVITY AND AGENCY THROUGH FAMILIAL TALES

Without any overt demand or plea for formal recognition, the narratives in *She Says* do not fit into the conventional genre of citizenship and recognition claims Hongkongers expect to hear from the South Asian community that portray them as victims of racism in need of sympathy and support from the mainstream citizenry.[101] In a rhetorical situation in which power relations are imbalanced and recognition is withheld for some, storytelling makes it possible for marginalized subjects to, as Jackson posits, "restore viability to their relationship with others, redressing a bias toward autonomy when it has been lost, and affirming collective ideals in the face of disparate experiences."[102] The narratives in *She Says* accomplish these goals by disrupting the dominant interpretive frameworks Hongkongers subscribe to: specifically, to challenge the assumption that the lives and interests of South Asians do not intersect

---

100. Ibid., 57.
101. Erni and Leung, *Understanding South Asian Minorities in Hong Kong.*
102. Jackson, *The Politics of Storytelling,* 37.

with theirs at all because South Asians are not readily intelligible as members of the nation-family.

The women featured in *She Says* are shown as subjects on their own terms—subjects who do not fit neatly into the cultural, gender, and political expectations Hongkongers have of South Asian women. This disruption unsettles how the audience perceives South Asian women: Instead of viewing them as helpless subjects who seek one-sided sympathy, the audience is prompted by the disruption to consider the women as agentic interlocutors who demand reciprocal engagement from them. In addition, by portraying the way race and gender intersect to produce specific material conditions and lived experiences, *She Says* produces a second kind of disruption in mainstream public discourse on ethnic minority and women's rights: It reminds not only the readers but also other advocacy groups that race and gender are not disparate but intersecting categories that ought to be addressed intersectionally.

The first few familial stories in the collection challenge the simultaneously racialized and gendered conceptions about South Asian women; namely, these stories undermine the neocolonial thinking that brown women who stay home as caretakers must have been disempowered by their sexist cultural traditions or the lack of educational opportunities in their home country. This assumption coheres with the dominant transnational neoliberal discourse on gender mainstreaming that defines an empowered woman as someone who is a member of the productive economy and is able to make a living wage.[103] Under this ideology, women who merely labor in the domestic sphere are seen as either oppressed, victimized, or not fulfilling their responsibility in the productive economy. Given the prevalence of neoliberal ideology and ethnocracy in Hong Kong, this narrative is often left unchallenged by the nation-state and advocacy groups. A few South Asian women, however, make use of *She Says* to assert how they would like to be seen outside of this dominant stock narrative.

Abeer's chapter begins with a portrait—printed as a two-page spread—of her standing in her living room. In the picture, Abeer—a young South Asian woman—wears a light-blue hijab and a patterned pastel-colored shalwar kameez; she looks directly at the camera and holds a faint yet confident close-lipped smile. The decorations of the living room behind her reveal that she lives in some form of affordable housing, with multiple big locks on the teal front door and multiple bills and letters pinned to the wall right above an old fuse box. This image posits an encounter between the audience and Abeer in a way that emphasizes Abeer's racial and cultural difference from

---

103. Dingo, *Networking Arguments.*

mainstream Hongkongers. Based on this image, the audience could easily see Abeer according to their preconceived notion of a brown woman—a stranger, or perhaps an exotic Other, who has little relevance to their own lives and experiences.

The narrative, however, troubles this presumed distance by enacting a rhetoric of proximity that invites the audience to reexamine their initial assumptions about Abeer and their relations with her. The narrative opens with a direct quote from Abeer: "Moving to Hong Kong was to secure a future, but I was not supposed to forget our culture, religion, and their limits on me."[104] This quote further marks Abeer's difference and distance from mainstream Hongkongers: Instead of claiming a sense of belonging to Hong Kong, as the South Asian citizenship petitioners examined earlier in this chapter did, Abeer unabashedly brings to the forefront her cultural background that does not fit into the national imaginary of mainstream Hongkongers.

Switching to a third-person narration, the essay then describes how Abeer came to reside in Hong Kong: her father, after having lived in the city for twenty years, brought Abeer and her sister to Hong Kong from India when Abeer was sixteen years old. Abeer was left to take care of her father and stepmother a year later when her sister went back to India for marriage. Here, the narrative diverges from the expected liberal representation of a brown woman victimized by her own culture and familial traditions. Recounting the years after her sister was gone, Abeer says, "It was not what I expected. I was preparing to be a housewife like my sister."[105] Instead of staying home as a caretaker, Abeer found a job as an interpreter for a social service organization: "I worked for a year taking basically no holidays. I loved it."[106] Abeer's professional position and her passion for her career challenge the preconceptions many audiences likely have toward South Asian Muslim women; it thus demands the audience look at the portrait again through a different lens—one that is inflected not by dominant representations and misrecognition of Muslim women, but by Abeer's own narrative that showcases her career drive. The passion and work ethic Abeer articulates cohere with the self-enterprising narrative that mainstream Hongkongers laud and subscribe to.[107] As Kun and Pun argue, in order to shift the economic responsibility from the state to individuals, the SAR government has always encouraged Hongkongers to devote themselves to their professional lives and to pull themselves up by their bootstraps by being resourceful and independent. Abeer's discussion of her job,

---

104. Wing-see Ngo, *She Says*, 21.
105. Ibid.
106. Ibid.
107. Ku and Pun, *Remaking Citizenship in Hong Kong*.

therefore, is readily intelligible to the mainstream audiences. While her story may reinforce values of neoliberalism, it nevertheless challenges the presumed distance between her and the audiences who often assume that they have little in common with South Asian Muslims. The troubling of distance prompts the audience to experience critical empathy rather than apathy or identification with Abeer.

A few other women in *She Says* also make use of familial tales to defy common racial and cultural stereotypes about South Asian women. Bushra, a Pakistani woman who completed a master's degree in business administration before she immigrated to Hong Kong, fondly recounts her father's courage in granting all seven of his daughters the opportunity to pursue higher education. In her portrait, Bushra wears a brightly colored floral khimar and sits on the ground next to a washing machine with her daughter leaning against her, the girl coyly yet directly staring at the camera with a mischievous smile. While this image fulfills the cultural and racial stereotype that Muslim women are confined to the domestic sphere by their culture, Bushra openly challenges this conception. She explains that while Pakistani women are usually not expected to appear in public interviews and photographs, she decided to participate in *She Says* with her four-year old daughter because she "want[s] to change how people perceive Pakistanis. [She] want[s] people to know that in Pakistan, education is considered important—and there are no restrictions for girls either."[108] Bushra continues by discussing the dreams she has for her daughter: "At least master's—hopefully in engineering or computer sciences. . . . But actually, I won't force her—like how I wasn't forced either. I'll let her choose."[109]

Bushra's narrative changes the typical subject position South Asians occupy: Instead of appealing to the mainstream Hong Kong audience from a position of lesser power, Bushra claims epistemic privilege and uses it to debunk common stereotypes.[110] While Bushra is speaking to mainstream Hongkongers, her narrative does not see successful persuasion or education of the audience as its main rhetorical purpose. Rather than attempting to convince the audience to relinquish their misconceptions, Bushra's narrative centers on the gratitude she extends to her father, the dreams she has for her daughter, and her own career aspirations and plans to overcome the alienization she experiences in Hong Kong.[111] Bushra's narrative, in other words, allows her to bear internal witness to the experiences and values that are

---

108. Wing-see Ngo, *She Says*, 38.
109. Ibid.
110. Narayan, "Working Together across Difference."
111. Wing-see Ngo, *She Says*, 38,

important to her and her loved ones. While to an extent this narrative is self-affirming regardless of the audience, by making clear her intention to debunk common misconceptions about Muslim women, Bushra demonstrates that she is fully aware of the public and political values of her intimate familial narrative. Bushra's chapter makes clear to the audiences that for them to be privy to Bushra's personal and familial life, they must hear it on her terms, even though it may unsettle their preconceived notions and prompt them to reconsider their assumptions.

In *She Says,* the women's senses of agency and self-empowerment are intimately connected to their familial relationships. As Jackson points out, "the source of the energy that both motivates and structures storytelling is the existential tension that informs every intersubjective encounter—a tension between being for oneself and being for another."[112] Stories are grounded in relationality among subjects, and the way these relations shape one's sense of self and perception of the world. Family, as a key social unit that informs human relationships and intimate bonds in both the public and private spheres, thus provides the backdrop for one's life story and the construction of one's selfhood. For example, Abeer's agency is demonstrated not only through her passion for her job but also by her status as a breadwinner for her family back in India. Soon after her sister left Hong Kong, Abeer's father and step-mother returned to India; after realizing that her family would likely never return to Hong Kong, Abeer found herself alone in a city with high living standards and very little money to her name. While struggling to pay rent, Abeer continued to work and remit most of her income to her father. Reflecting on her financial decisions, Abeer notes with a sense of pride, "When I became the breadwinner and was sending money back to my family, I was suddenly respected. I was the one supporting so many back in India."[113] The respect she received became a potent motivation for her to return to the workplace after becoming a mother. While Abeer's story mirrors the phenomenon of female migrant workers becoming the primary source of financial support for their family through remission—a phenomenon caused largely by a neoliberal framework that exploits gendered labor—in Abeer's story, she represents herself as someone who has made a conscious financial choice and has benefitted from the decisions she made amid circumstances beyond her control.[114] She is not in need of sympathy of rescue from the audience. By disrupting the conventional image of South Asian women as objects of pity

---

112. Jackson, *The Politics of Storytelling,* 47.

113. Wing-see Ngo, *She Says,* 21.

114. For more discussions on the labor of migrant female workers, see Chang, *Disposable Domestics*; Ehrenreich and Hochschild, *Global Woman.*

by embracing how the neoliberal script of productivity has contributed to her self-esteem and status, Abeer's narrative troubles the affective and social distance between her and the mainstream audience.

Abeer's story, however, does not adhere entirely to the ideologies and representations of neoliberalism either. Later in the narrative, Abeer challenges the neoliberal logic that brown women only become agentic and empowered if they work outside of the private sphere and participate as part of the productive labor.[115] She does so by emphasizing how much she values her husband and child, in conjunction with her professional ambition: That is, Abeer celebrates her labor in both the domestic and public spheres and does not see her decision to become a stay-at-home mother as disempowering. After recounting the difficult years during which she lived alone in Hong Kong to support her family in India, Abeer chuckles, "Nothing turned out the way I planned, and I got to plan nothing—except my marriage."[116] While Ngo does not provide any direct quotes here, she writes that Abeer described at length how she first met her husband as she cooed to their newborn daughter. At the time of the interview, Abeer had quit her job and was a full-time caretaker to her daughter. Despite the effusive affection she had toward her spouse and child, Abeer planned on returning to the workforce:

> A woman can handle many things and achieve many things. Being a housewife is very honorable. My time in Hong Kong is not enough. I've worked in NGOs, but I'd like to try the commercial world too. I want to be able to live independently, be able to support my family. To be a good housewife, a good mother and a good worker. There is still a long way to go in Hong Kong.[117]

In describing the intersections between her home life and her professional trajectory, Abeer once again brings to the forefront the intersubjective tension between being simultaneously subjugated and an agentic subject: She cannot plan for much that happens in her life, yet she still has some agency in making decisions about her familial relationships and, to some extent, how she wants to pursue her professional career.

Undergirding Abeer's hopefulness and openness about her future, however, is a different form of neoliberal feminism that encourages middle-class women to provide both domestic and productive labor because they suppos-

---

115. Dingo, *Networking Arguments*.
116. Wing-see Ngo, *She Says*, 21.
117. Ibid.

edly can "have it all."[118] While Abeer's story may not have completely escaped the dominant discourse of gender mainstreaming, it nevertheless troubles the assumptions held by the mainstream Hongkongers that brown women are different from them because they are subservient and dwell only in the domestic sphere. By debunking such misconceptions and by placing the emphasis on the familial love between these South Asian women and their family members, these narratives illuminate the social and emotional similarities between South Asian women and the Hong Kong audience. As Newendorp and local social scientist Siu-Kai Lau point out, Hongkongers "define themselves in relation to certain idealized views of the 'Chinese family,'" in which familial interests trump individual and broader social concerns.[119] The familial stories of South Asian women therefore illustrate to the mainstream audiences the commonality they share despite their cultural and racial differences.

The families presented in Abeer's and Bushra's narratives belong staunchly in the category of biological kinship; however, unlike the exclusionary usage of kinship in dominant Hong Kong citizenship discourse, these familial narratives evoke an almost universal love for spouse and children and the aspiration for loved ones to prosper. These stories invite an empathetic affective encounter between the audience and the women across difference through the care they extend toward their respective circle of concern. At the same time, rather than prompting the complete erasure of difference, these stories highlight the distinctiveness of each woman's experience and selfhood, not just from the mainstream Hong Kong audiences, but also from each other. In fact, the affective and ethical potential of these familial narratives stems exactly from their simultaneous particularity and universality: If a story is too individualistic, it risks erasing the shared structural forces and material conditions that contribute to such experiences. On the other hand, a universal story does very little to humanize the storyteller and highlight the narratable self of the subject whose stories are being told. What must be conveyed in these acts of storytelling, then, is the simultaneous separation and togetherness among the narrated subject, the narrator, and the audiences who are connected across difference within the web of human relationships and material conditions.

The interspace and closeness between the mainstream audiences and the represented South Asian women is cultivated partly through the emotional power of familial stories. Sairah's narrative about the death of her son illustrates how a deeply intimate and personal familial tale acts on and moves an audience across racial and cultural difference into an empathetic relation-

---

118. For critiques, see Rushkoff, "No, You Can't Have It All"; Slaughter, "Why Women Still Can't Have It All."

119. Siu-kai Lau, *Society and Politics in Hong Kong*; Newendorp, *Uneasy Reunions*, 182.

ship that does not require complete identification. Unlike Abeer, Bushra, and most other women featured in *She Says,* Sairah never articulates any sense of self-empowerment through work or conscious choices; rather, her narrative is filled with uncertainty and her lack of control over the unexpected circumstances in life. The narrative begins with a stark description from Ngo: "Her little boy told her he was thirsty, so she turned around to find a sip of water while he lay on the hospital bed. . . . And those were the last words she heard her little boy speak."[120] Sairah's son slipped into a coma unexpectedly. Sairah recounts seeing her son have violent seizures in the intensive care unit after she sent him to the hospital, and "he never woke up."[121]

While the audience is aware of Sairah's otherness because of her portrait (like Bushra, Sairah is wearing a khimar) and her discussions of Pakistan as her homeland, the recounting of her son's sickness and eventual death transcends racial and cultural difference, prompting the audience to move closer to Sairah. While particular to Sairah, her familial story and the grief she experiences highlight the uncertainty and looming loss in a human condition shared by all of us. Taken together, Sairah's identity as a Pakistani Muslim woman and her grief confound the audience's established emotional template for responding to her story and to her as a subject. According to the dominant imaginary of the nation-family, Sairah is a racialized alien subject who should always be kept at arm's length; her experiences and the emotions she expresses, however, render her human and close the affective and social distance between her and mainstream Hongkongers.

Represented most often as either helpless subjects who need rescuing or as violent, incomprehensible, and irrational men who threaten the safety of mainstream Hongkongers, South Asians are rarely portrayed in public discourse as having deep emotional bonds with their loved ones the way mainstream Hongkongers do.[122] Contrary to the dominant imaginary of South Asians, Sairah is not violent, nor is she asking the audience for help or acceptance. Instead, she communicates a grief that, while intelligible to the audience, does not fit neatly into dominant perceptions of the South Asian community and South Asians as persons with unique life stories. The audience cannot default to their usual political and emotional response based on their preconceptions

---

120. Wing-see Ngo, *She Says,* 57.

121. Ibid.

122. See Erni and Leung, *Understanding South Asian Minorities in Hong Kong.* In 2009, a Hong Kong police officer shot and killed an unarmed homeless Nepali man. Before Unison intervened, mainstream news reports praised the officer for his courageous act and described the victim as an insane and violent beast that could not be reasoned with. For a detailed account of the event and subsequent reporting and investigation, see Lai, *Colours of Justice.*

of South Asians. While sympathy could be an appropriate emotional reaction here, Sairah's narrative does not seek pity. In fact, unlike the political junk mail that Shuman critiques, Ngo and Unison do not mobilize Sairah's story of grief to garner donations or ideological support from the audience. What remains, then, is the opportunity for the audience to encounter Sairah as a unique individual not defined entirely by her racial and cultural difference, but whose familial story reminds the audience to consider the precariousness of their own lives, specifically how despite their relative political and racial dominance, they too are constantly acted upon by circumstances and forces beyond their control.

Despite the lack of an established emotional and political template to respond to Sairah's story about her grief, this chapter nevertheless betrays Ngo's desire to adhere to the liberal script of empowerment: namely, to portray her interview subjects as having successfully exercised their agency and competence to overcome structural disadvantages. After devoting the first four paragraphs of Sairah's narrative to chronicling her son's illness and medical journey, the narrative shifts into Sairah's reasons for immigration and discussions of her career and her general experiences in Hong Kong. It appears that Ngo is attempting to maintain consistency among the narratives by making sure to include details about Sairah's life in the city outside of her son's death. Ngo reports that Sairah works at a nonprofit as an interpreter to assist other ethnic minorities; despite Sairah's respectable profession, Ngo writes, "Life is hard when you're not familiar with the language, and is even harder when the host community isn't particularly friendly to foreigners with darker skin."[123] While Ngo does not didactically criticize the racism prominent and widely endorsed in mainstream Hong Kong culture, she nevertheless attempts to portray Sairah as a heroic figure who has achieved self-empowerment against societal odds and has defied the racial and cultural stereotypes against brown Muslim women in the public sphere. While Sairah may not be exceptional the way Zeman and other white tycoons are, Ngo nevertheless attempts to portray her as a different kind of exceptional neoliberal subject: a resilient and self-enterprising brown woman from a developing country who, despite personal tragedies and structural racism, manages to succeed in her professional life.

Sairah, however, rejects such a representation. Interrupting her discussion of Sairah's social and professional experiences in Hong Kong, Ngo writes, "However, when we asked her about her life and her dreams, Sairah didn't speak much about her work—even though she takes great pride in it and what she has accomplished. Her hands clasped, her voice soft, Sairah spoke of her

---

123. Ibid., 57.

son."[124] Sairah's refusal to follow Ngo's narrative template shifts her story from a critique of racism and a triumphant tale of liberal self-empowerment to one that emphasizes subjugation—not subjugation to the nation-state or the mainstream citizenry, but to the precariousness of the human condition and the unwavering sense of loss, grief, and love that comes with it. Sairah's son passed away after she and her husband took him on a long trip back to Pakistan, hoping that they would find a cure there. Sairah recounts the day when her husband lifted their son in his arms for a bath: "I took one look at my husband and I knew he was gone."[125] Instead of ending on an optimistic note of aspiration like most other narratives in the collections do, Sairah's story ends up with a solemn direct quote: "My dreams died with my son. Now I just want to take life day by day. I cannot look that far."[126]

Sairah's narrative is about the intimacy of motherhood and the love, trepidation, and grief that it carries. The demand for citizenship or recognition as a successful neoliberal subject has no place in her story. By forcing Ngo to recount a story that otherwise is untellable in this specific social context, Sairah compels the audiences to recognize the human condition shared by all, regardless of their relative social privilege. Sairah's narrative mobilizes deliberative empathy among the audiences because it refuses to let them settle on a comfortable distance: After witnessing Sairah's love and grief, the audience cannot easily turn away, but at the same time, they also cannot ignore the otherness of Sairah's brown body. What they could do with this constant troubling of proximity is instead to reconsider their affective, social, and ethical relations with Sairah and the interconnectedness between them.

## INTERSECTIONALITY AND SOLIDARITY
## ACROSS DIFFERENCE

While motherhood in Sairah's narrative is one about grief and the precariousness of lives, it emerges in other stories as a rhetorical instrument that invites solidarity among women across racial lines. Motherhood, in other words, is mobilized to close the emotional and perceived sociopolitical and ontological distance between the mainstream audiences and South Asian women. As a Nepali, Sangita's racial difference as a brown woman is never lost on the audience; yet, infused with her blunt sense of humor, Sangita's narrative of her childbirth and postpartum depression emphasizes not so much her racial

124. Ibid.
125. Ibid.
126. Ibid.

otherness but the economic, physical, and emotional challenges working-class women across races encounter in Hong Kong.

Sangita's narrative opens with a list of eclectic jobs she has held even though she is only in her early twenties: She has been a dance teacher, has worked at a law firm, and most recently is a licensed bobcat operator on construction sites. After discussing how she has learned to make do by developing diverse skill sets, Sangita quickly launches into her experience birthing her daughter:

> I was working that day [on the construction site], and when I got to the bathroom—usually people have their water break first, but I started bleeding first. And that day there was only men around! All of us were so young. I was taken to the hospital and it was so painful, I fainted at some point. They poured water over my face to wake me up! After giving birth I was exhausted. . . . And the first thing I woke up, I was like: I'm hungry, can you get me something to eat![127]

This vignette is intimate and visceral. It is exactly this viscerality—the pain, the hunger, the blood—that fully demonstrates Sangita's humanity in an embodied fashion. Like Sairah's story about the death of her son, Sangita's birth narrative captures a significant moment amid our human condition. By bearing witness to the experiences of life and death, the audience is inevitably implicated within "the web of human affairs" with subjects who are otherwise represented and seen as aliens through the dominant citizenship framework.[128] Confronted with Sangita's intimate viscerality, the audience must question the primacy of their current interpretive lens: How much valence should one give to a sociopolitical system that systematically devalues the lives of those who, despite their difference, inhabit the same set of human conditions?

Sangita's narrative about her bodily and social experience as a mother and a brown woman suggests the possibility for the cultivation of alliances across dominant racial and cultural divides. As feminist scholar Aimee Carrillo Rowe posits, "alliances are affectively charged sites of connection in which intimacy and power become entwined."[129] The basis of an alliance across difference, Carrillo Rowe argues, must always entail a politics of relations that sees experience, agency, and consciousness (understanding of lived experiences) as interconnected parts within networks of power.[130] Akin to Levinas's

---

127. Ibid., 47.
128. Arendt and Canovan, *The Human Condition,* 204.
129. Rowe, *Power Lines,* 4.
130. Ibid., 11.

alterity ethics that privileges being for others, a politics of relations urges us to move away from an individualized notion of the self toward a sense of longing and belonging with others based on the recognition that one's being is constructed via intersubjective relationships, that the self and self-interests are always transforming based on ongoing negotiations and deliberation with others.[131] As Carrillo Rowe poignantly states, "belonging precedes being."[132] The undergirding principle behind the politics of relations coheres with that of transformative deliberation: In both, the self is posited as always in flux, and subjected to change as it enters into relationship with others. There is no a priori being, but a constant process of becoming through relationality and engagement.

While the impulses to belong and to identify often follow established and seemingly fixed identities along national, racial, and cultural lines, Sangita's and Sairah's narratives suggest that it could be otherwise. Inviting the audience to enact deliberative empathy through the renegotiation of their proximity with South Asian women, these narratives posit that alliances need not and should not be built upon the identification of absolute sameness, familiarity, and symmetry. Rather, they could be powerfully fostered by simultaneously recognizing difference and shared conditions and interests. By focusing on their emotional and bodily experience as women and mothers while foregrounding their racial difference, Sangita and Sairah prompt the mainstream Hong Kong audience to practice what Carrillo Rowe calls differential belonging: forms of belonging that recognize the shifting and sometimes contradicting politics behind them and the performances and conditions such politics produce.[133] As Carrillo Rowe explains, differential belonging "allows us to move among different modes of belonging without feeling trapped or bound by any one in particular. The point is not to be correct, consistent, or comfortable."[134] Rather, this practice acknowledges that identities and one's perception of one's interests are constantly in flux as they are constructed in relations with others through transformative deliberation, or the mutual constructions of inter-est.[135]

Interpreted this way, differential belonging is similar to Arendt's concept of the interspace that acknowledges the simultaneous separation and overlapping interests among unique individuals; it also echoes Leela Gandhi's concept of an affective community founded on "invisible affective gestures that

---

131. Ibid, 27; Levinas, *Otherwise than Being.*
132. Rowe, *Power Lines,* 27.
133. Ibid., 28.
134. Ibid., 40–41.
135. Adams, "At the Table with Arendt."

refuse alignment along the secure axes of filiation to seek expression outside, if not against, possessive communities of belonging."[136] Contextualized familial tales that evoke deep affective connections and viscerality are productive in establishing relationships among interlocutors beyond the dominant interpretive framework of citizenship—a framework that seeks to annihilate difference within the mainstream nation-family, unless the difference, like whiteness and wealth, marks one as more superior than the existing citizenry.

While the life story of a working-class South Asian woman is typically not considered worth telling to the mainstream public, Sangita's narrative prompts the audience to adopt an intersectional approach while exercising deliberative empathy to consider the structural causes of Sangita's experience. After recounting her dramatic birth experience, Sangita reveals that she has struggled with postpartum depression: "Not everyone has courage to speak up about postpartum depression. . . . All mums could go through this, and it's important to share the experiences."[137] Continuing to advocate for women with depression based on her personal experience, Sangita's narrative shifts from the visceral, emotional details of motherhood to systematic discrimination. Acknowledging her Nepali identity, Sangita reflects that she has nevertheless experienced more discrimination as a woman than as a person of color. Treating race and gender as two separate, rather than intersecting, categories, Sangita continues:

> If I were a man, it'll be enough for me to get a secure job in construction. . . . But people think women are only good for low-class jobs. Even if I got my license they ask: can you really operate a bobcat? People always think, oh she's here for housekeeping, or she's here to make coffee. There is no advancement.[138]

While Sangita does not take an overtly intersectional approach here, her claim that women—like South Asians—are systematically disadvantaged posits that social injustice also influences those who identify as mainstream Hongkongers. Her narrative opens up a space that invites the mainstream female audiences to recalibrate how they define their positionality and interests vis-à-vis their relationship with Sangita's experience. As Arendt makes clear, given the way material contexts influence all those who are caught up in them, public politics are inherently heterogenous: While individuals may distinguish themselves as different from one another, their togetherness in this "world of things" never-

---

136. Gandhi, *Affective Communities*, 10.

137. Wing-see Ngo, *She Says*, 47.

138. Ibid.

theless binds them to act in relation to each other.[139] By deliberating together, the interlocutors' self-interests begin to turn into overlapping inter-ests that prompt all parties to see identities not as fixed but rather as co-constituted in relations. For racialized and doubly marginalized subjects like South Asian women, the cultivating of this interspace through familial and personal narratives is more productive for what Karma Chávez calls "coalitional moments" than the participation in mainstream citizenship discourse.[140]

If Sangita's narrative appeals primarily to working-class women and mothers, Puja's story makes clear that gender—particularly when it intersects with race—hinders the professional development and self-esteem of even educated, middle-class women. After overcoming the stigma among the Hong Kong Indian community to forgo marriage and study abroad at Harvard, Puja returned to Hong Kong and found that her race and gender put her at a disadvantage professionally. Puja recounts her experience as a barrister with a shrug: "Lay clients didn't value an Indian lawyer—especially a woman. This is true especially with Chinese clients."[141] She continues to explain that especially in criminal case, "Caucasian barristers were typically the first pick, followed by the Chinese ones. The brown-skinned female barristers seemed to be at the bottom of the pecking order."[142] The hierarchy Puja articulates mirrors the ethnocratic structure of Hong Kong's mainstream society. Puja has since left her job as a barrister and now teaches classes on race, gender, and law at a local university, where she continues to experience bias from her predominantly Hong Kong–Chinese students.[143] Puja's narrative challenges the common perception among the mainstream citizenry that the impact of racism would miraculously disappear from someone's life once they have achieved professional, publicly sanctioned success. By articulating the discrimination she continues to face as a brown woman in an ethnocratic society, Puja prompts the audience to rethink the stronghold race and gender as social categories and hierarchies have on one's life, despite one's individual efforts and accomplishments.

Currently, race and gender are treated as separate rather than intersecting identity categories by activists and advocacy groups in Hong Kong. In recent years, several women's rights groups have been established based on the understanding that gender disproportionately marginalizes brown women; as such, they have devised intersectional programs to address poverty and

139. Arendt and Canovan, *The Human Condition*, 168.
140. Karma Chávez, *Queer Migration Politics*, 8.
141. Wing-see Ngo, *She Says*, 75.
142. Ibid.
143. Ibid.

access to professional and education opportunities.[144] However, the oldest and largest advocacy groups for women in Hong Kong, such as the Hong Kong Federation of Women's Centres and the Hong Kong Federation of Women, continue to focus only on women of Chinese descent, including female mainland Chinese immigrants, who are heavily stigmatized by the mainstream citizenry. However, they do not provide any specific service directed toward South Asian women, whose needs are vastly different from Chinese immigrants'. Meanwhile, nonprofit organizations that serve ethnic minorities rarely emphasize structural obstacles encountered by women in that population. For example, Unison—the largest and most vocal advocacy group for South Asians in Hong Kong and the sponsor of *She Says*—promotes policy changes and social opportunities for the South Asian community at large, but it has not devoted any specific resources to serve the women in that population. By complicating the distance and proximity between the mainstream citizenry—particularly Hong Kong women—and the South Asian women in the anthology, *She Says* challenges the dominant perception that identity categories are always stable and exist as discrete entities. The intersectional narratives in *She Says* instead help generate room for the mainstream citizenry and activists to deliberate the shared interests between South Asian and mainstream Hong Kong women despite their differences, and how social resources and programs could be implemented in a way that takes into account intersecting identity categories and experiences.

## CONCLUSION

In this chapter, I have juxtaposed rhetorical acts performed by marginalized South Asians within the dominant citizenship discourse with those that lie outside the parameter of formal recognition by the nation-state. I have demonstrated how the former attempt, despite its complicity in perpetuating the familial interpretive framework for citizenship, has been largely unsuccessful in allowing South Asians to secure the recognition they seek from the nation-state, which includes but also transcends legal citizenship status; as Khan, Singh, and Kumta explain, citizenship status is significant because it serves as an ontological and affective validation for their sense of belonging and self-identity.[145] Citizenship, or formal recognition, in other words, cannot be severed from the deep yearning to be seen by others on one's own terms—to be

---

144. HER Fund and the Women's Foundation are the most prominent examples.
145. "Unclear Identity."

seen and acknowledged despite differences that should not and could never quite be erased.

It is exactly the state's refusal to fulfill this yearning that makes the rejections of citizenship such a "deep hurt" for South Asians in Hong Kong, as Kumta puts it in the interview.[146] The narration and subsequent circulation of the familial stories of South Asian women, on the other hand, sidestep the state and the citizenship apparatus and instead rearticulate this yearning as the desire to be recognized for one's humanity, on one's own terms. Rather than abiding by the interpretive framework of citizenship that always seeks to stabilize and uphold the dominant imaginary of the existing nation-family, the telling and retelling of stories from the margin produces an intersubjective space between the marginalized protagonists and the more privileged audience—a space that prompts interlocutors to acknowledge their simultaneous togetherness and separateness within the shared web of human conditions and materiality.

By deploying the rhetorics of proximity in their personal narratives, marginalized rhetors not only are able to reclaim their sense of unique selfhood through the acts of storytelling but also problematize the distance between them and their more dominant audience, prompting the latter to reconsider simultaneously the commonality and separation they share with those they consider Others under the dominant imaginary of the nation-family. Instead of responding to otherness with either exclusion or identification, the audiences are now prompted and given room to engage in a way that invites a rearticulation of their ethical and political relationships with marginalized subjects. These stories, therefore, serve as Arendt's proverbial table that brings together subjects from different positionality and provides them a space for transformative deliberation through which one's sense of self and interests are reexamined in relation to others'.

---

146. Ibid.

CHAPTER 3

# Uneasy Recognition and Proximity

## *Strangers in the Home*

IN 2014, Indonesian domestic worker Erwiana Sulistyaningsih publicized the horrendous abuse she suffered at the hands of her Hong Kong employer. After she was severely beaten and tortured for months, Sulistyaningsih was sent home with only a few dollars in her pocket.[1] While the abuse of domestic workers is not uncommon in Hong Kong and many other receiving countries of migrant women, Sulistyaningsih was the first to openly condemn her former employer in front of mainstream news media for the physical and emotional abuse she had suffered; she also allowed the media to release photographs of her wounds and critical physical condition in order to bring public attention to the exploitation and abuse of domestic workers.[2] While there are many previous cases of reported abuse, none of those victims talked directly to mainstream news media the way Sulistyaningsih did. Sulistyaningsih's public testimony thus became a watershed moment in migrant advocacy in Hong Kong. Her story made both local and international headlines, with *Time* condemning the Hong Kong government for allowing "modern-day slaves."[3] Sulistyaningsih's former employer was sentenced to seven years in prison, but years after the abuse, local newspapers and international media such as *Forbes* and the *Guardian* continued to report on the ongoing exploi-

---

1. Chiu, "Indonesian Helper, 23, in Critical Condition."
2. Parry, "Beaten, Hit with an Iron, Doused in Bleach."
3. Liljas, "Beaten and Exploited."

tation of migrant domestic workers in Hong Kong, referring to the system as "forced labour."[4] Sulistyaningsih's abuse not only highlights the precarious work conditions imposed on domestic workers but also provokes conversations about how the current labor system dehumanizes migrant women and erases their personhood.

Unlike the South Asian residents in Hong Kong whose ancestors arrived at the beginning of the colonial era, Southeast Asian migrant workers did not enter Hong Kong en masse until 1974, during the city's economic boom.[5] As of November 2017, there are 360,000 migrant domestic workers in Hong Kong—most of them female and from Southeast Asian countries like the Philippines, Indonesia, and Thailand.[6] The term *Filipino* in Hong Kong has become almost synonymous with *domestic workers*.[7] Southeast Asian women, regardless of their ethnicity or nationality, are commonly referred to by mainstream Hongkongers as *bun mui*—Filipina servant girls. South Asian women, in other words, are simultaneously racialized and gendered as *naturally* suited to perform domestic labor. As such, they are considered valuable by the Hong Kong government and mainstream citizenry only as servants who perform intimate domestic labor, and never as potential members of the nation-family.

Mainstream public discourse and immigrant policies make clear that migrant women are never considered incorporable; they thus, as I will later demonstrate, do not represent migrant women as people whose humanity deserves recognition beyond their scripted roles as workers.[8] Performing intimate labor in local families does not translate into admission into the nation-family. Because of their alien status, coupled with the intimate nature of their labor performed right in the homes of local employers, the behaviors and appearances of domestic workers are constantly scrutinized and treated with suspicion by mainstream Hongkongers.[9] The most popular online forum for parenting, Baby Kingdom, dedicates an entire discussion board for employers to complain about their domestic workers and to exchange tips on how to police their behaviors to make sure that they remain docile.[10] In public libraries, it is easy to find handbooks written for new employers, portraying incendiary and extreme scenarios in which domestic workers purposefully starve

---

4. In, "Helper Abuse Still Widespread"; Hampshire, "Forced Labour Common"; "'Nothing Has Changed.'"

5. *Vallejos v. Commissioner of Registration*, HCAL 124 (2010), 14.

6. Siu, "Hong Kong Will Need 600,000 Domestic Helpers in Next 30 Years.'"

7. Constable, *Maid to Order in Hong Kong*.

8. Ibid.; Constable, *Born Out of Place*.

9. Constable, *Maid to Order in Hong Kong*.

10. So, *Migrant Domestic Workers*.

their employer's children, steal valuables around the house, or seduce their male employers.[11] As I demonstrate in this chapter, such negative discourse and sentiments against domestic workers function in tandem with governmental control on citizenship and foreign gendered labor to strip migrant women of their humanity, so that their only role and identity in Hong Kong is defined by their undervalued domestic labor.

While formal citizenship and permanent residency status, as many critical race and immigration scholars have pointed out, do not necessarily entail full protection and recognition of humanity for the gendered and racialized bodies of migrant women, residency status in Hong Kong nevertheless is a critical factor in determining how precarious their life may be.[12] While South Asians discussed in the last chapter are subjected to systematic discrimination and racism, their permanent residency status in the SAR nevertheless affords them a degree of privilege: They could legally work anywhere in the city, they are free from the fear of deportation, and their children will automatically become Hong Kong permanent residents as well. Migrant domestic workers, however, are not only further down the ethnocratic structure in Hong Kong because of their race, countries of origin, and socioeconomic background, but they are also on the more precarious end of spectrum because of their immigration status.

As temporary guest workers who are categorically excluded by the Hong Kong Immigration Ordinance from ever obtaining permanent residency, their legal status and right to work in Hong Kong are always contingent upon their local employers. Without their jobs in Hong Kong, most migrant women will not be able to pay back the thousands of dollars they owe to employment agencies in their home countries, or to support their family members back home who rely on their remission.[13] Coupled with public discourse that chastises migrant women whenever they perform their identities and personhood outside of the script of the docile servant, migrant women's precarious immigration status and their subsequent economic dependency on their employers have severely limited their ability to advocate for themselves and to assert their humanity outside of their job function.

The fight for permanent residency status is seen as crucial by advocacy groups and unions for migrant domestic workers because it would entail the dismantling of the Foreign Domestic Helpers (FDH) Scheme, a strict set of

---

11. Ibid.

12. For second-class citizenship among African Americans and Latinx immigrants in the US, see Allen, *Talking to Strangers*; Alexander, *The New Jim Crow*; Plascencia, *Disenchanting Citizenship*; Constable, *Born Out of Place*.

13. Constable, *Maid to Order in Hong Kong*.

labor and immigration policies the Hong Kong government has in place to regulate migrant workers.[14] The FDH Scheme not only imposes restrictions on the workers' living conditions, employment, and length of stay but also regulates the affective ties migrant workers develop and maintain with, respectively, the SAR and their home country. Applied only to migrant domestic workers but not to skilled labor from Euro-American countries, the FDH Scheme makes it mandatory for domestic workers to reside in the homes of their employers. The material conditions created by the scheme render Southeast Asian women economically and socially dependent on their employers in Hong Kong, which promotes systematic exploitation of gendered, domestic labor through the transnational neoliberal economy.

Attempts made by advocates to alter the terms of the FDH Scheme have been largely unsuccessful.[15] As a result, legal appeals to claim migrant women's eligibility for permanent residency became an attractive option in the early 2010s: The permanent residency status would allow them to circumvent the control imposed by the FDH Scheme and to gain economic and political leverage over their employers. To accomplish that, domestic workers must demonstrate in court that they should be treated like other foreign nationals who enter Hong Kong legally. If migrant domestic workers could successfully become permanent residents, they could pursue different forms of employment and would be free to switch employers whenever they desire. In addition, they would also be able to sponsor their spouse, children, and parents to join them in Hong Kong. Gaining permanent residency status would free migrant women from the chokehold of the current labor and immigration systems that render their material conditions precarious and take away the opportunity for them to live as people who have their own intimate familial and sexual relationships outside of their job.

Because Hong Kong is a semiautonomous region rather than a sovereign state, and permanent residency in the SAR does not carry the same legal and political connotations as state citizenship, Hong Kong permanent residency status nevertheless is similar to formal citizenship in many ways, particularly in the economic and immigration freedom it affords to foreign nationals. While migrant domestic workers and the South Asian community are both racialized and marginalized in Hong Kong, the quest for migrant women to obtain permanent residency differs significantly from the naturalization

---

14. As Nicole Constable points out in *Maid to Order*, the term *foreign domestic helper* carries strong negative cultural connotations that justify the marginalization of migrant women. In my own analysis, I refer to these women as domestic workers, unless I am referencing the language of official legal documents or popular discourse among Hong Kong employers.

15. "'Nothing Has Changed.'"

cases examined in the previous chapter. As Nicole Constable points out, the processes and meanings of acquiring permanent residency and citizenship are politically and legally distinct.[16] While naturalization entails changing one's nationality to become a citizen of a different state, obtaining permanent residency status (e.g., the "green card" in the US) does not have such a requirement. Regardless of the subject's nationality, Hong Kong permanent residency denotes the right of abode in the SAR, namely, "the right not to have imposed upon him any condition of stay, and the right not to be deported or removed."[17] In addition, permanent residents, including the South Asian petitioners in chapter 2, are allowed to take up any forms of employment in the SAR, and are granted the right to vote in local elections and run for office at the district councils.[18]

Additionally, while South Asians are legally eligible to obtain Chinese citizenship under the Basic Law, migrant domestic workers are excluded categorically and explicitly from applying for permanent residency by an added provision in the Hong Kong Immigration Ordinance. The legal differences surrounding the two populations' claims to formal recognition reflect the disparate public attitudes mainstream Hongkongers have toward the two groups. While the mainstream Hong Kong public is receptive to the familial citizenship claims made by South Asian petitioners because of their community's long ancestral lineage in the city, migrant domestic workers are not privy to this rhetorical opportunity: Seen as foreign and welcomed in Hong Kong only to fulfill the SAR's labor need, migrant women are unable to gain the same kind of public sympathy if they mobilize familial claims of belonging.

Between 2010 and 2012, Hong Kong was embroiled in heated debates both in and out of the courtroom over whether migrant domestic workers should be granted permanent residency in the SAR after they fulfilled the mandatory period of continuous residence stipulated by the Basic Law. This two-year-long lawsuit was brought on by Evangeline Vallejos, a Filipina domestic worker who had been working in Hong Kong since 1986. While the Basic Law stipulates that foreign nationals who enter Hong Kong legally are eligible

---

16. Constable, *Born Out of Place*. While Chinese citizens or children born in Hong Kong to at least one Hong Kong permanent resident parent are immediately qualified for the right of abode, non-Chinese citizens above the age of twenty-one only qualify if they have established ordinarily residence in Hong Kong for seven continuous years prior to their application. Rather than following the *jus sanguinis* model like Chinese citizenship, the Hong Kong permanent residency system is based on a combination of the *jus sanguinis* and *jus soli* models: The status is inherited from one's parents, but it can also be achieved by actively demonstrating one's intention to establish residence in the SAR.

17. Immigration Ordinance Cap. 115, 2A.

18. Legislative Council Ordinance, Section 27.

for permanent residency after seven continuous years of ordinary residence, an impugned provision in the Immigration Ordinance categorically excludes domestic workers, along with "illegal immigrants, detainees and refugees," from being considered as "ordinarily residents" of the SAR.[19] By categorizing domestic workers as extraordinary residents—that is, persons not in Hong Kong "for a settled purpose"—this provision bars domestic workers from ever being eligible for permanent residency.[20] The counsel for Vallejos argued that the provision is unconstitutional as "ordinary residence" should be defined according to the subject's voluntary intention to settle in Hong Kong, rather than by the government's legally arbitrary addition to the Immigration Ordinance.[21] At the time of the lawsuit, approximately 300,000 domestic workers would have been eligible for permanent residency should Vallejos win the case.[22] The ruling about migrant workers' right of abode, therefore, had significant economic, cultural, and political consequences to the SAR government and the mainstream citizenry. Given the racialization of migrant domestic workers and the public sentiments of distrust and skepticism directed toward migrant women, the mainstream Hong Kong public was outraged by the workers' attempt to secure permanent residency.[23]

In the first half of this chapter, I contextualize the courts' judgments and Hong Kong's labor and immigration policies used to regulate migrant domestic workers within the neoliberal economic and political framework. I examine how the Hong Kong government exercises biopolitical and affective control over migrant domestic workers by regulating their physical and emotional connections with their employers and their own family in their home country. While family functions as a trope evoked by South Asian petitioners to demonstrate their emotional tie to Hong Kong, in this case family is evoked primarily as a social unit in the private sphere; I interrogate how it, despite its intimate and domestic nature, is co-opted by the nation-state to erase the personhood of migrant women. Analyzing the policies and laws that justify the categorical exclusion of migrant domestic workers from permanent resi-

---

19. Immigration Ordinance, Cap. 115, Section 2(4)(a) (1997).

20. Hong Kong Immigration Department, "Meanings of Right of Abode and Other Terms."

21. *Vallejos v. Commissioner of Registration*, HCAL 124 (2010).

22. Man, "In Hong Kong, a Setback for Domestic-Worker Rights"; Drew, "Maids Test Residency Rules in Hong Kong."

23. An opinion poll conducted during the lawsuit shows that local Hongkongers were concerned that allowing domestic workers to become permanent Hong Kong citizens would put pressure on the public welfare, education, and medical systems. Bradsher, "Hong Kong Court Denies Foreign Domestic Helpers Right to Permanent Residency." Ethnographic work on Hong Kong employers also suggests that there was a great deal of animosity directed toward domestic workers during the legal dispute. Constable, *Born Out of Place*.

dency, I trace the constraints and neoliberal economic ideologies imposed on non-normative subjects by mainstream citizenship discourse in the legal context. I argue that given the ways citizenship law and immigration policies are inflected by neoliberal practices and values, migrant domestic workers cannot fruitfully make use of legal discourse on formal recognition to assert and validate their personhood.

While arguing for formal citizenship in court may appear to be the most direct and efficacious rhetorical and political strategy for domestic workers to be recognized as subjects instead of economic tools, the dominant rhetorical and interpretive framework for citizenship in fact forecloses the opportunity for migrant workers to be seen as humans (a "who") beyond the economic and gendered duties they provide (a "what"). Indeed, as the court judgments made clear, during the two-year trial, the intention, desires, and personhood of domestic workers were rendered irrelevant in the courtroom, nor had this court case addressed any systematic exploitation entrenched in the labor policies surrounding migrant domestic workers. While the Court of First Instance ruled in favor of Vallejos, the Court of Final Appeal—much to the relief of the Hong Kong government and the mainstream public—overturned that ruling. If the central goal is for migrant women to escape their scripted role as disposable servants and be seen as persons with unique selfhood, my analysis of the judgments demonstrates exactly how participation in the legal citizenship discourse is counterproductive to that aim. As the court judgments make clear, legal recognition granted to migrant domestic workers would not result in a shift in the existing cultural and political scripts of citizenship in which only mainstream citizenry and skilled Euro-American immigrants are regarded as members of the nation-family. Participation in mainstream citizenship discourse via state-sanctioned rhetorical platforms, in other words, does not allow racialized and gendered transnational subjects to be recognized as persons whose interests and subjectivity intersect with those of mainstream Hongkongers.

Sulistyaningsih's shocking abuse was publicized two years after the court case concluded. While mainstream Hongkongers made it clear through numerous protests and petitions during the permanent residency trial that they did not think domestic workers deserve to be included into the nation-family, they were very quick to condemn Sulistyaningsih's former employer and express sympathy for workers who had been similarly abused.[24] While such sympathy was short-lived and has not led to any substantial policy

---

24. Drew, "Maids Test Residency Rules in Hong Kong"; Siu, "New Employee Abuse Victims Emerge."

changes on the labor conditions of domestic workers, it nevertheless motivated workers and their advocates to mobilize different rhetorical tactics to highlight their humanity beyond their role as maids.[25] Located outside of the dominant citizenship framework, these alternative rhetorical responses make use of personal narratives written by migrant women and transnational storytelling to reestablish the humanity of migrant domestic workers, and to cultivate a critical empathetic response among the local audience and solidarity between the workers and local Hong Kong women.

In the latter part of this chapter, I perform rhetorical analysis on *Wishing Well*, an anthology of personal narratives written by domestic workers, and *Migrant Domestic Workers: Strangers at Home*, a transnational ethnography written by a Hong Kong journalist who is herself an employer. I understand these texts as alternative rhetorical responses to formal citizenship claims and as ways to address the injustice migrant workers encounter outside of the model of formal recognition. I interrogate how storytelling and narratives provide rhetorical recourse for workers and their allies beyond dominant citizenship discourse. Particularly, I explore how the family—often a discursive and biopolitical mechanism for states to regulate marginalized bodies—is recuperated in storytelling as an affective site of invention for workers to illuminate their narratable self and personhood outside of the prescribed scripts of formal citizenship and gendered labor. In addition, the emotions associated with families prompt mainstream audiences to experience empathy toward the workers, instead of immediately resorting to the established feeling template of anger, suspicion, and defensiveness. As the center of conflicting affections, desires, and ideologies that connect the private and public spheres across transnational terrain, the family elucidates how the intimate lives of migrant domestic workers and local employers alike are impacted by structural and material forces beyond their control. Despite the power imbalance and the cultural and socioeconomic differences between the two, they nevertheless share and are harmed by the material conditions created by neoliberal logics.

Since storytelling is a performative act that, as Langellier points out, "*does something* in the social world," it matters not only whose stories are told but also how they are told.[26] For familial narratives to effectively evoke deliberative, instead of affective, empathy among mainstream audiences, they must highlight how the familial bonds and the experiences documented in the stories are grounded in a material context shared by both the narrated subject

---

and the dominant audience. Paying special attention to this criterion, I argue that *Wishing Well* perpetuates the emotional and social divide between the mainstream audiences and the workers by implicitly condoning the existing neoliberal labor and economic structure and by depoliticizing the narratives of migrant women. The audiences, as a result, are prompted to experience only momentary sympathy, pity, or affective empathy for the migrant women—none of which, as Spelman points out, are effective in prompting a more sustained concern, unease, and investment among the audience that would promote necessary internal deliberation.[27] On the other hand, by taking a transnational approach to unveil the shared material interests and struggles between domestic workers and their female employers in Hong Kong, *Migrant Domestic Workers* provokes the audience to experience deliberative empathy, thus cultivating the room for transformative deliberation. More importantly, *Migrant Domestic Workers* highlights the simultaneous difference and commonality between the two groups, which helps foster what Gandhi calls "dissident friendships" between domestic workers and local women that would help undermine an economic structure that binds them both.[28]

## CONTEXT AND HISTORY OF THE FDH SCHEME

Since the permanent residency lawsuit sought to free migrant women from the tight regulation of the FDH Scheme, the history and material ramifications of the scheme were highly relevant in Vallejos's lawsuit; in fact, they were used by Chief Justice Ma at the Court of Final Appeal as legal evidence that the SAR had never intended to admit migrant domestic workers as ordinarily residents for settlement purposes.[29] In this section, I interrogate how the neoliberal logics embedded within the FDH Scheme intersect with the construction of the nation-family and the mutation of the family as a social unit; I demonstrate how the Hong Kong government's regulation of affective ties and familial relationships is essential to the maintenance of its economic interests. In addition, I illustrate the ways in which the FDH Scheme obscures potential coalition moments between migrant women and their female employers, despite the fact that both are limited by gender expectations.

In their judgments, Justices Lam and Ma explained that the influx of migrant domestic workers began in the mid-1970s, when Hong Kong's

---

27. Spelman, *Fruits of Sorrow*.
28. Gandhi, *Affective Communities*, 10.
29. *Vallejos v. Commissioner of Registration*, HCAL 124 (2010); *Vallejos v. Commissioner of Registration*, FACV 19&20 (2012).

export economy was developing rapidly. In fact, exports from Hong Kong had increased from 54 percent of its GDP in the 1960s to 64 percent in the 1970s.[30] This economic boom created a growing middle class, and it also motivated and necessitated more women to become part of the productive labor force. As a result of women joining the workforce, the demand for domestic labor increased. Soon, the colonial Hong Kong government began to recruit migrant women from Southeast Asian countries to meet such needs. The demands for migrant domestic workers continued to increase over the years since the return of Hong Kong's sovereignty to mainland China. The Hong Kong government projects that by 2047, the demand for migrant domestic workers will rise to 600,000.[31] By outsourcing feminized and undervalued reproductive labor to migrant workers from developing countries, middle-class Hong Kong women are partially freed from their gender roles of staying in the domestic sphere to pursue higher-paying jobs within the productive economy. At the same time, the import of migrant domestic workers further privatizes reproductive labor, which in turn allows the Hong Kong government to skimp on providing necessary public infrastructures for care work.[32] The FDH Scheme, in other words, was born out of and is now sustained by the neoliberal economic ideology that diminishes the government's role in social support, while outsourcing domestic labor to marginalized transnational subjects. Due to the lack of public support in caregiving, middle-class Hong Kong women often have to choose between being a stay-at-home caregiver and hiring a full-time domestic worker so that they can continue to participate in the productive economy and enjoy the economic freedom and power that comes with their employment.

While the decision to hire a stranger—a stranger who has been vilified by mainstream news media, no less—to live in one's home to perform some of the most intimate labor may seem perplexing to many, the demand for domestic workers is fueled by a neoliberal economy in which domestic work is undervalued and not supported by the state; families, therefore, have few alternative options.[33] In Hong Kong, to qualify as a "middle-class family" that is eligible to hire a migrant domestic worker, the family only needs to prove to the government that the household generates at least HK$15,000 (approximately US$1,912) a month.[34] Given Hong Kong's notoriously high living standard, a household income of HK$15,000 would not allow for a middle-class

---

30. Schenk, "Economic History of Hong Kong."
31. Siu, "Hong Kong Will Need 600,000 Domestic Helpers in Next 30 Years."
32. So, *Migrant Domestic Workers.*
33. Parreñas, *The Force of Domesticity.*
34. GovHK, "Hiring Foreign Domestic Helpers."

lifestyle at all. As a result, while local employers are relatively wealthier than the migrant women imported to Hong Kong from developing countries, many of them still struggle economically. Their financial struggle is compounded if their family consists of young children or elderly people in need of care. Without public support, families with two working adults often have to resort to expensive private day care or nursing homes. Child care for toddlers averages about HK$3,121 (US$400) a month.[35] Since the minimum wage of a domestic worker is only HK$4,410 (US$562) a month, it is more cost-efficient for a Hong Kong family to hire a live-in maid to perform caregiving and other domestic work, such as cleaning and cooking. That way, the employer's family can continue to be a dual-income household without having to pay any exorbitant fees for caregiving.

Because hiring a domestic worker is sometimes the only economically viable option for a local working- or middle-class family to make ends meet while fulfilling the needs of everyone in the household, the needs and personhood of the worker are often dismissed. For example, while illegal and exploitative, it is not uncommon for employers to share their domestic workers with extended family members or have domestic workers work at their family business.[36] These practices allow local employers, who themselves may be struggling economically, to maximize the use they could get out of migrant bodies.[37] Given their competing economic interests, the relationship between migrant domestic workers and many mainstream local employers, particularly female employers, is always a contentious one: From the employer's perspective, if she does not utilize the labor of the domestic worker to the fullest extent, she herself may have to shoulder more economic and domestic responsibilities than she is willing to.[38]

Despite such common exploitative practices, due to the ever-increasing economic disparity between developed and developing countries, even educated middle-class Southeast Asian women are motivated to participate in this transnational labor flow. Being a domestic worker in wealthy locations like Hong Kong, Singapore, and Dubai carries more potential for upward mobility than white-collar jobs in their home country.[39] The remissions from migrant domestic workers, in turn, contribute not only to the economic well-being of their own family but also to their home country's national econo-

---

35. Ka-kuen Lau and Bland, "The Cost of a Family in Hong Kong."
36. Constable, *Maid to Order in Hong Kong.*
37. Ibid.
38. Ibid.
39. Ibid.; Lan, *Global Cinderellas*; Parreñas, *Servants of Globalization.*

my.[40] The Philippines, for example, receives over $21 billion from remittances annually, and the country's economy is dependent upon this ongoing stream of income.[41] Southeast Asian governments, therefore, are invested in further exporting their high-skilled female citizens to pursue low-skilled positions abroad, despite the fact that many receiving countries have in place strict labor and immigration laws designed to exploit cheap, imported domestic labor.[42] In a recent campaign, the Filipino government referred to its two million migrant domestic workers as "the national hero."[43] Filipina and Southeast Asian women from other exporting countries are welcomed as valued members of their nation-family when they participate in a transnational economic framework that marginalizes and often dehumanizes them.

On the other hand, in order to maximize the profit margin from importing domestic labor, receiving countries enact a simultaneous inclusion and exclusion of migrant bodies: While they admit migrants into the state, receiving countries do not and cannot incorporate migrant women as members of the nation-family because once they are recognized as members, they cease to be disposable and interchangeable economic instruments and instead become subjects that could make demands on the state. As Charles Lee points out, it is in the receiving countries' interests to "actively *include* them as an immanent part of their biopolitical order—as disposable and exploitable labor—to foster and optimize their own sovereign production of liberal citizenship."[44] The inclusion of migrant domestic workers for the labor they provide is necessary to the nation-state so that the mainstream citizenry can remain hopeful that they can achieve the "good life" under the current government administration.[45] However, the mainstream citizenry, while benefitting from this labor arrangement, is also trapped in what Berlant refers to as "cruel optimism" as the import of domestic labor would not in the end provide them liberation from the neoliberal economic system that leaves them feeling perpetually precarious, anxious, and uneasy.[46]

Hong Kong's FDH Scheme is created to simultaneously include and exclude migrant domestic workers: Migrant women are incorporated into Hong Kong only insofar as they service the families of the existing citizenry.

40. Lagman, "Moving Labor"; Parreñas, *Servants of Globalization*.

41. Lagman, "Moving Labor," 2.

42. Ibid. Indonesia is one of the few Southeast Asian countries that has banned the export of its citizens to twenty-one Middle Eastern countries due to rampant abuse and exploitation. Whiteman, "Indonesia Maid Ban."

43. Lagman, "Moving Labor," 2.

44. Charles T. Lee, *Ingenious Citizenship*, 81.

45. Berlant, *Cruel Optimism*, 3.

46. Ibid., 24.

However, they are never seen as potential members of the nation-family. As mentioned repeatedly by the justices who heard Vallejos's case, in 1990 the Immigration Department issued a document titled "Explanatory Notes for the Standard Employment Contract," which explicitly states, "Domestic helpers and other semi-skilled persons are not admitted to Hong Kong for settlement. They are admitted only for specific employment that is for a specific job with a named Employer, and for a limited period."[47] The characterization of migrant domestic workers as economic instruments rather than persons was further solidified in 1986 when the Sino-British Joint Liaison Group clearly defined what Hong Kong permanent residency status means in preparation for the return of Hong Kong's sovereignty to China in 1997. After making amendments to the Immigration Ordinance on who would have the right of abode in Hong Kong after the return of sovereignty, the Chinese government submitted a document to the Hong Kong Executive Council titled "Note on Conditions of Stay for Foreign Domestic Helpers." In addition to reiterating that domestic workers are not admitted so that they can settle in Hong Kong, this document also clearly explains that restrictive FDH Scheme immigration and labor regulations are in place specifically to deter migrant women from ever wanting to reside permanently in Hong Kong.[48]

To render the migrant women's life precarious in Hong Kong so that they will not harbor the desire to settle, the FDH Scheme ensures that the workers' legal status—and in turn, their economic opportunities—in Hong Kong are completely dependent upon their local employer. Local employers are free to terminate a contract at any time. Without a contract, workers will be deported within two weeks. If they are terminated prematurely, domestic workers are prohibited from signing a new contract with a different employer without first returning to their home country. Because migrant domestic workers often have to pay an exorbitant amount of money to agencies in their home country, and sometimes also in Hong Kong, to secure employment, they are commonly in significant debt before they begin working.[49] The economic obligations they have back home, coupled with such debts, motivate migrant women to stay with their existing employer and maintain good relationships with them, sometimes even at the expense of their own mental, emotional, and physical health. The employers, after all, hold the power to return them to their home country poorer than when they first left.[50]

---

47. Cited in *Vallejos v. Commissioner of Registration*. HCAL 124 (2010), 15.

48. Ibid., 23.

49. Constable, *Maid to Order in Hong Kong*.

50. For ethnographic and more extensive discussions of how agencies exploit migrant women, see Constable, *Maid to Order*; Parreñas, *Servants of Globalization*.

Policies in the FDH Scheme—which are much more restrictive than the regulations imposed on skilled migrants, who are most often white Euro-Americans—are set up to police not only the physical bodies of migrant women but also their desires, affective ties, and intimate familial relationships. Such affective regulations include the mandatory week-long "home leave" and the prohibition on the sponsorships of dependents: Migrant domestic workers are required by Hong Kong law to return to their home country before they begin a new two-year standard employment contract, and they are not allowed to bring any dependents with them to Hong Kong.[51] As the explanatory note submitted by the Chinese government explains, these two practices are "designed to ensure that [migrant workers] will maintain genuine links in their own country."[52] Implicit in these policies is the assumption that migrant women would not want to settle permanently in Hong Kong if they are barred from transporting their affective ties and families to the city. Migrant women, in other words, are not supposed to have a home life of their own in Hong Kong for as long as they are serving their employer's family.

The mandatory home visits, on the other hand, allow migrant domestic workers to rekindle relationships with their own family members, particularly the children they have left behind. These visits function simultaneously as affective and political reminders for migrant women that their home is not in Hong Kong but elsewhere. Despite the great sorrow they experience from separating from their family, many Southeast Asian women choose to become migrant domestic workers to better provide for their children back home.[53] However, because domestic workers often cannot afford to spend their money and time on long international phone calls, the young children they left behind sometimes forget about their mothers or grow up having fraught relationships with them.[54] For workers with adult children, they may spend more emotional energy deepening the affective ties they share with their employer's family, rather than spending the time and resources to maintain their familial relationships back home.[55]

The mandatory home visits under the FDH Scheme provide rare opportunities for migrant women to reconnect with their family members and witness firsthand how their remittances have contributed to the improved living standard of their loved ones. Because of the economic draw of their jobs in Hong Kong, migrant women are unlikely to resettle back home. Rather, after

---

51. *Vallejos v. Commissioner of Registration*, HCAL 124 (2010), 16.
52. Cited in ibid., 23.
53. Constable, *Maid to Order in Hong Kong*.
54. Ibid.
55. Ibid.; So, *Migrant Domestic Workers*.

seeing how their labor abroad has helped promote their family's well-being, many women become more encouraged to return to Hong Kong and continue to participate in a transnational labor and citizenship model that only values them as economic instruments.[56] While the mandatory home visits illustrate how the Hong Kong government makes use of the women's familial affective ties to exercise biopolitical control transnationally and to further its own neo-liberal economic interests, the women's home country also benefits materially from this arrangement. Both nation-states have much to gain from the careful regulations of the women's familial relationships. The intimate ties of gendered and marginalized bodies are far from private in the transnational arena.

The emotional impact of the home visits is striking because domestic workers are not allowed to have their dependents with them in Hong Kong. While the official justification of that policy is that it helps prevent an influx of immigrants that would overwhelm the city's public welfare and education systems, the policy also serves the purpose of affective regulation. First, it makes clear to migrant women that Hong Kong is not a place for settlement: They are only wanted in the city because of the labor they provide, and thus the government bears no responsibility or concerns toward their emotional needs, desires, and personal relationships. Second, by forcing migrant women to forsake the opportunity to care for their own children in exchange for greater economic opportunities in Hong Kong, this policy imposes a high opportunity cost to becoming a domestic worker. Women who have made the decision to nevertheless become one are very committed to successfully completing their employment contract in Hong Kong because only their income could justify the grief they experience from leaving their children behind to take care of someone else's.[57]

As many migrant women reflect in their own writing, they are able to endure the harsh working conditions in Hong Kong because they remember what they have already given up and how much they must contribute economically to their family so that they can be good mothers from afar.[58] Since migrant women cannot directly care for their children, the primary way they can perform motherhood is through the financial capital they gain by providing emotional and reproductive labor to someone else's family. Given this emotional motivation, migrant domestic workers are eager to maintain good relationships with their local employers by fulfilling even their unreasonable demands. This policy not only prevents the influx of what the state considers to be inferior, racialized bodies that would decrease the quality of

---

56. Constable, *Maid to Order in Hong Kong*.
57. Ibid.
58. *Wishing Well.*

the nation-family, it also produces a condition that promotes workers' dependency on their local employers. The power imbalance between the worker and the employer exists at the geopolitical, economic, and also emotional levels.

The exploitation of labor by local employers is made even easier by the live-in rule implemented by the Hong Kong government in 2003 to prevent workers from moonlighting and competing with local Hongkongers in the housekeeping industry.[59] The mandatory live-in policy dictates that domestic workers must reside right in the homes of their employers. This rule exemplifies how home and family in the private sphere are regulated heavily by the state in a way that transports the distinction between citizens and aliens into an intimate space. The home environment created by the live-in rule also exacerbates conditions for exploitation because there is no distinction between professional and personal boundaries between the employer and the worker. Due to high property prices, most homes in Hong Kong are small: The size of an average apartment is only 475 square feet. As a result, 70 percent of domestic workers share a room with their employer's children, while others are sometimes relegated to sleeping on mats on the floor or in tight, uninhabitable spaces such as storage cabinets or the bathroom.[60]

Because the close proximity between the employer and the worker constantly threatens to undo the boundary between them, many employers implement strict rules around their home to demarcate the power difference between them. For example, workers are also often barred from occupying the living room or sharing meals with the employer's family.[61] Despite the emotional labor domestic work demands, this legally enforced spatial arrangement in the private sphere makes clear that migrant women are in Hong Kong and in their employer's home just to perform labor but not to be incorporated as part of the nuclear or national family. The blurring of private home space and professional workplace leads to easy exploitation: Because domestic workers lack the power and resources to physically remove themselves from work, it is not uncommon for employers to expect workers to be available for chores and caregiving around the clock.[62] If "home" is understood to be a private place for refuge, then the domestic worker has no home in Hong Kong—the home

59. In October 2017, Filipina domestic worker Nancy Lubiano challenged the live-in policy in court on the grounds that it promotes servitude. The High Court ruled in favor of the government, stating the constitutionality of the policy. Phoebe Ng, "Domestic Helper Loses 'Live-In' Court Challenge."

60. Hollingsworth, "Sleepless in Hong Kong."

61. Constable, *Maid to Order in Hong Kong*; Lan, *Global Cinderellas*.

62. Constable, *Maid to Order in Hong Kong*.

space is exactly the migrant worker's workplace, where her and her family's economic well-being is at stake.

While the mandatory live-in policy is meant to control the citizenship status, labor, and bodies of migrant domestic workers, it inadvertently also alters the intimate relationships local Hongkongers—particularly women—have with their family members. The familial framework of citizenship, in other words, is not only at work at the discursive level, but it also extends materially to regulate both local and transnational familial relationships. Drawing from her research and firsthand experience living with a migrant domestic worker as an employer in Hong Kong, sociologist Annie Chan observes that because of the live-in policy, neither the domestic worker nor the employer truly feels at home, despite the spatial demarcations employers set within their home: There is simply not enough space in a tight Hong Kong apartment for the worker and the employer to carve out separate spaces to perform their identities outside of this intimate economic arrangement.[63]

Based on her interviews with fifteen pairs of middle-class local couples who employed full-time domestic workers, Chan argues that the live-in policy is a system that "pitches women against women" and results in two losers: Not only do migrant domestic workers lose by having to live under constant unease and the fear of exploitation, but local female employers also feel pressured and under siege because they sense the need to defend their domestic roles and authority as wife and mother against a competitor.[64] Because of the constant presence of a strange woman in their own home, local female employers feel that they must compete with the domestic worker for affections from their own children, while worrying that their husband may become sexually attracted to the worker.[65] Meanwhile, Chan observes that male employers are unhindered by the pressure their wives feel because they see domestic work as belonging to the feminine realm: If they have any requests for the domestic workers, they expect their wives to execute their demands.[66] In other words, male employers never see domestic workers as competitors who threaten to take over their position in the household, but merely as subordinates. The anxiety among female employers that they will be replaced, in fact, is more often shared by the domestic workers who struggle to maintain intimacy with their own children and spouses back home: Because of their extended absence, migrant workers must rely on others to care for their children and

---

63. Kammerer, "When Hong Kong Flats Are the Size of a Parking Space."
64. Cited in So, *Migrant Domestic Workers*, 62.
65. Ibid.; Constable, *Maid to Order in Hong Kong*.
66. Ibid.

brace themselves for the news that their husband has taken up other lovers.[67] The pressure migrant domestic work places on intimate familial relationships similarly affects both the workers and their female employers.

The shared concerns and emotional experiences between migrant domestic workers and local Hong Kong women, however, do not lead to a sense of solidarity or coalition across difference. Due to the perceived competitions in intimate familial relationships and the economic role domestic workers play in the neoliberal economy and in the home of their employers, Chan points out, "female employers and migrant domestic workers are never partners. In the eyes of the female employer, this is a zero-sum game: 'if migrant workers are granted more rights, it means more household chores and more economic burden for me.'"[68] Despite the government's official reasoning that migrant domestic workers would alleviate the workload of local women in the private sphere, Hong Kong female employers experience a great deal of tension from having to, in the intimate space of their own homes, simultaneously manage and compete with women who are otherwise peers whose familial pressure, intimate concerns, and desires echo their own.

While some employers are uncomfortable enforcing a stark division between themselves and their domestic workers, they often realize that despite their attempts to welcome the workers as a part of their family, the affective ties they hope to share with their migrant domestic workers are always already fraught with social expectations on how employers and workers ought to relate to one another. These relationships are inflected by the vast transnational economic and power differential between them that uncomfortably blurs the line between familial and professional.[69] Constable recounts a joke she hears often among Filipino domestic workers in Hong Kong, in which the familial is used by employers as a trope to justify labor exploitation:

A Filipina domestic helper arrives in Hong Kong at the home of her new employer. The employer says to her, "We want to treat you as a member of the family." The domestic helper is very happy to hear this. On Sunday, the helper's day off, her employer says to her, "You must work before you leave the house on Sundays because you are a member of the family." And the employer adds, "And you must come home in time to cook dinner for the

---

67. Ibid. Parreñas refers to the phenomena in which "a privileged woman pays a migrant woman to perform her housework, and she in turn passes on her own household work to a woman left behind in her country of origin as a 'care chain.'" "The Reproductive Labour of Migrant Workers," 269.

68. So, *Migrant Domestic Workers*, 63; translations mine.

69. So, *Migrant Domestic Workers*.

family." "But sir, ma'am, I would like to eat with my friends today, because it is my day off," says the helper. "But you are a member of the family," says her employer, "and because you are a member of the family, you must eat with us."[70]

As this joke illustrates, familial relationships between workers and employers cannot be taken at face value under the FDH Scheme. The system has perverted the affective connotations of family so that being a family member no longer means that one is treated with respect and care. Rather, as Mary Romero points out, such familial analogies are used by employers to mask exploitation and to ensure ready access to the worker's emotional and physical labor.[71] For employers and workers, the family is no longer the center of intimate affective ties, but is instead always imbued with calculation about one's labor and economic interests.

As a result, despite the best intentions among certain employers, the FDH Scheme forecloses the opportunities for domestic workers to become part of a local family or the nation-family via affective ties. The lack of such intimate ties, in turn, helps justify and perpetuate xenophobic attitudes against migrant women that permeate public and legal discourse regarding their right to permanent residency. The mainstream public is unsympathetic to the workers' claim to permanent residency status because, as Constable points out, most Hongkongers see migrant women as either good or bad workers: The former "are those who are willing to be *only workers* and who treat the work as their life, whereas 'bad workers' are those who demand recognition of their rights as workers while expressing political subjectivities that go well beyond that of worker."[72] The key rhetorical and political task for migrant women and their advocates, therefore, is to undo the dominant perspective that migrant women do not deserve respect and recognition for their personhood and humanity outside of their role as domestic workers.

Given the hostility between workers and employers bred by the FDH Scheme, it is not surprising that local employers were outraged when the Court of First Instance initially ruled that migrant workers should be granted the right to permanent residency. After the ruling, public animosity toward migrant domestic workers rose to a historic high—so high that the Hong Kong government's decision to appeal the ruling was justified and welcomed.[73] Exclusions enacted by the familial framework of citizenship have come full

---

70. Constable, *Maid to Order in Hong Kong*, 112.
71. Romero, *Maid in the USA*.
72. Constable, *Born Out of Place*, 19.
73. Ibid.

circle: By imposing regulations on affective familial ties and arrangements at the state and transnational levels, the Hong Kong government has inadvertently also influenced the dynamics within local homes. The tension that permeates among local Hong Kong families, in turn, helps justify exclusionary citizenship policies that render those who perform the most intimate reproductive labor disposable strangers to the nation-state. The immigration and labor policies imposed on migrant domestic workers by the Hong Kong Immigration Department not only illustrate the ways in which home and family are regulated at the transnational level to keep economically marginalized and racialized bodies out of the nation-state but also demonstrate how the exclusion of migrant women from formal inclusion is made possible by the devaluation and privatization of feminine reproductive labor at large.

## ORDINARY RESIDENCE AND THE CONSTITUTIONALITY OF STATE IMMIGRATION CONTROL

Given this sociopolitical and economic backdrop, the odds were stacked against migrant domestic workers who hoped to regain their personhood via legal appeal to their right to permanent residency. The limitations of such citizenship discourse and formal recognition, however, are best illustrated in the judgments penned by the three justices who heard the case at various levels of the court system. Focusing on the judgment handed down by Justice Johnson Lam at the Court of First Instance, I demonstrate that despite his favorable ruling toward the workers—which was later overturned—his judgment nevertheless condones the use of governmental power to categorically exclude migrant workers from citizenship so that they can continue to provide the state and the nation-family with cheap domestic labor. Legal citizenship discourse, in other words, does not provide room for migrant workers to challenge the existing interpretive framework of the neoliberal nation-family that renders them nothing more than economic instruments.

Legally, the case hinges upon how *ordinary residence* ought to be interpreted, and whether it is constitutional for the Hong Kong government to unevenly execute the SAR's permanent residency law. According to the Immigration Ordinance, ordinary residence is defined by one's lawful and voluntary settlement in Hong Kong.[74] Gladys Li, the counsel for domestic worker Evangeline Vallejos, submitted to the court that the added provision in the Immigration Ordinance that categorically excludes domestic workers from ordinary

---

74. Hong Kong Immigration Department, "Meanings of Right of Abode and Other Terms."

residence violates Article 24(2)(4) of the Basic Law, an article that generously stipulates *all* foreign nationals, as long as they have entered and remained in Hong Kong legally, are eligible for permanent residency after they have met the seven-year ordinary residence requirement. Li also argues that the provision is discriminatory because it only applies to unskilled migrant labor from developing countries.[75]

On the other hand, Lord Pannick, representing the Hong Kong government, argued that based on Article 154(2) of the Basic Law, the SAR government is given the authority to exercise immigration control on foreign nationals regarding their entry, stay, and departure. According to Pannick, this article on immigration control should be taken into account when interpreting Article 24(2)(4): Despite the generous criteria for permanent residency outlined in the article, the Basic Law still grants the Hong Kong government the power to determine who should and should not be a permanent resident."[76] The provision, Pannick argued, is therefore constitutional. Pannick also posited that the definition of ordinary residence should not be determined by the subject's voluntary desire to settle in Hong Kong; rather, it should be interpreted as whether the nature of the subject's residence is "out of ordinary."[77] Referencing the precarious material and living conditions produced by the FDH Scheme, Pannick concluded that the residence of migrant domestic workers in Hong Kong is summatively out of ordinary. Since no one except domestic workers has to abide by the strict set of immigration and labor policies imposed by the scheme, no one else in the SAR lives the way migrant workers do; as a result, Pannick argued, the existence of domestic workers in Hong Kong is extraordinary. By arguing that ordinary residence should be determined by whether the subject lives according to the norm, Pannick made use of the precarious conditions created by the FDH Scheme to justify the continual categorical exclusion of migrant domestic workers from formal recognition. Whether such policies are discriminatory and exploitative was, on the other hand, legally irrelevant to Pannick and the court.

Based on the arguments presented by both parties, the case was largely a debate about contesting legal interpretations on two Basic Law articles, respectively, on how ordinary residence should be interpreted, and whether the SAR government has the legislative power to implement selective immigration policies that exclude certain populations from permanent residency, even after they have fulfilled the terms stipulated in the Basic Law. Far from allowing domestic workers to appear and participate in the public realm of deliberation

---

75. *Vallejos v. Commissioner of Registration,* HCAL 124 (2010).

76. Ibid., 33.

77. Ibid., 29.

as unique subjects with interests that overlap with the mainstream citizenry's, the legal parameter set by the court illustrates the limit of formal citizenship discourse in granting migrant women recognition for their humanity. At the center of this trial is the Hong Kong government and its power to regulate alien bodies, rather than the rights of migrant workers. Indeed, the personhood of the migrant domestic workers, their desire to work in Hong Kong without the fear of exploitation, and the affective ties they cultivated in Hong Kong after decades of working in the city are all rendered irrelevant. While permanent residency status could ameliorate the exploitation faced by many migrant domestic workers by making their material conditions less precarious, focusing solely on formal citizenship nevertheless recenters state authority and the state's role in exercising biopolitical control to assure the coherence and material interests of the existing nation-family.

Legal discourse on permanent residency reifies the dominant interpretive framework of citizenship, through which the neoliberal economic and political interests of the nation-state are prioritized over the subjectivity and personhood of migrant domestic workers. In his argument, Pannick posited that despite the general criteria for permanent residency outlined in Article 24(2)(4) of the Basic Law, the Hong Kong legislature should still be authorized to "define and clarify what are the *exceptional cases* where a foreigner's residence in Hong Kong falls outside the scope of 'ordinary residence.'"[78] The "exceptional cases" here refer to situations that concern the prosperity of Hong Kong and the well-being of the mainstream citizenry. Situated within a context in which Hong Kong's economy is dependent upon privatized, gendered, and affordable reproductive labor, Pannick's argument in effect demanded that the court grant the legislative branch of the government the authority to exercise neoliberal exceptions regarding the residency status of migrant domestic workers.[79]

As Aihwa Ong argues, while the mainstream citizenry and marginalized subjects are all governed by neoliberal technologies at the transnational and state levels, the economic and political benefits that the citizenry enjoys are built upon the labor of marginalized bodies who are cast out of the nation-family and the formal citizenship framework. Marginalized populations, like migrant workers, are therefore "exceptions to neoliberalism": They are stripped of rights and excluded from enjoying the high living standards and economic development created by the market-driven policies they help support with their labor.[80] By advocating for state regulation outside of the Basic

---

78. *Vallejos v. Commissioner of Registration*, HCAL 124 (2010), 33; emphasis mine.
79. Ong, *Neoliberalism as Exception*.
80. Ibid., 4.

Law to prevent migrants from threatening the economic interests of the SAR, Pannick's argument exemplifies how dominant citizenship discourse perpetuates the primacy of neoliberal ideologies and state power.

While Justice Lam of the Court of First Instance rejected Pannick's argument, Justice Cheung of the Court of Appeal decided otherwise: He penned that given that Hong Kong permanent residency provides "a highly valuable status and rights, . . . naturally one expects the Basic Law to intend a more cautious if not different approach" to determine who is eligible for such a status.[81] Treating Hong Kong permanent residency, which carries similar political connotations as formal citizenship, as an exclusive, highly revered and desired status symbol, Justice Cheung's decision highlights the connections between legal interpretations of the Basic Law and the dominant interpretive framework of citizenship: Only those who are deemed economically or racially worthy for inclusion would be granted legal access to the inner circle of the nation-family.

It is, therefore, unsurprising that the judgments handed down by the Court of Appeal, and later the Court of Final Appeal, relegate the personhood and interests of migrant women in order to protect the political power of the Hong Kong government and the economic prowess of the nation-state. Justice Cheung of the Court of Appeal posited that the founders of the Basic Law likely "intended to leave it to the legislature to define, within bounds, what 'ordinarily resident' means according to its best judgment, which would no doubt be dependent on, amongst other things, policy considerations and the ever-changing political, economic and social conditions prevailing for the time being."[82] The Hong Kong government, Cheung continued, therefore possesses the power to adapt what *ordinary residence* means to "meet the changing needs of society."[83] Never seen as members of the Hong Kong society and ineligible to participate in elections of legislative members, migrant domestic workers and their needs were immediately rendered irrelevant by Cheung's judgment. The SAR government, on the other hand, was granted the political power to freely interpret what the city needs and to make categorical exceptions to permanent residency as it sees fit. Migrant domestic workers, therefore, became exceptions to the Basic Law. As Carl Schmitt and Giorgio Agamben posit, while those who are deemed citizens and members of the nation-state remain inside the juridical order, marginalized Others are stripped of legal and political protections.[84] As Schmitt puts it, "[The sovereign] has monopoly over this

---

81. *Vallejos v. Commissioner of Registration*, CACV 204 (2011), 18.
82. Ibid., 11.
83. Ibid., 29.
84. Agamben, *Homo Sacer*; Schmitt and Strong, *Political Theology*.

last decision. Therein lies the essence of the state's sovereign, which must be juridically defined correctly, not as the monopoly to coerce to rule, but as the monopoly to decide."[85] While Hong Kong is not a sovereign state, this case nevertheless illustrates how the judicial branch works in tandem with the executive branch to defend the dominant interpretive framework of citizenship that readily relegates marginalized transnational subjects so that the state can protect its economic interests while the existing citizenry maintains their superiority over racialized Others. Migrant domestic workers, in other words, are preemptively prevented from gaining recourse through the juridical context.

While unstated in Cheung's judgment, the Hong Kong government's primary concerns at the time of the lawsuit were twofold: to maintain Hong Kong's status as a leading transnational financial hub, and to appease the mainstream citizenry who had become increasingly disgruntled over mainland China's influence over the SAR that challenged its semi-independent status. Established to help strengthen China's economic power in the global market, the SAR was immensely important to Beijing during its nascent years. In 1997, Hong Kong accounted for 16 percent of China's GDP, even though it contained only 0.5 percent of China's population.[86] Hong Kong's economic prowess has translated into political leverage for the SAR to remain semiautonomous within China's sovereignty. However, as China's economy became increasingly more powerful transnationally, Hong Kong's importance to Beijing began to wane.[87] In order to maintain its relevance and political leverage, the SAR government must ensure a substantial economic growth every year. The pressure to remain competitive in a transnational market economy necessarily entails limiting the scope of formal citizenship. To put it differently, in order to maximize Hong Kong's GDP, the SAR government must import a substantial number of migrant women to provide affordable reproductive labor, while at the same time ensuring that they remain outside of the nation-family and therefore will not put stress on the public welfare system.

On the other hand, the increased political encroachment of mainland China and its looming economic power since the 2000s have caused fear and anxiety among mainstream Hongkongers about their national identity and sociopolitical status. While Hongkongers used to liken mainland Chinese people to country bumpkins because of China's slow economic development during Hong Kong's colonial era, many upper-middle-class mainland Chinese people now possess more economic and therefore political power than

85. Schmitt and Strong, *Political Theology*, 13.
86. Don Lee, "Hong Kong"; Ong, *Neoliberalism as Exception*.
87. Don Lee, "Hong Kong."

mainstream Hongkongers.[88] The sense of superiority Hongkongers feel and their position within the ethnocratic hierarchy is being actively undermined by China's looming power. The exclusion of migrant domestic workers from Hong Kong permanent residency, therefore, not only serves economic purposes but provides material proof that despite the threatening presence of wealthy mainland tourists and investors, mainstream Hongkongers still hold significant sociopolitical and economic power over others.

In the wake of the trial, a cartoon was circulated widely among social media platforms, particularly Facebook groups set up by outraged Hongkongers. The cartoon depicts what would happen if domestic workers were to obtain permanent residency. Split into two frames, the image on the left depicts the current situation: A local Hong Kong woman sits comfortably in her living room while barking orders to the domestic worker. The image on the right, however, shows how the power dynamic would switch once the worker attains permanent residency: The worker is now relaxing on the couch and ordering the local Hong Kong woman to do chores. In the second scenario, the Hong Kong woman is forced to respond to the migrant woman as "boss." This cartoon depicts the anxiety and anger mainstream Hongkongers have toward migrant women who dare to challenge the existing ethnocratic hierarchy and makeup of the nation-family. It also highlights how the animosity Hongkongers harbor toward migrant women is intimately connected to their anxiety about social status and power in everyday life.

Given such status anxiety, the desire among mainstream Hongkongers to exclude migrant domestic workers aligns with the SAR government's overarching economic and political agenda. This is a rare alliance between the two as the Hong Kong public has grown increasingly more resistant to the Beijing-appointed SAR administration. By ensuring that migrant domestic workers remain excluded from the nation-family, the Hong Kong government can simultaneously appease the mainstream citizenry while protecting its own economic and political interests. When the Court of Final Appeal ruled in the end that the government was free to exercise immigration control according to the perceived needs of the Hong Kong society, it in effect sanctioned the privileging of the state's economic and political interests and the mainstream citizenry's national anxiety over the protection of vulnerable, marginalized transnational subjects. At the end of the two-year lawsuit, not only did migrant domestic workers not gain permanent residency, but they became even more vilified by the mainstream public for attempting to usurp a place in the nation-family that was never meant for them.

---

88. Yam, "Affective Economies and Alienizing Discourse."

## BEYOND THE CITIZENSHIP FRAMEWORK:
## PERSONAL NARRATIVE AND ETHNOGRAPHY

The courts' judgments and the public backlash against migrant domestic workers demonstrate how formal citizenship is structured in a way that privileges the nation-state's economic interests and the current power hierarchy between the existing citizenry and those who are outside of the nation-family. Reinforcing the dominant interpretive framework of migrant women as workers but not people, legal citizenship discourse forecloses what Karma Chávez calls "coalitional moments" between migrant domestic workers and their local employers that "occur when political issues coincide or merge in the public sphere in ways that create ways to reenvision and potentially reconstruct rhetorical imaginaries."[89] Coalitional moments, and the prospect for transformative deliberation to occur across power difference, are obscured by formal citizenship discourse that delineates members of the nation-family from aliens according to race, social class, and gender. Further, they are also hindered by the neoliberal transnational caregiving system that entangles intimate familial relationships with high-stakes economic considerations. In an economic and political system that privileges productivity, migrants and local women are pitched against each other, with the latter always acting as the manager of the former so that neither party can see the other as a person outside of the economic and labor context.

To combat this dehumanization in a transnational economy that actively exploits gendered labor, it is important to, as Mohanty argues, cultivate "a notion of political solidarity and common interests, defined as a community or collectivity among women workers across class, race, and national boundaries that is based on shared material interests and identity and common ways of reading the world."[90] For Mohanty, women workers include not only women who work for a wage but housewives as well because their emotional and domestic labor should be properly recognized. In addition, because First and Third World women both operate under the logics of transnational capitalism and neoliberalism, there is, as Mohanty argues, "a political basis for common struggles" across social class and race.[91] Such solidarity across difference allows for the recognition of shared interests between the two parties, while prompting the interlocutors to remain attuned to the significance of different lived experiences, histories of oppression, and positionality among allies.

---

89. Karma Chávez, *Queer Migration Politics*, 9.
90. Mohanty, *Feminism without Borders*, 145.
91. Ibid., 167.

For female employers in Hong Kong to recognize the common material interests and desires they share with their domestic workers, they must first see migrant workers as humans who have a unique narratable self and life stories outside of their labor role, stories that are worth listening to and feelings and experiences that intersect with or echo their own. Only then could local Hong Kong women enact deliberative empathy and interrogate the ways in which they have colluded in a system that also entraps them. By recognizing their intersubjectivity with migrant domestic workers, local Hong Kong women could, from a relative position of power, subsequently consider how they could enact a different form of relations with domestic workers—one that creates coalitional moments across difference and decenters the framework of formal citizenship that actively alienizes and exploits marginalized gendered subjects.[92]

In the following sections, I examine two texts that make use of storytelling as an alternative rhetorical strategy to engage the mainstream Hong Kong audience: *Wishing Well,* an anthology of personal narratives, poetry, and photographs composed by domestic workers, and *Migrant Domestic Workers: Strangers at Home,* a transnational ethnography of migrant workers and local employers written by acclaimed Hong Kong journalist Mei-Chee So. I argue that these two texts illustrate the different ways in which family functions as a topos for both migrant domestic workers and their local allies and thus makes room for emotional responses outside of the dominant emotional template of defensiveness and anger. The familial, in other words, is not always tethered to the exclusionary conception of the nation-family. Rather, stories about the migrant women's familial relationships could help mitigate the dehumanization produced by mainstream citizenship discourse. Telling such stories also provides migrant women the opportunity to appear in a plural public discursive space as their unique selves, outside of their job functions.

However, while *Wishing Well* offers migrant women the opportunity to represent themselves and their life stories using their own words, the anthology's overarching goal is to mitigate the hostility Hongkongers have toward domestic workers and to promote the start-up employment agency that sponsored and published the text. As a result, these narratives tend to rehash normative familial tropes that are readily intelligible to the company's targeted audience (potential employers), and the usage of these tropes emphasizes the workers' individual agency in a way that forecloses the opportunity to interrogate how structural forces, such as the transnational neoliberal economy and oppressive state immigration policies, support the uneven distribution

---

92. Karma Chávez, *Queer Migration Politics,* 9.

of power and labor. By allowing the audience to read the workers' narratives without considering how they themselves are implicated within the same web of economic and political forces, *Wishing Well* evokes emotions that are unlikely to promote transformative deliberation among mainstream readers. While *Wishing Well* effectively humanizes migrant domestic workers and highlights the shared humanity and womanhood between migrant and local Hong Kong women, it falls short on prompting mainstream audiences to transform the sympathy, pity, or affective empathy they experience into more critical and deliberative interrogation of the transnational care chain and economic system. Without experiencing deliberative empathy, the audiences are never prompted to consider how they are implicated in the socioeconomic system that causes the marginalization of migrant women, nor are they encouraged to see how their self-interests overlap with those of the domestic workers.

In contrast, So's ethnographic investigation reveals how structural economic and political forces transform intimate familial dynamics in local Hong Kong homes and in the homes Filipina workers have left behind. Part transnational ethnography and part life history interviews, *Migrant Domestic Workers* reveals how the familial ties and life stories of workers and employers intertwine and how they are all embedded within the same neoliberal economic, social, and geopolitical network. By portraying employers as individuals who are subjugated to socioeconomic and political forces beyond their control and workers as simultaneously exploited and empowered by this transnational labor practice, *Migrant Domestic Workers* challenges binary portrayals of these two groups as oppressors and victims, and instead highlights the networked economic and sociopolitical forces that connect them across difference. By doing so, *Migrant Domestic Workers* calls for the enactment of deliberative empathy among the readers, and for workers, advocates, and employers to participate in deliberative acts through which they acknowledge each other's humanity, difference, and the intersecting interests they share.

## PERSONAL NARRATIVES AND THE LIMIT OF THE INDIVIDUAL

Four years after the lawsuit on permanent residency concluded and two years after Hong Kong made international headlines for the abuse of Indonesian domestic worker Sulistyaningsih, HelperChoice, a start-up that seeks to replace exploitative employment agencies, published *Wishing Well* as an e-book. The anthology contains eighteen portraits, personal narratives, and poems selected from submissions to a writing competition HelperChoice organized with Coconuts, a Southeast Asian news website. This context is significant as it influences the kinds of narratives collected in *Wishing Well* and the way migrant writers tell their stories. In my analysis, I treat HelperChoice as the primary rhetorical agent as it selected and curated these acts of storytelling, and thus decided what kinds of narratives are tellable.

Described by *Bloomberg* as "the LinkedIn for domestic helpers," HelperChoice provides a free online platform for migrant women to post their employment profiles and directly apply for jobs posted by employers in Hong Kong, Singapore, Dubai, Qatar, Saudi Arabia, and Kuwait.[93] HelperChoice brands itself as a social enterprise because the online platform it provides allows migrant women to bypass exploitative employment agencies that put them in debt before they even start working. Touting itself as an ally and advocate for migrant domestic workers, the company, however, never discusses the labor conditions in the countries it works with, despite ample reports on the rampant abuse and exploitation domestic workers face there.[94] Despite its brand as a socially conscious enterprise, HelperChoice nevertheless profits from and remains largely silent about the transnational division of labor that promotes the dehumanization and exploitation of marginalized gendered bodies.

As an e-book published and advertised only by HelperChoice, *Wishing Well* does not have a wide audience in Hong Kong. It nevertheless still serves multiple key rhetorical functions: First, it provides migrant domestic workers the opportunity to speak publicly about their lives in their own words, and second, it helps boost HelperChoice's ethos as a company that intends to create social change. In the foreword she writes for the anthology, the founder of HelperChoice, Laurence Fauchon, describes her experience relocating to Hong Kong as an international banker from France, and becoming "fascinated by these women and their joyful personalities."[95] Fauchon founded HelperChoice after realizing that the "charming lady from the Philippines" who helped take care of her daughters had been illegally exploited by her employment agency. While Fauchon mentions the difficult work environments many domestic workers face, she mostly expresses sympathy at an individual level and her curiosity about domestic workers as a collective group with few internal distinctions; Fauchon then uses such sympathy to highlight the impor-

---

93. "Meet HelperChoice.com, the LinkedIn for Domestic Helpers."

94. Benach, Muntaner, Delclos, Menéndez, and Ronquillo, "Migration and 'Low-Skilled' Workers"; Constable, *Maid to Order in Hong Kong*; Parreñas and Silvey, "Domestic Workers Refusing Neo-Slavery in the UAE."

95. *Wishing Well*, 4.

tance of her start-up in protecting migrants' rights. As I mentioned in my introduction, sympathy reinforces the power hierarchy between the privileged subject and the suffering Other. Sympathy, in other words, is ineffective in prompting critical and sustained transformative deliberation that examines the structural causes of suffering.

In the conclusion of her foreword, Fauchon explains that she hopes *Wishing Well* will "encourage employers to treat their domestic helpers better. . . . They are loving people and faithful workers who deserve to be treated as such."[96] By reinforcing the distance between employers and workers using an us-versus-them approach, this statement not only essentializes migrant women as a gregarious and friendly group whose identity is defined primarily by their job as helpers but also sanctions the overwhelming authority employers have over domestic workers. Fauchon's statement suggests that it is up to the employers to free the workers from the working conditions they are in; domestic workers, on the other hand, must rely on their luck in landing an understanding employer. In taking this approach, Fauchon obscures how local employers—particularly Hong Kong women—are also negatively impacted by the transnational transaction and devaluation of gendered labor. Fauchon's statement forecloses the opportunity for mainstream audiences to reflect on the shared sociopolitical structures and realities between them and the migrant workers. There is, therefore, little room for transformative deliberation and the potential of coalition across difference.

Given Fauchon's foreword, the targeted audience—mainstream Hong Kong public and employers—is primed to read the anthology as stories about the challenges individual migrant women encounter in their experiences as domestic workers, and more importantly, as evidence that HelperChoice is doing the much-needed humanitarian work of supporting these workers. Fauchon's foreword suggests that wealthy white social entrepreneurs like her are already creating initiatives to protect migrants, and that they are able to do so without implicating local employers or influencing their current lifestyle. Fauchon is reinforcing a white savior narrative rather than cultivating the opportunity for the audience to experience critical, deliberative empathy in relation to the workers' narratives and lived experiences. As a result, while the audience is invited to experience sympathy and pity—or even affective empathy— after reading the workers' narratives, the framing of *Wishing Well* nevertheless encourages the readers to remain comfortably within their existing conceptual framework about their privilege and distant relationship with migrant workers. As Spelman points out in her reading of Arendt, none of those emotions

---

96. Ibid., 6.

have a productive place in political life across difference: While sympathy and pity reinforce the distance between the privileged audience and the sufferer, affective empathy (Arendt refers to it as *compassion*) does not open up any room for the audience to entertain uncertainties and alternative responses.[97] As a result, none of these emotions promote transformative deliberation, nor do they, as Spelman argues, "allow the sufferer a particular face or a particular voice."[98]

The introductory chapter of the anthology, penned by local anthropologist Ju-chen Chen, offers a more productive way of engaging with the narratives. Functioning as a cultural intermediary between the mainstream Hong Kong audience and domestic workers, Chen remarks:

> While we enjoy different income levels and social standing in Hong Kong, my informants and I actually share similar core concerns. We both wonder how to achieve a "better" life than what we have, how to provide the best for our children and how to juggle our roles of working professionals, wives, and mothers. On the level of common humanity and womanhood, we are not that different after all.[99]

Chen's statement invites local women to see domestic workers as people who share similar interests based on their shared gender and humanity. Chen's introduction counters the framework Fauchon puts forth by encouraging the audience to reflect on common concerns and desires as women, rather than remaining in the scripted cultural and socioeconomic roles of workers and employers. In order to highlight the personhood of migrant women outside of their job, Chen divides the eighteen entries in *Wishing Well* into two sections: The first, "Portraits," features writings that fit neatly into dominant national and sociopolitical narratives of the model migrant domestic worker. Narratives in the second section, titled "Whispers," "showcase FDWs outside the workplace and tease out identities other than the worker, resembling a bustling chorus of whispers."[100]

Analyzing texts from both sections, I demonstrate that while these narratives help cultivate a recognition of the migrant women's humanity and highlight the emotional and bodily harm caused by exploitative labor practices,

---

97. Arendt and Schell, *On Revolution*; Spelman, *Fruits of Sorrow*. Arendt defines compassion as a form of "co-suffering" in which the audience is so moved that they bear the suffering of the other; this description echoes my definition and usage of *affective empathy*.

98. Spelman, *Fruits of Sorrow*, 67.

99. *Wishing Well*, 8.

100. Ibid.

most of them end on a celebratory note of personal redemption, suggesting that despite the hardship imposed by the labor system, the women nevertheless emerge more empowered and fulfilled than they were before. Because of such upbeat closures, the audience may stop short of enacting deliberative empathy to critically reflect on the structural causes of the workers' suffering and how they themselves are implicated within such systems. Rather than prompting the audience to engage in internal deliberation based on the empathetic responses they have toward the narratives of the migrant women (i.e., deliberative empathy), *Wishing Well* instead reinforces the existing distance and hierarchy between the two groups by emotionally rewarding the mainstream audiences for feeling momentary compassion toward the workers.

The entries in the first section—texts that support the dominant representations of migrant domestic workers—embody the values and state narratives sending countries like the Philippines use to facilitate gendered transnational labor migration. While these narratives celebrate the labor of migrant women, they nevertheless prioritize the women's productivity over their personhood and individual life stories. Using "we" to stand in for all domestic workers in Hong Kong, Jing Jing—the author of the first article, "Superstar"—makes use of readily intelligible tropes to celebrate the affective qualities and virtues of the model migrant women. Composed only of sentences that begin with imperatives like "we need to," or "we must," the second paragraph of "Superstar" details the qualities a domestic worker ought to possess to fulfill her duties:

> We need to be strong when facing each challenge in our everyday dealings with our employers and job responsibilities while at the same time thinking about the situations we have left back home. We have to have greater patience, discipline and self-control. We must also adjust to a new culture that's far different from our motherland's. Furthermore, we have to be selfless and great multi-taskers in order to complete our daily workloads.[101]

As Lagman points out, in addition to physical labor, migrant domestic workers also have to constantly engage in "affective management" of their emotional responses to their employers and to different household situations.[102] While in her writing, Jing supposedly has the freedom to deviate from the social script she is expected to perform, this introduction demonstrates that

---

101. Jing, "Superstar," 10.
102. Lagman, "Moving Labor," 5.

she continues to represent herself and other domestic workers in a way that meets the expectations of the mainstream Hong Kong readers.

In the next paragraph Jing describes how migrant women are motivated to work in Hong Kong because of the intimate familial ties they have back home, but she does so in a way that flattens the emotional complexities of domestic workers. Describing the desires of the collective "we" to provide healthy food, homes, and education to their families, Jing repeats the common representation of migrant women as in need of humanitarian assistance from their employers just to fulfill basic needs. At the end, Jing adopts the liberal narrative of female empowerment via productive labor. Asserting the agency of migrant women ("But wait! We take these jobs not because we don't have a choice, but instead, we embrace them with reason and purpose"), Jing ends her essay by proclaiming that migrant domestic workers are "even the heroines of [their] loved ones who in one way or another idolize [them] as superstars!"[103] The emphasis on being the heroine echoes the Filipino state's narrative. In 2006, the Filipino state launched the Supermaid training program to prepare women for domestic work abroad; rife in the advertisements of this program are representations of Filipina women as "ideal maids and ideal worker heroes."[104] Referring to migrant women as heroes capable not only of domestic labor but of supporting their nation-state, the Filipino government actively encourages its female citizens to work abroad despite exploitative policies in the receiving countries so that these women will bring more capital in the form of remittances.[105] Based on neoliberal economic logics like the FDH Scheme in Hong Kong, the Filipino national hero narrative inadvertently supports the scheme and the essentialist notion that Filipinas are ideal domestic workers by nature and can only thrive through the economic support of local employers.[106]

Despite how harmful celebratory hero narratives could be in perpetuating exploitative labor practices, *Wishing Well* nevertheless includes several entries that reinforce such representations. In "Sadness to Smile," Joanna—her smiling portrait printed right above her essay—recounts that she used to be ashamed of the word "helper" because "for some, it's the cheapest kind of job one can have."[107] However, without delving any deeper into her feelings of shame and homesickness, Joanna quickly shifts into a celebratory mood: "The more I thought, the more I realized the important role helpers play in society,

---

103. Ibid.
104. Lagman, "Moving Labor," 2.
105. Lagman, "Moving Labor."
106. Constable, *Maid to Order in Hong Kong.*
107. Joanna, "Sadness to Smiles," 25.

even when it is unnoticeable or meaningless to some."[108] After describing the chores a domestic worker completes each day to ensure a smooth life for her employer, Joanna writes that "they are the people that turn illness to health and sadness into smiles."[109] Echoing the hero narrative used in the Supermaid program in the Philippines, Joanna reinvents the label "domestic helper" to celebrate the economic and domestic productivity of migrant women. While it is possible and valid for migrant women to feel celebratory about their labor and economic participation, by including predominantly essays that fulfill the social expectations of mainstream Hongkongers, *Wishing Well* is missing the opportunity to prompt the audience to critically interrogate the precarious labor conditions migrant women experience, and the shared interests and humanity that connect Hongkongers with migrant women amid the web of neoliberal economic practices.

In addition to the national hero narrative, Joanna—like Jing in the first entry—also draws on the liberal trope of female empowerment and autonomy:

> But for now I feel blessed and thankful that as a domestic helper I can provide well for my family. . . . And I live my life without depending on others. . . . But as long as Hong Kong keeps helping me fulfill my goals, I will keep on being a responsible and hardworking helper worthy of trust, even a dreamer![110]

While both Joanna and Jing evoke the family and the affective ties migrant workers have outside of their job, they do so in a way that reinforces the Filipino state narrative of gendered labor migration, rather than asserting their personhood and lived experiences within the system. Keenly aware that they are submitting to a writing contest run by an employment platform based in Hong Kong, Joanna and Jing highlight their identity as first and foremost helpers. They also express gratitude for the economic benefits and financial empowerment provided by their employments. By highlighting female empowerment through the women's participation in the neoliberal labor migration, these narratives allow the mainstream audience to feel not only unimplicated but perhaps even morally righteous in their role as employers, as they are represented as those who empower migrant women and help feed their otherwise impoverished families. Frontloading largely celebratory narratives such as Jing's and Joanna's in the anthology, HelperChoice effectively promotes and protects its own brand. By using domestic workers' own words

---

108. Ibid., 26.
109. Ibid.
110. Ibid.

to portray the benefits of gendered labor migration, HelperChoice frees itself from the potential criticism that, despite its social entrepreneurial agenda, the company nevertheless still participates in and benefits from a labor system that perpetuates a transnational power imbalance.

Entries collected in the second section of *Wishing Well*, as Chen points out in her introduction, present a more intimate view of the domestic workers' lives, particularly the conflicting affective ties they have developed, respectively, with the children they left behind and the children they are paid to care for. These narratives expose exploitative labor conditions and capture parts of the complex emotions and familial lives migrant women have because and outside of their jobs. Most of all, they call for an empathetic response from the mainstream audience by demonstrating how migrant women share the same goodwill, love, and longing for their children as local employers have for theirs. These narratives help counter dominant discourse in Hong Kong that often portrays domestic workers as conniving and lacking in common decency. However, this section continues to fall short in evoking deliberative empathy among its audiences: The readers are not prompted to interrogate the existing injustice that bolsters the migrant domestic worker system or to consider migrant women as potential allies rather than as unfortunate individuals who deserve pity and sympathy.

Despite how candid these narratives are in revealing the intense emotional and physical labor demanded of domestic workers (as one writer puts it, "It is torture that we have to pretend to be happy and energetic while taking care of our wards"), most of them end on a redemptive note in which the workers realize the value of their sacrifice and appreciate the outcome so much that they optimistically choose to remain in the migrant domestic labor system.[111] For example, in her narrative "Love Begets Love," Cleirmarie recounts the day she first left her husband and two young daughters to go work in Hong Kong. In great detail, Cleirmarie describes the emotional turmoil and heartbreak she experienced as she hugged her husband for the last time in Manila. After waiting for six hours at the Hong Kong airport for her new employer, she was immediately ordered to work: "I was introduced to at least seven members of the family, even though in my contract there were supposed to be three family members only. They were so hostile—no smiles, no handshakes."[112] After tolerating food insecurity and verbal abuse from her employers, Cleirmarie asked to be let go and was hired by a different family quickly after. Cleirmarie's descriptions of the treatment she suffered at the hands of her first employer,

---

111. Tumbaga, "Is it Worth it?," 34.
112. Cleirmarie, "Love Begets Love," 32.

which included having to survive on a food budget of HK$20 (US$2.50) a week and constantly being shamed, are vivid. While her employer's behaviors, as Constable's ethnographies show, are extremely common, the mainstream audience is prompted by Cleirmarie's narrative to reflect on the effects of these acts: Instead of a body that performs domestic labor, the domestic worker at the receiving end of such treatments is in fact a living person with complex emotions, intimate familial relationships, and a unique life story.[113] Cleirmarie's vivid description of her suffering not only humanizes her but also evokes pity among the readers. Unlike deliberative empathy, which unsettles the audiences in a way that prompts them to reexamine the material contexts of suffering and how they themselves are implicated, pity encourages them to distance themselves from the objects of such sympathy. As Susie Linfield argues, pity is a "maddening guise of generous virtue" that would not cultivate the necessary solidarity across difference through shared interests.[114]

Cleirmarie's narrative also takes on a redemptive note quickly after she describes her suffering, painting a picture that the maltreatment she received was just a matter of bad luck. Describing her second employer in very fond words, Cleirmarie writes that "for as long as they need me, I will be happy to work for them."[115] While Cleirmarie mentions the two daughters she tearfully left behind at the beginning of the narrative, her motherly love is now directed toward her employer's son: "My ward was nine months old when I started working. He will soon turn 4. I am happy to say I have enjoyed looking after him and watching him grow up to be a smart and lovable little boy. He loves me and I love him more."[116] In addition to her enjoyable work environment and the familial ties she has cultivated with her new employer, Cleirmarie's biological family is also thriving because of her job: "Now, my family is happy because they can have whatever they want. They were even invited by my employers to visit Hong Kong. That was one of the happiest days of my life, seeing them so happy."[117]

As this narrative suggests, the familial ties Cleirmarie shares with her family have not been lost at all; in fact, Cleirmarie has gained even deeper and more fulfilling affective connections through her relationship with her employer's son. While Cleirmarie's narrative makes use of intimate familial ties to highlight her humanity, it does so in a way that reinforces the image of the ideal maid: a domestic worker who is able to put aside her longing for

---

113. Constable, *Born Out of Place*; Constable, *Maid to Order in Hong Kong*.
114. Linfield, *The Cruel Radiance*, 128.
115. Cleirmarie, "Love Begets Love," 32.
116. Ibid.
117. Ibid.

her own children to love her employer's child like her own—only then does a worker deserve the happy ending Cleirmarie chronicles. What the audience is unlikely to realize from reading a redemptive narrative such as this is how the workers' family members back home cope with their loss, and how spousal and familial relationships in the sending countries are significantly altered in negative ways by the transnational care chain.[118] The redemptive tale of one individual, in other words, is not effective in prompting the audience to consider how transnational lives and families are impacted at a systematic level by the outsourcing of care across economic strata.

Cleirmarie ends her narrative by thanking God for giving her "the best employers," which in turn allows her to provide for her family. This concluding sentence reinforces the existing ethnocratic and socioeconomic hierarchy that draws the line between mainstream Hongkongers and migrant domestic workers, rendering the former more powerful and righteous. The audience's preconceptions about domestic workers and their relationship with them are left unchallenged. While sympathy, and later, affective empathy are evoked, what is missing is an invitation for the audience to consider the migrant worker system from a structural perspective and reflect on how and why migrant women deserve a seat at the table to deliberate how the system has impacted the intimate, familial aspects of all their lives.

Cleirmarie's redemptive ending is by no means singular in the anthology: Several other narratives, including ones that openly grieve the workers' broken familial relationships back home, end on an optimistic and triumphant note that highlights how grateful the writers are for being able to provide for their family, and for gaining strength and faith through the hardships they have encountered as domestic workers. The essays and poems featured in *Wishing Well* fulfill a readily intelligible narrative of a strong woman from a poor country who lifts herself and her family up from poverty through labor and perseverance. This narrative constitutes what Robert DeChaine calls "humanitarian doxa": a terministic screen through which the mainstream public understands concepts such as humanitarianism, development, victims, and heroes.[119] It reinforces negative stereotypes about Southeast Asian countries and essentialist neoliberal representations of migrant women as empowered through transnational domestic labor; it also posits that the suffering migrant women face can be solved by personal perseverance and the benevolence of individual employers. The structural causes of poverty, and the geopolitical power imbalance between sending and receiving countries, on the other hand,

---

118. Madianou and Miller, *Migration and New Media*; Parreñas, *Servants of Globalization*.
119. DeChaine, "Ethos in a Bottle," 77.

are both omitted so that these narratives seamlessly cohere with the dominant audiences' existing worldview, rather than challenging the audiences' perceptions of the transnational care chain. *Wishing Well* therefore functions more as a marketing campaign that promotes HelperChoice as a socially responsible business under a neoliberal economic framework than as an artifact that promotes deliberative empathy and the opportunity for coalitions between mainstream Hongkongers and migrant domestic workers.

## TRANSNATIONAL ETHNOGRAPHY: CONNECTING THE PERSONAL WITH THE STRUCTURAL

First published in 2015—around the same time as *Wishing Well*—So's book *Migrant Domestic Workers: Strangers at Home* was released and promoted by one of the largest publishers in Hong Kong. Prior to the publication of *Migrant Domestic Workers,* So was already an acclaimed journalist who had written numerous award-winning books and long-form articles on marginalized populations and taboo topics such as death and sexuality. Because of So's reputation, *Migrant Domestic Workers* enjoys a wide readership and has been reprinted twice in less than two years. Targeting mainstream Hongkongers as her audience, So's foreword makes clear the intricate affective, economic, and sociopolitical connections between migrant domestic workers and local employers, thus paving the path toward transformative deliberation.

Unlike Fauchon's foreword in *Wishing Well,* which essentializes Southeast Asian migrant women and reinforces the division between employers and workers, So's foreword immediately asks the audience to interrogate how they and migrant domestic workers are all affectively and economically implicated in the web of transnational caregiving and outsourced domestic labor. Entitled "Starting From One out of 33,000 . . . ," So's foreword reflects on her position as one of Hong Kong's 33,000 employers who hires a live-in migrant domestic worker. Beginning from her own experience and insecurity as a *feminist employer*—a seeming oxymoron under the current FDH Scheme—So foregrounds the intricate connections between the personal and the transnational and systematic. Using "I" as the pronoun to stand in for local employers who share her positionality, So explicates how she and women like her are represented by mainstream media as Sulistyaningsih's abusers; by dedicated parents as irresponsible mothers who expect domestic workers to fulfill the duties of a maid, cook, caregiver, and teacher; and finally, by academics as perpetrators of transnational exploitation who "have not stood arm in arm on the feminist frontline with migrant workers to struggle against the patriarchy, but have instead bound the workers tighter with the same rope we ourselves are bound with."[120] Putting aside such negative representations, So explains that she, like most other local employers, is in fact also only a human attempting to balance the needs of her family and work in a situation where there are few choices and resources available. Because of the lack of public support for caregiving, many local families must rely on domestic workers to fill the gap.[121] As So points out, on the one hand, based on rumors they have heard from others about the cunning ways of migrant workers, local women are wary that the stranger in their own home would mistreat their loved ones. However, on the other hand, after seeing abuse cases like Sulistyaningsih's, many employers have become more self-conscious of their behaviors and vow not to become an abuser.[122] Caught in polarizing public narratives about workers and employers, local women are thus at a loss as to how they ought to act and feel. The tension between workers and employers, So points out, is inevitable not only because of cultural difference and the labor contract that divides the two but also because the two parties must constantly negotiate how to relate to each other as humans amid demanding familial and career responsibilities within the spatial constraint of a small Hong Kong apartment.[123]

By reflecting on her positionality, vulnerability, and privilege as an employer and mother, So acknowledges that power is relative within the neoliberal economic and social network: While local female employers have more financial and cultural capital than domestic workers, they nevertheless exist within the same neoliberal framework. It is, therefore, unproductive to villainize all female employers because such sweeping critiques tend to focus on exploitation at the individual level, while omitting the structural causes of exploitation at the state and transnational levels. So's discussion of her own unease allows mainstream readers to lower their defense, and to examine their own complex assumptions and feelings as employers who rely on a cultural and racial Other to perform intimate familial work. To identify the cognitive, emotional, and cultural barriers that prevent coalition-building between workers and employers, So wonders what causes mainstream Hong Kong women, who are loving parents and have themselves experienced the deep affective bonds one shares with one's children, to act so callously toward the women who share the same roof and help care for their loved ones.[124] So's observation points to a dissonance that the audience may not previously have

---

120. So, *Migrant Domestic Workers*, 9.
121. Ibid.
122. Ibid.
123. Ibid.
124. Ibid., 17.

realized: that while they likely see themselves as compassionate people and parents, most of them have never questioned why they are unable or unwilling to extend the same kind of understanding to those who perform the most intimate labor for them, even though they share with the migrant women similar positionalities as mothers and woman workers. Such a schism, So points out, stems from most employers' willful ignorance of how the workers' own families and the familial and parental structures of their home countries have been drastically altered by gendered labor migration.[125] In order to cultivate any solidarity across difference through shared interests, therefore, it is necessary for the mainstream audiences to experience empathy in a way that prompts them to critically assess the structural causes and consequences of the outsourcing of care work.

Divided into five sections, *Migrant Domestic Workers* adopts a transnational feminist theoretical framework that effectively "address[es] the multiple and interlocking kinds of power relations that affect women's lives within and across national boundaries."[126] My analysis focuses on the first three sections because they best highlight the shared socioeconomic and political forces that materially and affectively connect migrant women to their female Hong Kong employers. The first section, titled "Our Home: Drawing a Line within False Intimacy," centers on the employer's perspective: why they decide to hire a live-in foreign domestic worker, how they navigate conflicting but intersecting lines of intimacy and labor relations, and how their familial dynamic has been influenced by the worker's presence. Among the families So observes and interviews, most employers, particularly those who were raised by domestic workers themselves and those who are cognizant of the exploitative nature of the FDH Scheme, express their initial desire to include the domestic worker as part of their family. These employers, however, quickly realize that despite their good intentions, the physical proximity and intimacy they share with their domestic worker are not enough to erase the barriers established by the economic nature of their relationship and the inherent power imbalance between a middle-class local family and a migrant woman whose family's well-being hinges upon her employment contract. As one employer puts it, "Now I understand: the labor relation between us is always going to be there. You will never sever ties with your family members; however, no matter how deep your emotional bond is with your foreign worker, you can always still end the contract."[127] This realization makes clear how local families and domestic workers are structurally prevented from relating to each other emotionally

---

125. Ibid.

126. Stone-Mediatore, *Reading across Borders*, 126.

127. Cited in So, *Migrant Domestic Workers*, 43.

outside of the labor context. It also illustrates that affective and familial ties are always conditioned by material conditions and neoliberal logics that entrap both citizens and aliens.

In her interview with So, acclaimed local playwright Candace Chong recounts that she has always found the strict household rules local employers impose on domestic workers ridiculous. While many employers restrict the spaces domestic workers could inhibit in their home—for example, forbidding domestic workers from sitting on the couch, or demanding that they take their meals alone in the kitchen—Chong invites her worker, Okah, to eat at the same table and share the same toiletries with Chong's family.[128] However, as So observes, Okah has drawn invisible lines that divide Chong's spacious home into spaces she can inhabit and spaces that are meant only for Chong and her family; while Okah is welcome to use the living room, she was trained by the vocational school in Indonesia to reside mainly in her own room and in the kitchen. Chong reflects:

> From [Okah's] perspective, she may find it necessary to always be cautious about how she interacts with us. . . . What I am trying to say is, even though we are treating her really nicely right now, who knows what's going to happen in the future? She may worry that she would fall into a trap when she relaxes. Honestly, I also don't think that our relationship is equal—I am asking her to work after all.[129]

Chong's lament reflects how the systemic power imbalance creates an uneasy home space for both the employer and the worker. As So opines, "An unhealthy system inevitably breeds unhealthy familial and labor relations."[130]

Showing the readers an aerial view of the situation that many of them are likely already familiar with, So's interviews with local employers make clear the complex dance between employers and workers as they continuously navigate a living arrangement that is suffused with power imbalance, mutual suspicion, and conflicting intimacy and familial bonds. While there are domestic workers who do not always fulfill all their job responsibilities and employers who are not always the most understanding, absent in these interviews are the archetypal conniving migrant women and cruel local women. Rather, what So shows in this first section is the ways in which local families and migrant women are bound together in a stifling living arrangement and a labor system that uncomfortably blurs the line between home and workplace.

---

128. So, *Migrant Domestic Workers*.
129. Ibid., 24.
130. Ibid., 64.

By highlighting the interconnectedness of their positions and lived experiences, So helps cultivate what Carrillo Rowe calls "coalitional subjectivity," in which an audience member "sees her oppression and privilege as inextricably bound to others and when she cannot envision her existence and politics as separate from others' existence and politics."[131] Here, coalitional subjectivity is cultivated alongside deliberative empathy, evoked by the candid portrayal of the interviewees' home lives. Prompted to reflect critically on the structural causes of these fraught familial dynamics—which likely resemble their own— the audience could experience deliberative empathy through the employers' stories and begin to consider how the same set of socioeconomic forces has led to similar uneasy relationships in their own lives. This critical empathetic response helps pave the path toward the second and third sections of the book: "Their Home: Familial Relationships at the Other End of the Phone" and "From Family to Structures. From Exploitation to Change."

Shifting the focus from the employers' families to the homes migrant women have left behind, the second section consists of So's interviews and ethnographic work in San Miguel, the Philippines. By juxtaposing familial stories she collected from the Philippines with narratives from local Hong Kong employers that the audience is already familiar with, So turns familial storytelling into a form of "political praxis" that asks the audience to reconsider their relationship with migrant workers.[132] This "fusion of stories," as Shari Stone-Mediatore puts it, prompts the audience to draw on familiar narrative matrices and story images to interpret and respond to subjects, relationships, and phenomena they once deemed alien.[133] Through the juxtaposition of similar yet different narratives, the storyteller and the audience enter into an intersubjective relationship in which they consider how their lifeworlds intertwine in ways that were previously obscured by the power structure or by differences in positionality. The act of storytelling and listening, in addition, promotes an affective encounter between interlocutors that moves them toward one another and prompts them to acknowledge the personhood of each other beyond their prescribed relationships within the dominant neoliberal and geopolitical context.

With Remy Borlongan, a former domestic worker in Hong Kong and the founder of the Asian Domestic Worker Union, as her key informant and guide, So interviewed and visited with families that have been directly impacted by the transnational gendered labor migration, focusing specifically on the children and husbands who have been left behind. Interwoven

---

131. Rowe, *Power Lines*, 10; Karma Chávez and Griffin, *Standing in the Intersection*, 11.
132. Langellier, "Personal Narratives," 267.
133. Stone-Mediatore, *Reading across Borders*, 41.

among these interviews are So's conversations with and observations of Borlongan's personal life since she retired from her work with the union. So's ethnographic writing, coupled with the photographs Robert Godden takes of the informants and their homes, paints a vivid picture of Filipina women as wives, mothers, advocates, and community members—they each have a life story and complex experiences that most Hongkongers have not previously considered. By directing the audience's attention to the women's family members as well, So reveals that despite cultural and geopolitical differences, these families experience desire, longing, disappointment, and love the way mainstream Hongkongers do. Through these familial vignettes in San Miguel, So invites the readers to consider the palpable emotional and familial consequences of gendered labor migration in a locale that is economically and affectively intertwined with Hong Kong.

Twenty-six-year-old Jhun Agdeppa, nicknamed Jun Jun, is one of So's interview subjects. Left behind by his mother for over twenty years, Agdeppa lives in the village with his father, younger sister, and a local maid as part of the transnational care chain.[134] Agdeppa's relationship with his father has always been distant and tense. Agdeppa recounts that because his family had not hired a new maid to replace the former one, when he was twelve he was once forced to spend the night sleeping with his sister in his father's office in the army base. He was starving, yet he dared not ask his authoritarian father for food. What So and the audience know but Agdeppa doesn't, however, is that on that same night, his father, Elbrent, was struggling not to cry in front of his children because he felt so lonely and incompetent as the sole caretaker.[135] Despite the tuition his mother paid for him to attend university, Agdeppa decided to quit school and soon found himself spending most of his time on alcohol and video games. He then enlisted in the armed forces, but got into a drunken car accident before his training even began. Now he spends most of his days playing cards and drinking. Answering So's questions about the role he wants his mother to play, Agdeppa responds, "I hope that she could come back to discipline me. I tried disciplining myself, but it didn't work. It would only work if she tells me what to do in person." So's interview with Agdeppa ends on a seemingly mundane note: After answering all of So's questions, Agdeppa reveals that he agreed to the interview only because he wanted to find out if his mother had asked So to bring him the new pair of sneakers she had gotten him for his birthday. Nonchalantly, Agdeppa says, "She showed me those shoes on Skype the night before you guys came. . . . Those are my

---

134. Parreñas, "The Reproductive Labour of Migrant Workers."
135. So, *Migrant Domestic Workers*.

birthday presents. My birthday was on June 16—it has passed a long time ago already."

So's interview with Agdeppa challenges the dominant narrative that migrant domestic workers are national and familial heroes whose labor brings their families nothing but prosperity and fulfillment; it also reveals to the readers how familial relationships in the Philippines are as complex—if not more so—as the ones they experience in their lives in Hong Kong. The readers must consider migrant workers and their family members as subjects whose interests deserve attention. Agdeppa's lack of ambition and his childlike desire for the pair of new sneakers suggest that despite migrant domestic workers' intention to provide a good education for their children so that they can gain upward mobility, their financial contribution is not always sufficient. What is lacking, as So demonstrates through her interview with Agdeppa, is the familial connection and guidance a parent could provide only when she is able to maintain physical and emotional closeness with her children. Through her interview with Agdeppa and other children who have struggled with the absence of their mothers, So debunks the misconception that migrant women and their families always benefit from the women's employment in Hong Kong. Unlike the narratives anthologized in *Wishing Well,* these ethnographic portrayals of the migrant women's families ask the audience to reconsider whether the transnational care chain and gendered labor migration are justifiable given the emotional and social tolls they take. So does not allow the audience to sit comfortably in the momentary pity or sympathy they feel toward Agdeppa and others like him, but actively prompts the readers to engage in a more critical evaluation of the labor system they participate in.

Agdeppa's tense relationship and misunderstanding with his father, in addition, shows how the absence of a key female family member impacts familial dynamics: As So demonstrates in her ethnography in San Miguel, men, socialized to be masculine, are struggling to take on a primary parenting and caregiving role in the domestic sphere.[136] In addition to Elbrent, who struggles with connecting with his children as a single father, So interviews other men who have since become the main caretakers of their children. Some children of migrant domestic workers themselves, the husbands left behind lament to So the loneliness they experience and the simultaneous understanding, longing, and jealousy they feel toward their wives, who sometimes spend as much as decades abroad. While these emotions are not the same ones Hong Kong employers experience on a daily basis, they nevertheless are readily intelligible to the audience, prompting them to recognize these subjects as

---

136. Ibid.

people who possess complex feelings and desires, rather than as disposable brown bodies devoid of shared humanity. It is possible to humanize marginalized subjects without allowing the mainstream audience to indulge or wallow in their feelings of pity or affective empathy toward them.

In addition, these vignettes demonstrate to the audience that transnational gendered labor migration influences the familial and social structures in both Hong Kong and the Philippines: While local Hong Kong women are jealous of their domestic workers gaining too much attention from their husband and children, the husband and children of the workers also suffer from similar jealousy. Given the financial and sociopolitical constraints surrounding care work, however, none of them could free themselves from these corrosive emotions. The families of Hong Kong employers and Filipina migrant women, in other words, are interconnected in the transnational economic and affective network. By inviting the reader to observe and reflect on such intimate interconnectedness, So helps cultivate deliberative empathy that acknowledges positional differences but nevertheless takes into account the shared humanity across power hierarchy and the similar ways in which Hongkongers and workers navigate the fraught familial relations and affective ties amid the larger neoliberal political and economic system.

Scattered throughout So's interviews with different families is the oral history she collects from her host, Borlongan. Borlongan's life story not only reveals how transnational economic inequality undermines the dignity and personhood of Southeast Asian women but also demonstrates that Filipinas have unique narratable selves that transcend their job function as domestic workers. By exposing the readers to the life story of a former domestic worker, So asks that they see migrant women as a *who* instead of a *what*—as a distinct subject whose humanity and personhood lies beyond the economic functions she fulfills. Because she is an activist, Borlongan's narrative defies the dominant cultural script that portrays Filipina as the ideal, docile maid, and it also challenges the neoliberal construction of feminist empowerment through participation in the transnational gendered labor market. Rather than feeling empowered by the money she earned in Hong Kong and the new financial stability she gained, Borlongan demonstrates in her narrative the dehumanizing nature of labor exploitation and the messiness of affective familial connections that cannot be translated into financial terms.

Before she became a domestic worker, Borlongan was a student leader who vehemently resisted the Marcos regime. The same year Marcos was overthrown, Borlongan's husband lost his ability to work in a car accident. In order to pay for his medical bill and to support the family, Borlongan was forced to become a migrant domestic worker in Hong Kong. She recounts that a few months into her new job, her employers, without informing her, went traveling and locked her inside the apartment alone with limited food for a week, expecting her to finish painting the apartment walls while they were away. When her employers returned, they threw Borlongan their dirty laundry as if nothing out of the ordinary had occurred. Borlongan, at the time, did not say a word about this incident. Asking Borlongan to explain how she—a former leader of the resistance movement who in 1983 was on the frontline to protest Benigo Aquino Junior's assassination—could tolerate such exploitative and dehumanizing treatments, So inadvertently prompts the readers to reflect on the essentialist stereotypes mainstream Hongkongers hold about Filipina: namely, the assumptions that they are only capable of doing undervalued domestic labor, and while street-smart, they rarely possess a sense of moral righteousness.[137] At the same time, So's question also demands the audience to consider how Hong Kong's FDH Scheme dehumanizes rather than empowers migrant women the way dominant neoliberal narratives suggest. In response, Borlongan answers, "I really needed the money. Also, my older sister had already warned me that I could not act the way I used to in Hong Kong: I should never resist. I thought this was the norm in Hong Kong—I was fine about it as long as [the employer] didn't hit me."[138] Borlongan presents the audience with a dissonance: Far from bringing the worker and her family joy and prosperity, being a domestic worker in Hong Kong could be more treacherous and demoralizing than participating in a resistance movement against a dictatorship.

Borlongan's answer may not evoke immediate affective empathy—most middle-class Hongkongers have not experienced similar events and likely cannot embody the fear, indignation, and resignation Borlongan felt at the time— but the audience nevertheless must engage in a critical reflection about the conditions and structural causes that have led to Borlongan's dehumanization in Hong Kong, to the point when her unique life story and experience were rendered entirely irrelevant. So's subsequent discussions of Borlongan's advocacy work as one of the key founders of Hong Kong's first migrant domestic worker unions further highlights migrant women's political capacity beyond the domestic sphere. Specifically, So's discussions of the union illustrate that migrant domestic workers possess epistemic privilege that local Hongkongers do not, and they therefore deserve a seat at the deliberative table to reenvi-

---

137. As Constable points out, Hong Kong employment agencies perpetuate different stereotypes about migrant workers from different countries: While Filipina women are considered intelligent and often conniving, Indonesian women are often described as innocent and simpleminded. Constable, *Maid to Order in Hong Kong*.

138. Cited in So, *Migrant Domestic Workers*, 113.

sion a system in which migrant domestic workers are seen not only as economic instruments, but rather as potential allies with local women who could
cultivate a dissident friendship "based on shared politics, rather than shared
identities."[139]

In addition to detailing Borlongan's experience of exploitation and resistance as a domestic worker, So also evokes deliberative empathy and explores
the possibilities of a dissident friendship between Borlongan and the readers
by discussing Borlongan's relationship with her transgender daughter Jeppoy,
particularly how Borlongan has repeatedly advocated for Jeppoy in front of
school officials. Jeppoy and Borlongan's story resembles the narratives So has
recorded in her other book, *Our Queer Children*, which documents how nine
Hong Kong parents negotiate their children's non-normative sexualities, particularly in dealing with the pressure and stigma imposed by the mainstream
public. While Jeppoy's transition and the way Borlongan supports her have
seemingly little to do with the topic of migrant domestic workers, the vignette
of the parental relationship between the two against oppressive social stig-
mas makes clear that Filipino families and Hong Kong families alike experience similar social pressures—that despite their geopolitical, cultural, and
economic differences, they nevertheless are caught up within the same web
of human affairs, attempting to provide the best for their loved ones against
stigma and oppression. If the readers experience any empathy for Borlongan,
it is the kind of uneasy empathy that does not allow them to co-suffer with
her, but rather prompts them to acknowledge the unsettling simultaneous
sameness and difference between them and Borlongan.[140]

While Borlongan's and other individuals' familial stories are compelling
and effective in generating empathy from the audiences, focusing only on the
personal is inadequate in prompting the audience to consider the political and
economic dimensions of the injustice of the migrant domestic labor system.
This connection between the political and systematic and the personal and
intimate is key in promoting deliberative empathy in a way that cultivates
coalitional moments. As Rowe points out, "We must reckon with the ways in
which power relations are reproduced and potentially rewritten within these
intimate sites of our belonging because our loyalties produce and are produced by a range of possible material and political conditions. This reckon-
ing entails scrutinizing the modes of power and empowerment that drive our
affective ties, and which those ties make possible."[141] Prompted to consider how

---

139. Chowdhury and Philipose, *Dissident Friendships*, 14.

140. For discussions on the ethical and political limitation of co-suffering, see Spelman,
*Fruits of Sorrow*, 67.

141. Rowe, *Power Lines*, 2.

various forms of familial relations—the bonds they share with their nuclear family members, the uneasy economic and affective ties they have with their domestic workers, and the often fraught transnational relationships migrant women have with their loved ones back home—are produced by overlapping structures of power, the audience must grapple with how their subjectivity intersects with that of the workers amid their shared material and ideological contexts in ways that unsettle politically ineffective pity or affective empathy.

In the third section, So interviews stakeholders from different social sectors at both the local and transnational levels to reveal the structural causes of labor exploitation and the initiatives workers and advocates are taking to address the power imbalance. In addition to showcasing how workers are collaborating with local advocates through organizations such as the Asian Migrant Credit Union and Helpers for Domestic Helpers, a pro bono legal clinic for migrant women, So also invites the audience to critically examine how local employers are being harmed by existing labor practices. For example, a former employee at a Hong Kong domestic worker employment agency confides in So that agencies purposefully provide very little support to employers when they experience conflicts with their domestic workers; rather, agencies often encourage employers to fire their current worker and hire a new one so that the companies can continue to generate profit through the transactions. As the informant tells So, "The employment agency has no sense of obligation at all towards its clients' family."[142] While many local employers see employment agencies as their ally, So reveals that perhaps it is wiser and more pragmatic for them to establish a coalition with the migrant workers rather than with a company that is driven to profit from both ends. So's interview allows the audience a glimpse of the material inter-est that binds mainstream Hongkongers and domestic workers together despite their difference. While the potential of this coalition moment is driven primarily by the employers' self-interests, as Adams argues, "self-interest can promote a practice of coalition discourse that accommodates diverse truths and centers their constitution on material culture."[143] By situating these truths, together with the different identities and positionalities that produce them, within overlapping material contexts, interlocutors could begin to understand how their interests connect with those of others; they are thus motivated to make use of these differences to form new alliances and sociopolitical models that would best benefit themselves and their allies. While the first two sections primarily evoke

---

142. Cited in So, *Migrant Domestic Workers*, 285.
143. Adams, "At the Table with Arendt," 2.

feelings of uneasy critical empathy, this section gives the audience material reasons to engage in more internal deliberation about the kinds of emotional, economic, and political relationships that would most benefit them.

To close, So and Godden—the photographer—document the lives of domestic workers in Hong Kong outside of their jobs through photographs and personal narratives. While these narratives and some of the women's portraits resemble those featured in *Wishing Well,* none of them have a tidy, redemptive ending. Rather, they demonstrate the bonds migrant women have built with each other, their intimate but sometimes fraught relationships with their employers, and the many difficult decisions they have made throughout their diasporic experience. None of the women, however, see themselves as heroes of their nation or of their families because they are keenly aware that the economic stability they bring home comes with a hefty emotional price tag. While the entries in *Wishing Well* mostly conform with the audience's expectations of migrant domestic workers and with the image of the ideal servant, the personal narratives in *Migrant Domestic Workers* directly confront the audience's assumptions that domestic workers ought to be treated with caution because they are here to usurp the resources of Hongkongers. Addressing the 2012 lawsuit on domestic workers' right to permanent residency, Thai domestic worker Phobsuk Gasing tells So, "You think we are going to be greedy for the HK$2–3,000 the government gives out [for public welfare]? Life in Hong Kong is not cheap! We could buy our own house and land if we go home. We'd be much happier that way."[144] Another worker, Shiella, exclaims:

> Some people said that we were going to steal jobs from Hongkongers, or that we would bring our family over to take advantage of social welfare and the taxpayers' dollars. But I thought, "It isn't easy to live in Hong Kong, particularly the rent! You guys should know how much we make!' We are fighting for permanent residency only because we want to resist against the discrimination—why is it that only domestic workers are excluded from the right of abode?[145]

By speaking directly to the audience and asking them to reexamine their assumptions, these narratives jostle the readers out of their existing interpretative framework and any self-comforting feelings of sympathy, and instead

---

144. Ibid., 359.
145. Ibid., 364.

demand they see the workers as humans and political subjects who deserve to "co-appear" in the space of deliberation while maintaining their difference.[146]

So's *Migrant Domestic Workers* is best described as a cacophony of stories from subjects who occupy different positionalities. Unlike the uniform ideology mounted by entries in *Wishing Well* or the legal arguments made in court during the case on domestic workers' right of abode, So presents what Stone-Mediatore calls a "community of storytellers," composed of migrant women, local employers, and their respective families, to "make a claim about the world without ending debate."[147] By situating these narratives within the broader geopolitical and socioeconomic context, So's text invites the audience to see these narratives not as competing universal arguments about the phenomenon, but as specific ways in which subjects from different positionalities make sense of the world and of their experiences. By presenting these narratives as open-ended stories, So also engages the audience in active interpretation and deliberation to, as Stone-Mediatore cogently puts it, "explore the lived significance of strange affairs and consider how their own lives might be situated within the web of actions and reactions that make up those affairs."[148] The cacophony of transnationally situated stories invites audiences to enact empathy not by stepping into the shoes of the storytellers or the protagonists, but by reflecting on their own position and the roles they play amid the network of power that connects them all. This invitation to enact deliberative empathy echoes the kind of political inquiry and participatory civic culture that political theorists such as Arendt and Benhabib advocate for, a culture that encourages deliberation, discovery, and constant reinvention of inter-ests rather than sameness and consensus.[149]

## CONCLUSION

The lawsuit, *Wishing Well*, and *Migrant Domestic Workers* are rhetorical responses to the transnational structural injustice that has led to the systematic exploitation and dehumanization of migrant domestic workers in Hong Kong. As I have demonstrated in my analysis, each of these responses stems from and reinforces different ideological and interpretive frameworks, and not all of them are conducive to the cultivation of coalition across difference

146. Cavarero, *Relating Narratives*, 89.
147. Stone-Mediatore, *Reading across Borders*, 62.
148. Ibid., 63.
149. Arendt and Canovan, *The Human Condition*; Benhabib, *Situating the Self*.

through the awareness of intersubjectivity and inter-ests. Legal attempts to secure permanent residency for domestic workers, though on the surface appearing the most politically efficacious measures, circumscribe the mainstream citizenry and migrant women into the existing interpretative framework in which the former functions as the economic sponsor and manager of the latter. Within this framework, despite the intimacy domestic workers share with local families through their labor, they will never be deemed worthy for inclusion by the nation-family, as demonstrated by Hong Kong's Immigration Ordinance and the way the three judges interpreted the Basic Law. The public outrage and backlash against domestic workers at the time further highlights the inadequacy of formal citizenship in fostering a deliberative space in which mainstream Hongkongers and migrant women—despite their difference—would engage with each other as equal interlocutors, both having the ability to contribute to each other's overlapping inter-ests. In order to cultivate such a productive deliberative space in which alterity and difference is not a hindrance but a necessity for change, mainstream Hongkongers must first recognize the humanity of migrant women outside of their identity as domestic workers and acknowledge that their lives and material conditions are intertwined with the workers' within the same neoliberal economic web. Staunchly anchored in an ideological framework that values familiarity and penalizes poor, racialized and gendered bodies, formal citizenship is unable to bring forth such recognition.

Outside of the dominant framework of formal citizenship and arguments, personal narratives and acts of storytelling carry the potential to generate empathy, prompting the audience to see the narrated subject as a subject whose lived experiences remind the audience of their intersubjectivity.[150] The use of personal narratives, however, is never free of ideology. Stories, for example, could be co-opted to further political goals that perpetuate or reinforce the existing power hierarchy.[151] The personal stories anthologized in *Wishing Well* illustrate how narratives from migrant women could be used to generate sympathy or affective empathy among the readers, yet at the same time allow the audience to remain comfortably within the dominant ideological framework that highlights the divide between mainstream Hongkongers and domestic workers and willfully underplay the structural exploitation inherent within the FDH Scheme.

---

150. Jackson, *The Politics of Storytelling.*
151. Shuman, *Other People's Stories.*

While *Wishing Well* allows migrant women the rhetorical opportunity to represent themselves as people possessing identities outside of their job functions, it nevertheless reinforces the readily intelligible image of Southeast Asian women as dedicated mothers and wives who are only suited for undervalued work in the domestic sphere. Instead of asserting the unique narratable self of each migrant woman, these familial narratives reinscribe them within their gendered roles and within the dominant narrative of the Filipino nation-family: By fulfilling their duties as overseas domestic workers, these women are helping support the Filipino nation-state, while allowing both the Filipino and Hong Kong governments to skimp on providing public support for caregiving. Benefitting from the neoliberal market in which domestic work is outsourced transnationally, HelperChoice is able to boost its own ethos with *Wishing Well*. By choosing to include primarily narratives that end on a redemptive and uplifting note, HelperChoice presents transnational gendered labor migration as a path toward empowerment for poor Southeast Asian women; such empowerment, however, is contingent upon middle-class Hongkongers and the continuation of the FDH Scheme. As a result, while the anthology does allow for the circulation of migrant women's voices in the mainstream public, it falls short on prompting mainstream Hong Kong audiences to reflect on the intersubjective existence they share with migrant domestic workers, and to critically reexamine how they differentially belong to each other outside of seemingly fixed identity categories as they are all implicated within the same web of neoliberal logics.

In order to generate the sense of "differential belonging" and "coalitional subjectivity" between mainstream Hongkongers and domestic workers, the former must first enact critical empathy and reckon with the significance of the migrant women's lived experience and how the women's interests are intimately tied to the self-interests of local employers. Foregrounding familial narratives and experiences from local employers, So invites the readers to enact deliberative empathy and to critically consider how they could promote their self-interests by reexamining the existing labor and social system. So, however, does not allow the readers to think of Hongkongers' self-interests as confined to a fixed identity category based on the interpretive framework of citizenship that marks migrant women as outside of the nation-family. Rather, by juxtaposing familial narratives from employers with stories told by domestic workers and their family members, So productively transforms the nascent affective empathy she generates into a more critical and deliberative form that prompts the audience to consider the emotional and social commonalities between local and Filipino families—both having to participate in the outsourcing of domestic labor in order to best provide for their loved ones.

Focusing on the shared material and emotional consequences of neoliberal policies, *Migrant Domestic Workers* demonstrates that sameness and difference need not exist as contradictory, binary terms. Hongkongers' self-interests, in fact, are intertwined with the interests of migrant domestic workers. Such realization of the intersubjective nature of interests is key to the cultivation of alliances across difference because, as Lyon posits, "when interlocutors go beyond personal interests and commit to finding inter-ests, they acknowledge the narratability, the sequence, of another's life and the possibility of inter-ests they enter the in-between."[152]

---

152. Lyon, *Deliberative Acts,* 92.

# CHAPTER 4

## The Limits of Deliberative Empathy

*Chinese Maternal Tourism and*
*Contesting Familial Claims*

WHILE THE South Asian community and the Southeast Asian domestic workers are systematically marginalized in Hong Kong partly because of their race, the controversy surrounding the influx of mainland Chinese immigrants illustrates that subjects can be marginalized and denied formal recognition even when they share the same race and ethnicity with the mainstream citizenry. Formal citizenship is a mechanism used not only to marginalize those who are phenotypically different but also to exclude those who lack significant cultural and financial capital. In 2001, against the wish of the Hong Kong government and the mainstream public, the Court of Final Appeal made a controversial ruling and granted permanent residency to all children born to mainland Chinese parents in Hong Kong. Soon after, pregnant mainland women began crossing the border to give birth in Hong Kong, so that their children could enjoy the socioeconomic benefits and cultural capital the SAR and the Hong Kong passport offers.[1] Because neither parent of these children is a Hong Kong permanent resident, these children are coined by Hongkongers and local media as *neithers*.[2] The influx of *neithers* peaked amid a period of constant sociopolitical conflict between the Hong Kong public and the mainland Chinese government. Between 2006 and 2012, over 100,000 pregnant

---

1. Yam, "Affective Economies and Alienizing Discourse."
2. The literal translation of the Chinese term for these children is *double negative* (雙非).

women from mainland China gave birth in the SAR, causing significant public outrage among mainstream Hongkongers, which subsequently prompted the Hong Kong government to ban Chinese maternal tourism in 2013.[3]

Since China intensified its attempt to integrate Hong Kong politically and ideologically into the dominant Chinese nation-state during the early 2000s, Hongkongers have grown wary of any actions and signs that suggest China's increased interference encroaches upon the "One Country, Two Systems" framework guaranteed by the 1984 Sino-British Joint Declaration.[4] Since 2003, Hongkongers have been staging large-scale protests—culminating in the recent Umbrella Movement—to demand universal suffrage independent from Beijing, and also political, cultural, and ideological autonomy from mainland China.[5] Meanwhile, China has implemented a set of revised travel and economic policies that deepen Hong Kong's financial dependence on China by bringing in a tremendous number of mainland tourists, investors, and capital to the SAR.

The physical presence of mainlanders in the SAR has thus become a constant reminder of China's looming political and economic power. As a result, despite the fact that the children born to mainland parents are legal permanent residents of the SAR, during the 2010s Hongkongers were quick to make emotional and political claims that represent all maternal tourists as invaders of the Hong Kong nation-family, and the *neithers* as alien bodies undeserving of legal and national membership in the SAR because of the threat they pose to the welfare of *true* Hong Kong families. As the deep sense of anxiety and unease Hongkongers felt toward China's increased political and economic encroachment circulated and was transferred onto the bodies of mainlanders, negative emotional responses against Chinese maternal tourists quickly gained valence in the local affective economy, effectively silencing alternative and more humanizing representations of this population.

As a result, despite attempts made by Hong Kong journalists and Chinese mothers to portray maternal tourists as struggling parents who share the same concerns for their children as local Hong Kong parents do, these alternative representations have failed to elicit deliberative empathy from mainstream Hongkongers. Acts of storytelling and familial narratives, in other words, do not always generate the necessary emotional response from the mainstream

3. Yu-Wah Lam, "Number of Mainland Pregnant Women Rushing to Give Birth at the ER More Than Doubled Last Year," *Wenweipo*, last modified January 6, 2012, http://paper.wenweipo .com/2012/01/06/HK1201060007.htm.

4. Yam, "Education and Transnational Nationalism."

5. Gruber, "The (Digital) Majesty of All under Heaven"; Yam, "Education and Transnational Nationalism."

audience to motivate transformative deliberation or to cultivate solidarity across difference through shared interests. The enactment of deliberative empathy requires the dominant subject to modulate their affective and emotional responses with critical reflections and deliberation on their relationships with others and the structural forces that bind them together. As such, we cannot interrogate the rhetorical conditions that limit deliberative empathy without considering the affective economies that constitute the mainstream citizenry's lifeworld, particularly in relation to their perception of the stability of the nation-family and their own familial units.

In this chapter, I first examine the citizenship and familial discourse between Hong Kong and China from 1997 to 2013, demonstrating how the family as a social unit and a metaphor for the nation-state has impacted the emotional and political relationships between mainstream Hongkongers and the mainland Chinese people. Mobilized in the late 1990s by the Chinese government as a trope to stabilize the nation-state, the family as a metaphor incited public fear among Hongkongers who resisted the ideological agenda of the Chinese Communist Party.[6] As a social unit, the family was nevertheless intimately connected to the construction of postcolonial Hong Kong as a nation distinct from mainland China. Mainland Chinese families, therefore, were used—first by the Hong Kong government in the late 1990s and by the mainstream Hong Kong public in the early 2010s—as figures to fuel existing contempt and anger and to justify exclusionary practices against Chinese immigrants.

Beginning with an analysis of a monumental court case in 1998 on the residency status of mainland-born children to Hong Kong parents, I argue that dominant citizenship discourse proffered by the Hong Kong government prior to the ruling pitches local Hong Kong families against mainland Chinese families, reinforcing the impression that the welfare of local families would be significantly harmed by the influx of Chinese immigrants. The claims of family reunion made by mainland-born children, on the other hand, were deemed less significant by the mainstream citizenry and the Hong Kong government than protecting the well-being of Hong Kong families. By mobilizing its political power to decide what forms of family deserve legal recognition, the Hong Kong government was able to satiate the mainstream public's desire to maintain an exclusionary nation-family, while sidestepping the need to expand the SAR's social welfare system; thus, it was able to also protect its own neoliberal economic interests. This case demonstrates that in formal citizenship discourse, only normative families who fulfill the nation-state's neoliberal

---

6. Pan, Lee, Chan, and So, "Orchestrating the Family-Nation Chorus."

interests and imaginary are protected. I also examine how after the court's ruling, the Hong Kong government and mainstream news media mobilized and intensified the panic and fear among Hongkongers during the early 2000s to prevent the influx of poor Chinese families into the SAR. Attached to the bodies of mainlanders, these negative emotions continued to circulate and remain salient over a decade later, even though a significant number of Chinese immigrants and visitors are now upper middle class.

I then trace the ongoing political and rhetorical effects of these emotional resonances in subsequent sections by interrogating the exclusionary and nationalist claims produced by mainstream Hongkongers against the *neithers* and their Chinese parents between 2013 and 2014. These alienizing tropes were so affectively powerful that they triggered the feeling of fear among mainstream Hongkongers—a fear that suggests their survival and the survival of their kin were at stake. Since Hongkongers produced, circulated, and engaged in citizenship discourse most actively on social media, I analyze a wide range of internet writing and popular printed materials, which often carry immense rhetorical and emotional force to propel sociopolitical actions. In particular, I study how Hongkongers and mainstream media mobilized fear, anger, and disgust and deployed animalist tropes to render mainland Chinese people—particularly as families—an abject aggregate that does not deserve any empathy or room in a shared deliberative space. By examining how alienizing tropes and emotions constitute a powerful emotional pedagogy that renders more humanizing emotional representations impermissible and inexpressible, this analysis illustrates the conditions that limit the enactment of deliberative empathy.

## BACKGROUND: ONE COUNTRY, TWO IDENTITIES

Under the British colonial administration, Hong Kong experienced tremendous economic success beginning in the 1970s by participating in the liberal-capitalist system.[7] Around the same time, eager to build up its international reputation as a benevolent regime, the colonial government under Governor MacLehose expanded the social welfare system in Hong Kong and established an independent commission to eradicate corruption; these policies dramatically enhanced the quality of life of Hongkongers.[8] The colonial government later allowed and encouraged Hongkongers to participate in the elections of

---

7. Carroll, *A Concise History of Hong Kong.*
8. Ibid.

district officials and members of the Legislative Council. Unlike their peers in mainland China who at the time were struggling economically and socially because of the Cultural Revolution, Hongkongers were thriving and as a result subscribed to a cultural and national identity built upon capitalist achievement, relative freedom, economic prosperity, and political stability.[9] Most of all, Hongkongers began to define themselves as belonging to the British colony, rather than to China at large. Hongkongers, while ethnically Chinese, saw themselves as culturally, politically, and socially distinct from their more "backward" peers in mainland China.[10]

The distinction Hongkongers drew between members of their own nation-family and Chinese residents who were deemed culturally inferior was reinforced during the late 1970s and early 1980s, when an increasing number of Chinese nationals immigrated to Hong Kong under Deng Xiaoping's more relaxed sociopolitical policies.[11] Between 1978 and 1980, 193,300 legal and 161,800 undocumented Chinese immigrants were granted permanent residency in Hong Kong.[12] Given that most undocumented immigrants who arrived in Hong Kong were poor, uneducated, and in need of public support, the colonial government and mainstream Hong Kong media portrayed this new population as damaging to the social welfare of *rightful* Hongkongers. Although Hong Kong has always been within the border of mainland China, Hongkongers historically perceived themselves as belonging to a superior nation-family separate from that of the mainland Chinese people.

Since Hongkongers and their mainland Chinese counterparts share the same ethnic, historical, and cultural lineage, mainland Chinese people operate as the abject within the Hong Kong national and cultural imaginary: Mainlanders are uncomfortably close and familiar to Hongkongers, "who they are supposed to be radically different from."[13] As philosopher Shannon Sullivan points out, because the abject "troubles sharp, clear boundaries between subject and object, self and other," the dominant subject must painstakingly mark the distinction between themselves and the abject Other to prevent the dissolution of boundaries.[14] Indeed, during the 1970s, the mainstream Hong Kong public began to racialize mainland Chinese people and portrayed them as undeserving of care and concern. As Jaspir Puar and Donovan Schaefer point out, racialization is not only tied to what historically has been considered

---

9. Ku, "Hegemonic Construction, Negotiation and Displacement."
10. Ku, "Immigration Policies."
11. Newendorp, *Uneasy Reunions.*
12. Burns, "Immigration from China and the Future of Hong Kong," 664.
13. Sullivan, *Good White People,* 30.
14. Ibid., 32.

"race."[15] Rather, it refers to processes of social formation that "disdain an out-sider—national, religious, class—as a savage."[16] The social imaginary of main-land immigrant as lowly and uncivilized was solidified in 1979 when a popular Hong Kong TV show debuted the character Ah Chian. As Hong Kong media scholar Eric Kit-Wai Ma points out:

> Ah Chian is dirty in the actual sense of the word. . . . The character of Ah Chian is heavily imbued with references, both verbal and visual, to garbage, dirt, feces, urine, vomit, sweat, and nasal discharges. His dirtiness is exces-sive when seen in retrospect, but seemed to be very natural to the producers and local audiences at the time the serial was launched.[17]

Because of the show, newcomers from mainland China are to this day referred to by mainstream Hongkongers as *Ah Chian*. This representation of mainland-ers as culturally inferior continues to linger and is often mobilized by main-stream Hongkongers to justify their continual exclusionary sentiments against mainlanders.[18] Lacking self-discipline and low in productivity, Ah Chian—standing in for mainland Chinese immigrants—signaled the kind of lawless-ness and instability Hongkongers associated with the Chinese government.[19]

Because of the negative associations Hongkongers had about mainland China and Chinese nationals, prior to the return of Hong Kong's sovereignty in 1997, the British colonial government restricted the immigration of main-land Chinese people into Hong Kong, despite the fact that many of them had family members in the city.[20] For instance, while prior to 1983 any Chinese nationals born in Hong Kong would automatically be granted the right of abode, the colonial government revised its immigration regulation so that only children born to *two* Hong Kong permanent residents would be granted permanent residency as a birthright.[21] In addition, the British Nationality Act of 1981 restricted the right of abode to women married to Hong Kong perma-nent residents; prior to the act, spouses of Hong Kong permanent residents would automatically receive permanent residency. These restrictive immigra-tion policies made it difficult for cross-border families to legally reunite with their loved ones. Spouses and children in mainland China sometimes had to

15. Puar, *Terrorist Assemblages*; Schaefer, *Religious Affects*.
16. Schaefer, *Religious Affects*, 122.
17. Ma, *Culture, Politics and Television in Hong Kong*, 67.
18. Yam, "Affective Economies and Alienizing Discourse."
19. Newendorp, *Uneasy Reunions*.
20. Ibid.
21. Ibid.

wait one to two decades to obtain the necessary legal documents to join their family in Hong Kong.[22]

Although these restrictive policies were harmful to many families, they were much appreciated by mainstream Hongkongers who dreaded the return of the city's sovereignty to China in 1997.[23] In order to appease the anxious Hong Kong public who at the time were emigrating out of the city at an alarming rate to avoid being under Beijing's rule, the Chinese government agreed that Hong Kong would be designated as a Special Administrative Region (SAR) with a legal, political, and economic system—modeled largely after that of the United Kingdom—independent from China's control.[24] Proclaiming the "One Country, Two Systems" principle, the late Deng Xiaoping promised the Hong Kong public in 1984 that "Hong Kong's current social and economic systems will remain unchanged . . . [and China's] policies with regard to Hong Kong will remain unchanged for 50 years."[25] Deng's claim, therefore, served to maintain a sense of stability and security in Hong Kong before the formal transition of sovereignty.

Under the "One Country, Two Systems" principle, the postcolonial SAR government is charged with a seemingly contradictory task: It must guarantee that the living standard and values of Hongkongers remain the same prior to the return of sovereignty, while showing its allegiance to Beijing by gradually integrating Hong Kong into China's sovereignty. Selected by a small committee of 1,200 members handpicked by Beijing, the chief executive of Hong Kong has always been seen by the Hong Kong public as a proxy of the Chinese government. At the time, however, they must demonstrate—or at least maintain the appearance—that they are committed to protecting the rights and interests of local Hongkongers. Because of this contradiction, the ethos of the chief executive and the SAR government at large has always been under fire by prodemocracy advocates in Hong Kong.

Angered by the SAR government's intent to legislate an antisubversion law in the name of national security, half a million Hongkongers participated in a prodemocracy and anti-China march in 2003.[26] Since then, each year during July 1—the handover anniversary of Hong Kong—hundreds of thousands of protestors flood the streets, demanding democracy and the protection of political freedom under Chinese rule.[27] The 2003 march, which coincided with

---

22. Ku, "Hegemonic Construction, Negotiation and Displacement."
23. Newendorp, *Uneasy Reunions.*
24. Ong, *Flexible Citizenship.*
25. "Deng Xiaoping on 'One Country, Two Systems.'"
26. Jennifer Ngo, "July 1 Protest Is Hong Kong's Taste of Democracy," 1.
27. Ibid.

the transition of power within the Chinese Community Party, prompted Beijing to tighten its political and ideological control on Hong Kong to ensure that the SAR would be more fully integrated into the Chinese state.[28] Because of Hong Kong's special political and legal status within China's sovereignty, the Chinese government engages in what Ong calls "zoning technologies" to ensure that the SAR functions as a semi-independent enclave that nonetheless retains intimate economic ties with the mainland.[29] For Beijing, the economic ties between China and Hong Kong serve the political purpose of eventual ideological integration.

In 2003, the Chinese government implemented the Individual Travel Scheme to deepen Hong Kong's economic dependence on China. Under this policy, mainland Chinese from twenty-one select cities can visit Hong Kong and Macau for up to a week by applying for a simple visa permit. Prior to this policy, the entry of mainlanders into Hong Kong was highly restricted, while Hongkongers could visit mainland China with relative ease. As a result of the scheme, the number of mainland Chinese tourists who frequented the SAR increased exponentially throughout the next decade. In 2014, 47 million visitors from mainland China traveled to Hong Kong—a number that was six times larger than the local population of the city.[30] This huge influx of mainland visitors inadvertently altered the cultural and socioeconomic landscape of the city. Coming from China's growing upper middle class, many mainland tourists who visit Hong Kong possess a great deal of economic capital and have a high demand for the luxury goods sold in the city. As a result, both local and transnational businesses in the city began catering almost exclusively to mainlanders by using Mandarin Chinese and simplified Chinese characters instead of the local Hong Kong variant. Such economic and linguistic changes are jarring and unsettling to Hongkongers as they not only reflect the erosion of local culture but also signal the social power mainlanders can wield. While mainlanders have been historically represented by popular Hong Kong media as country bumpkins, such representations and distinctions between mainlanders and Hongkongers no longer ring true as many mainland visitors now possess more economic—and therefore political and cultural—power than local Hongkongers.[31] As Ming Chan explains, Hongkongers are concerned that the SAR's increased economic reliance on China would "result in the HKSAR's being more fully absorbed into the PRC mainland orbit, not just in

28. Yam, "Education and Transnational Nationalism."
29. Ong, *Neoliberalism as Exception,* 103.
30. Reuters, "Beijing to Limit Hong Kong Visits by Mainland Chinese."
31. Ma, *Culture, Politics and Television in Hong Kong.*

the nominal political sense, but also into its powerful, much larger, but less liberal social and cultural loci."[32]

The bodies of mainland visitors, therefore, have become a constant reminder for Hongkongers of China's superior economic status and the looming threat that the still semi-independent SAR will soon lose its autonomy and cultural superiority and become "colonized" by mainland China.[33] While mainland visitors has contributed significantly to Hong Kong's economy, Hongkongers commonly regard them with contempt and anger, sometimes hurling insults in public to mainland visitors.[34] In 2014, such anger translated into protests and violent clashes between Hongkongers and mainlanders that provoked harsh remarks from both the Chinese and SAR governments.[35]

The influx of mainlanders into the SAR has led to an enhanced sense of anxiety among Hongkongers as the space they consider home is becoming increasingly unfamiliar. As Sullivan points out, the dominant group often becomes much more anxious about interacting with the Other if there are no longer any explicit legal, political, or cultural barriers that demarcate the two.[36] Journalist Te-Ping Chen explains that because the number of mainland visitors significantly outnumbers the local population, they have overwhelmed the already crowded streets of a very small city; because of the purchasing power of mainlanders and their propensity to consume European luxury goods, many smaller local stores have been priced out of the market, giving way to flagship brand name boutiques like Rolex and Louis Vuitton. Chen further elucidates, "It has come to a point *where residents don't feel like the city is theirs anymore*—you walk out on the street [and] you hear Mandarin being spoken instead of the local dialect of Cantonese. . . . There is an increasing sense that Hong Kong is being swept up and assimilated into mainland China that people are really unready for."[37] Chen's descriptions elucidate the Hongkongers' new social anxiety that stems from an eroding social position, and the fear of feeling like a stranger in one's own home.

The dominant affective states Hongkongers feel toward China—and by proxy, mainland Chinese visitors and immigrants—are ones saturated with

---

32. Chan, Ming K. "Introduction: The Hong Kong SAR in Flux." In *Crisis and Transformation in China's Hong Kong*, Ming K. Chan and Alvin Y. So, eds. pp. 3–19.

33. Szeto, "Identity Politics and Its Discontents."

34. Naomi Ng and Chan, "Hong Kong to Chinese Shoppers"; Ying-kit and Jing, "2 in 3 Hongkongers Want Curb on Mainland Chinese Visitors."

35. Yam, "Grassroots Tactics and the Appropriation of State Nationalist Rhetoric."

36. Sullivan, *Revealing Whiteness*.

37. Chen, Interview with Mariko Sanchanta.

anxiety and unease. Such anxiety stems partially from their eroding social position and the fear of feeling like a stranger in one's own home. More importantly, however, such anxiety is induced by China's overwhelming political and economic dominance over the SAR.

## FAMILIAL TIES AND THE LIMIT OF FORMAL CITIZENSHIP

Such history and tension between mainland China and the mainstream Hong Kong public have significantly impacted the way Hong Kong permanent residency is legally defined in relation to Chinese nationals. Even after the return of Hong Kong's sovereignty to China, there remains a clear legal distinction between Hong Kong permanent residency status and Chinese citizenship. While Article 24(2)(1) of the Hong Kong Basic Law generously grants that (1) Chinese citizens born in Hong Kong before or after 1997 and (2) children born in the mainland to Hong Kong parents are all eligible for permanent residency, the Hong Kong government amended the Immigration Ordinance on July 1, 1997—the day Hong Kong officially became part of China—to significantly restrict Chinese nationals' access to permanent residency of the SAR.

Under the revised Immigration Ordinance, a Chinese national born in Hong Kong would only be granted permanent residency if at least one of her parents was a permanent resident in the SAR at the time of her birth.[38] In addition, only institutionalized forms of parental and familial relationships were recognized under this amendment: If the child was born out of wedlock to a Hong Kong father, the child would not be granted permanent residency, unless the father subsequently married the mainland mother.[39] For children born in mainland China to Hong Kong parents, their permanent residency status would not be legally recognized by the SAR government unless they first obtained an exit permit from the mainland Chinese government and then used the permit to enter the SAR.[40] The wait for the exit permit, however, was notoriously long and the process was not always affordable due to corruption among mainland officials.[41] As a result, eager to reunite with their parents, many mainland-born children entered Hong Kong without the required legal documents, and thus were not granted the right of abode in the SAR.

In this section, I examine a monumental lawsuit in 1999 brought on by children who had at least one Hong Kong parent but were denied permanent

---

38. Immigration (Amendment) (No. 2) Ordinance 1997.
39. Ibid.
40. Ibid.; Immigration (Amendment) (No. 3) Ordinance 1997.
41. Newendorp, *Uneasy Reunions.*

residency in the SAR under the new immigration amendments. In my analysis of this case, I first illustrate how biological familial ties are constructed concomitantly with the nation-family. I then demonstrate how despite the salience of the familial trope within mainstream citizenship discourse, families that are marginalized culturally and socioeconomically often cannot seek recourse within the dominant political and legal context, in which the state's concerns over its neoliberal interests and power trump the familial and citizenship claims made by marginalized subjects.

In 1998, a year after the return of Hong Kong's sovereignty to China, over 5,000 mainland Chinese claimants who were deemed "illegal immigrants" by the Hong Kong Immigration Department filed a lawsuit seeking the right of abode in the SAR.[42] All of these claimants were immediate family members of current Hong Kong permanent residents. At the center of this case was four claimants whose fathers were Hong Kong permanent residents; all four had entered Hong Kong without the necessary exit permit, and one of them was born out of wedlock.[43] Because of these circumstances, their application to permanent residency was denied under the amended Hong Kong Immigration Ordinance.[44] Advocates of the claimants argued that based on the immediate familial connections the claimants had with Hong Kong permanent residents, they should be entitled to legal recognition.[45] The claimants and their advocates specifically posited that it was their *moral right* to be reunited with their family members.[46] Outside of popular local discourse, the claimants' legal counsel argued in court that the restrictions imposed by the Immigration Ordinance were unconstitutional and therefore should be dismissed. In January 29, 1999, the Court of Final Appeal ruled in favor of the claimants, affirming the right of abode for all mainland-born children to at least one Hong Kong permanent resident (including those born out of wedlock) as a constitutional right.[47] This ruling was highly disputed by mainstream Hongkongers and the executive branch of the SAR government because there were approximately 300,000 such children in the mid-1990s who would be eligible for permanent residency.[48]

---

42. Ibid., 52.
43. Buddle, "The Right of Abode Cases That Shook Hong Kong"; Newendorp, *Uneasy Reunions*.
44. Newendorp, *Uneasy Reunions*.
45. Ibid.
46. Ku, "Hegemonic Construction, Negotiation and Displacement."
47. Ibid.
48. Newendorp, *Uneasy Reunions*, 52.

While legally, this case hinged upon the constitutionality of the Immigration Ordinance instead of the moral claims the claimants made about their right to reunite with their family members, Chief Justice Li of the Court of Final Appeal nevertheless took the latter into account: In his judgment, he repeatedly mentioned the familial ties between mainland Chinese people and Hongkongers, and the importance of protecting family units.[49] In the opening of his judgment, Chief Justice Li reckoned that "throughout history, residents in Hong Kong have had family ties in the rest of China," and these ties had only grown only stronger since mainland China adopted the Open Door Policy in 1978 that allowed a freer flow of capital and labor between Hong Kong and its surrounding burgeoning Chinese cities.[50]

Under the Open Door Policy, coastal Chinese cities surrounding Hong Kong and Macau were designated as Special Economic Zones (SEZs) that could participate in the capitalist, free market economy with fewer governmental constraints.[51] Close to the two then-European colonies Macau and Hong Kong, the SEZs allowed the Chinese government to benefit economically from transnational capitalism while, as Ong points out, continuing to ensure the stability and power of the ruling Communist Party.[52] The increased economic ties between mainland Chinese cities and Hong Kong inevitably led to the creation of family units across borders. Because of the gendered division of labor, middle- and working-class men from Hong Kong traveled across borders for work most frequently. Many of these men developed romantic relationships with mainland Chinese women—some legitimized by formal marriage, while some were extramarital affairs—thus giving rise to a large group of mainland-born children with only one Hong Kong parent.[53] Between 1995 to 2005, the Chinese government allowed approximately 55,000 Chinese citizens to immigrate to Hong Kong legally every year by issuing them exit permits: Over 85 percent of these individuals were the wives and children of local Hong Kong men.[54] Because of the quota set on the exit permit by the Chinese government, the wait to legally immigrate to the SAR was long.[55]

While the Open Door Policy was implemented at a time when China was more concerned about its economic development in the international market than the ideological incorporation of Hong Kong, the policy nevertheless cre-

49. *Ng Ka Ling v. Director of Immigration*, FACV 14 (1998).
50. Ibid., 3.
51. Ong, *Neoliberalism as Exception*.
52. Ibid.
53. Newendorp, *Uneasy Reunions*.
54. Ibid., 3.
55. Newendorp, *Uneasy Reunions*.

ated biological families that helped pave the path toward the eventual integration of Hong Kong into the "big Chinese family."[56] For Hongkongers, the immigration restrictions were a necessary gatekeeping mechanism to prevent mainland Chinese people and their children from contaminating the existing Hong Kong nation-family. Instead of acknowledging the commonality they shared with mainlanders, mainstream Hongkongers espoused alienizing sentiments against Chinese nationals that only intensified after the return of sovereignty in 1997.[57]

Hongkongers' denouncement of their mainland counterparts contrasted dramatically with China's state nationalist rhetoric that drew heavily from the familial trope.[58] Around 1997, the Chinese government made heavy use of the familial imagery, describing Hong Kong as returning to the "Chinese family," "coming home," and finally reuniting with other members of the Chinese nation-state who share the "same blood."[59] However, despite Beijing's repeated attempts to mobilize familial tropes to incorporate Hong Kong ideologically into the dominant Chinese nation-state, the anti-Chinese sentiments among mainstream Hongkongers made clear that the Hong Kong public did not see themselves as sharing the same affective familial ties with the Chinese nation-state or with the mainland Chinese people. The concern expressed by mainstream Hongkongers toward the residency status of mainland-born children in the court case thus stemmed not only from their contempt for poor Chinese people who might soon be immigrating to the city but also from their determination to maintain a high degree of autonomy from China after the return of sovereignty. For mainland-born children, however, the Immigration Ordinance reinforced a border that prevented many of them from reuniting with their parents and siblings. At work here were conflicting definitions and performances of family at the state, local, and individual levels. While Beijing deployed familial tropes to ensure to coherence of the Chinese nation-state, mainstream Hongkongers and the SAR government were mobilizing restrictive immigration policies to demarcate their own nation-family as separate from China's.[60] Cross-border families, on the other hand, were stuck in this battle of competing national imaginaries.

When the 5,000 mainland-born children filed a lawsuit against the Hong Kong government, their residency status became—at least on the surface—a

56. Pan, Lee, Chan, and So, "Orchestrating the Family-Nation Chorus," 338.

57. Lu and Hunt, "As Hostility Grows, Some Chinese Say so Long Hong Kong."

58. Chan and So, *Crisis and Transformation in China's Hong Kong*; Mathews and Lui, *Consuming Hong Kong*.

59. Pan, Lee, Chan, and So, "Orchestrating the Family-Nation Chorus," 336–37.

60. Ku, "Hegemonic Construction, Negotiation and Displacement," 260.

legal rather than an emotional or a social matter. The autonomy granted to Hong Kong under "One Country, Two Systems" gives the judiciary branch independence not only from Beijing but also from the executive branch of the SAR government. Eager to uphold such independence, the Court of Final Appeal was placed in a difficult position in this case. On the one hand, it ought to rule according to the Basic Law, which many consider to be the "mini constitution" of Hong Kong; doing so would require the court to denounce the amendments made on the Immigration Ordinance, thus signaling the court's autonomy from the executive branch of the SAR government. On the other hand, ruling in favor of the claimants would inevitably send the message that Hongkongers and mainland Chinese people belonged to the same nation-family.[61] This second implication would make it more difficult for the SAR in the future to maintain and assert its autonomy from China.

Chief Justice Li acknowledged this tension in his judgment: Admitting mainland-born children to Hong Kong parents as permanent residents, he stated, "may be an example of the derogation from the Region's high degree of autonomy but it is one sanctioned by Article 22(4)."[62] Chief Justice Li's statement makes clear that while the court ruled in favor of the claimants, it nevertheless did not see them as rightful Hongkongers. Rather, these children were seen as an extension of mainland China, and their incorporation therefore would erode Hong Kong's autonomy and distinctiveness from China. While the court was willing to remove the legal barriers that marked these children as strangers outside of the Hong Kong nation-family, it did not engage in what Michael Walzer refers to as the "second admissions process" to fully accept these mainland-born children as members.[63] As Walzer points out, "the nation club or family is a community different from the state."[64] In other words, the claimants could receive permanent residency to the SAR, yet remained ostracized by the nation-family.

The distinction between formal recognition and second admission to the Hong Kong nation-family was particularly stark in this case because despite the fact that mainstream Hongkongers shared similar racial, cultural, linguistic, and historical backgrounds with their mainland counterparts, Hongkongers had—with the help of the revised Immigration Ordinance—categorically severed the affective connections they once shared with the mainland Chinese people before the political divide between colonial Hong Kong and Communist China. The connections were instead replaced by contempt and fear over

61. Ibid.
62. *Ng Ka Ling v. Director of Immigration*, FACV 14 (1998), 55.
63. Walzer, *Spheres of Justice*, 52.
64. Ibid.

mainlanders whose bodies now symbolized contaminants. As Sullivan rightly points out, "it is intimacy and familiarity, not foreignness, that tends to produce anger and hostility towards others."[65] That is to say, closeness between the dominant subject and the Other does not remove aversion; rather, such intimacy could reinforce alienizing sentiments and the desire among dominant subjects to sever any positive affective connections with the Other.

Complete severances, however, were not feasible between Hongkongers and mainlanders because of the many biological families that were separated by the mainland–Hong Kong border. By ruling in favor of the claimants, the court demonstrated that the framework of formal citizenship privileges biological familial ties over other intimate claims of belonging, such as those performed by South Asian residents outside of the kinship network (see chapter 2). In response to the immigration restriction placed specifically on mainland children born out of wedlock to a Hong Kong father, Chief Justice Li stated in the judgment that excluding a child because of her parents' marital status is unconstitutional. Citing the legal relevance of the International Covenant on Civil and Political Rights (ICCPR), Li stated, "First, both the Basic Law and the ICCPR enshrine the principle of equality, the antithesis of any discrimination. . . . Secondly, Article 23(1) of the ICCPR recognizes that the family is the natural and fundamental group unit of society and is entitled to protection by society and the State."[66] Advocating for equal treatment for all children, Li argued that excluding only "illegitimate children of fathers . . . would not be conducive towards achieving some measure of family union."[67] Finally, Li emphatically pointed out, "a child born out of wedlock is no more or less a person born of such a resident than a child born in wedlock."[68] In other words, biological kin ties trumped the institution of marriage in the realm of formal recognition. After this particular ruling went into effect, all mainland-born applicants were required to undergo a genetic test to prove that they were indeed biological children of at least one Hong Kong permanent resident.[69]

The comparison between the judgment handed down in this case and the judgment regarding migrant domestic workers (see chapter 3) is also relevant as both groups share intimate connections with local Hong Kong families and they both argued that they had been unjustly discriminated against by

---

65. Sullivan, *Revealing Whiteness*, 40.

66. *Ng Ka Ling v. Director of Immigration*, FACV 14 (1998), 73.

67. Ibid., 74.

68. Ibid.

69. Legislative Council Secretariat, "Issue of Right of Abode in the Hong Kong Special Administrative Region of Persons Born in the Mainland to Hong Kong Permanent Residents," Appendix III.

the Immigration Ordinance. While Chief Justice Li emphasized the value of equality and anti-discrimination when ruling on mainland-born children, the judgment rendered in the migrant workers' case reinforces the Hong Kong government's right to discriminate against any aliens as it sees fit.[70] While the workers argued that the discrimination they were subjected to by the Immigration Ordinance was unconstitutional, the Court of First Instance immediately dismissed the claim as legally irrelevant.[71] Equality, in other words, is afforded only to those who share biological kin ties with the existing citizenry, and whose value is thus not measured only by their economic productivity. As Wingard argues, aliens who are immediate family members of an established citizen-subject are seen by the state and the public as less suspect: "The notion that immigrants are caring, heterosexual families, *just like us,* works rhetorically as a means to create identification through affect."[72] As such, while biological families composed of both citizens and aliens may still be marked by the nation-state as different, they nevertheless become intelligible as subjects deserving of protection from the state. This selective recognition, however, only applies to nuclear families that fit the dominant imaginary of what a family looks like. As Mae Ngai points out, in order to more effectively regulate the composition of immigrants admitted to the nation-state, immigration policies based on familial bonds often restrict the definitions of family to only nuclear family units comprising two heterosexual parents and their offspring.[73]

This narrow definition of family dismisses the affective and sometimes practical ties shared among those who are not part of the nuclear family, yet nevertheless share a familial bond. For example, despite the fraught labor relationships between domestic workers and employers, many workers do experience a deep familial tie their employers' family after sharing a home for decades.[74] These ties, however, were not considered relevant in court or in the dominant citizenship discourse. The desires and emotional well-being of subjects who are not related by blood are dismissed, and these subjects are subsequently denied formal recognition by the nation-family. The differences between how the Hong Kong judiciary system responded to the familial and equality claims espoused, respectively, by mainland-born children of Hong Kong parents and migrant domestic workers highlight the way formal citizenship privileges sameness based on a biological understanding of familial ties.

---

70. *Ng Ka Ling v. Director of Immigration,* FACV 14 (1998); *Vallejos v. Commissioner of Registration,* FACV 19&20 (2012).

71. *Vallejos v. Commissioner of Registration,* HCAL 124 (2010).

72. Wingard, *Branded Bodies,* 42.

73. Ngai, *Impossible Subjects*; Ngai, "The Dark History of Defining 'Family.'"

74. So, *Migrant Domestic Workers*; Constable, *Maid to Order in Hong Kong.*

Legal citizenship and the formal recognition it grants cannot be separated from a biological and racial logic that justifies selective exclusion.

The privileging of biological kin ties in Hong Kong's legal citizenship discourse, in fact, extends even to subjects who are part of the mainstream nuclear family structure. In a later ruling, the Court of Final Appeal decided that unlike children who were born in mainland China to Hong Kong parents, children adopted by Hong Kong permanent residents would remain ineligible for the right of abode, as the court interpreted the phrase "born of" in the Basic Law as referring only to biological parent-child relationships.[75] The DNA tests to prove a child's biological lineage and the court's subsequent ruling on adopted children demonstrate that the court's conception of the family is defined solely by biological kin ties. Claimants who are not related by blood to existing members of the Hong Kong nation-family are therefore excepted from legal recognition.

After the court ruled against the right of abode for adopted mainland children, fourteen-year-old Agnes Nga-yin Tam made headlines for being the casualty of this judgment. Adopted by her Hong Kong parents during infancy, Tam was brought to Hong Kong from mainland China on a temporary visitor's permit in 1996. At the time of the ruling, Tam had been living on the expired permit but was unaware of her perilous residency status. In fact, Tam did not realize that she was adopted and the consequences of her background until the court case.[76] After the ruling, images of Tam fleeing the courtroom in tears were widely circulated, together with testimonies from her friends, neighbors, and teachers advocating for her right to stay in Hong Kong. As a result of ongoing public pressure from the mainstream public, the director of immigration granted Tam the unconditional right to remain in the SAR on "humanitarian grounds."[77] Tam's case and experience were not dissimilar from those of Maggie Cheung—the Pakistani woman adopted by Hong Kong parents whose naturalization request was granted only after she obtained overwhelming support from mainstream news media (see chapter 2). Even though the fictive kin ties in both cases were subsequently recognized by the state, they remain the exceptions. By granting Tam and Cheung legal recognition outside of the courtroom, the Hong Kong government was able to appease the public and appeared benevolent without setting any legal precedents to accept more racialized subjects of that category into the nation-family.

---

75. Legislative Council Panel on Security, "Immigration Policy on Adopted Children," LC Paper No. CB(2)179/01–02(03); Newendorp, *Uneasy Reunions.*

76. Newendorp, *Uneasy Reunions.*

77. Ibid., 55.

## NEOLIBERAL INTERESTS AND STATE POLITICAL POWER

Despite the sense of obligation Chief Justice Li felt toward protecting what he deemed to be "natural and fundamental" family units in the case of mainland-born children, the judgment he penned focused not on the importance of familial bonds, but on the reasons why the court possessed the authority to rule on this case independently of the mainland Chinese government.[78] In fact, as the case continued to develop after Li's ruling, it quickly became clear that family reunification was not the crux of this debate. Rather, the claimants' contested permanent residency status served as a catalyst for the executive branch of the Hong Kong government, the SAR's judiciary system, and Beijing to assert their power over one another and to defend their respective political and economic interests, which did not always overlap. In the end, instead of allowing the claimants to reunite with their Hong Kong parents and be integrated into Hong Kong as rightful members of the nation-family, Chief Justice Li's judgment backfired and intensified the exclusionary sentiments among mainstream Hongkongers toward mainland Chinese people. Using negative public sentiments as a justification, the executive branch of the Hong Kong government invited Beijing to interfere and overturn Li's ruling, effectively reinforcing Beijing's dominance over the SAR. The aftermath of the ruling made clear that in matters of formal citizenship, the Hong Kong and Chinese governments' neoliberal and political interests trumped the familial desires of marginalized subjects.

In 1997, just two years before the litigation reached the Court of Final Appeal, Hong Kong's economy took a significant hit during the Asian economic crisis. As a result, many working- and middle-class Hong Kong men lost their jobs and struggled to sustain the families they had created in mainland China.[79] Still scrambling to help repair the economy at the time of the court case, the Hong Kong government had no interest in taking in these mainland-born children of Hong Kong residents who could not yet contribute to the economy but would immediately rely on of the social welfare and public education systems. As Ong points out, in a neoliberal economy, immigrants are deemed desirable and thus incorporable only when they can participate in the productive economy and be self-sufficient without public support.[80] The claimants in this case were mostly from working-class families that did not possess much financial or cultural capital in Hong Kong.

---

78. *Ng Ka Ling v. Director of Immigration*, FACV 14 (1998), 73.

79. Newendorp, *Uneasy Reunions*.

80. Ong, *Buddha Is Hiding*.

Given these circumstances, for the Hong Kong government, it was less important to legally reunite the children with their Hong Kong parents than to ensure that Hong Kong would remain economically competitive after the financial crisis. As a result, the Hong Kong government was dismayed by Li's ruling, which would prompt an influx of undesirable immigrants from China. Because the government had lost the case at the highest court in Hong Kong, it could no longer appeal the ruling. To bypass the judiciary restrictions, the chief executive of the SAR at the time, against vehement critiques from the court and the Hong Kong Bar Association, requested the case be sent to the National People's Congress (NPC)—China's national legislature—for reinterpretation. Sharing similar economic concerns as the SAR administration and eager to undermine the autonomy of Hong Kong's judiciary system, the NPC reinterpreted the relevant article in the Basic Law and ruled in favor of the Hong Kong government, thus overturning the judgment handed down by the supposedly independent Hong Kong court system.

The case morphed fully into a competition between Beijing's political power and the court's judiciary autonomy the moment the chief executive of the SAR determined singlehandedly that this case concerned affairs with the mainland Chinese government, and thus fell under the jurisdiction of the NPC. As the chief executive stated in his public report, "the HKSAR is no longer capable of resolving the problem on its own."[81] By taking up the SAR government's plea for help, Beijing was not only performing its paternal role over Hong Kong but was also asserting that its authority transcended the autonomy of the Court of Final Appeal. In its three-page decision statement, the NPC did not at all acknowledge the judgment handed down by Chief Justice Li, nor did it address the claimants' concern of family reunification. Rather, it plainly stated that "the interpretation of the Court of Final Appeal is not consistent with the legislative intent [of the Basic Law]."[82] The brief yet determining statement makes clear that despite the autonomy granted by the Basic Law to the SAR judiciary system, the executive branch of the Hong Kong government, and most of all, Beijing, have overwhelming political power in defining the terms of citizenship.

For Beijing, this case had little to do with family reunification. Rather, it was about protecting China's international reputation as the new leader of

---

81. Tung, "Report on Seeking Assistance from the Central People's Government in Solving Problems Encountered in the Implementation of the Basic Law of the Hong Kong Special Administrative Region of the People's Republic of China."

82. Standing Committee of the Ninth National People's Congress, "The Interpretation by the Standing Committee of the National People's Congress of Articles 22(4) and 24(2)(3) of the Basic Law of the Hong Kong Special Administrative Region of the People's Republic of China."

Hong Kong and about asserting Beijing's political authority over the newly incorporated SAR. Before the return of Hong Kong's sovereignty and in the years since, the Chinese government has always emphasized how it has helped the SAR maintain its "stability and prosperity."[83] Since the Asian financial crisis took place the same year Hong Kong was returned to China, the Chinese government did not want to appear as if the handover had caused the economic demise of the SAR. As a result, Beijing was eager to help protect the SAR government from any additional economic burden, even if the burden was in the form of mainland-born Hong Kong children who were separated from their parents.

In addition to helping protect the Hong Kong government's neoliberal interests and China's reputation, the NPC's reinterpretation of the Basic Law also allowed Beijing to assert its political dominance over a supposedly autonomous judiciary system. According to the Basic Law, the Hong Kong judiciary system has the power to adjudicate independently of mainland China and the executive branch of the SAR government—unless the cases "(i) concern affairs which are the responsibility of the Central People's Government; or (ii) concern the relationship between the Central Authorities and the Region."[84] This case fell under a gray area because one of the contested provisions in the Immigration Ordinance did concern the Chinese government: For mainland-born children to Hong Kong parents to qualify as permanent residents of the SAR, the provision requires that they first obtain an exit permit from the Chinese government prior to entering Hong Kong. Chief Justice Li argued extensively in his judgment that this provision is unconstitutional because those individuals are always already rightful permanent residents of Hong Kong, and thus they should never be subjected to any immigration procedures in mainland China.[85] Because of that, Li submitted, the case concerning mainland-born Hong Kong children should be adjudicated independently by the Court of Final Appeal instead of by the NPC.

While Li ruled the provision to be unconstitutional and thus subject to removal from the Hong Kong Immigration Ordinance, it was in Beijing's interest to keep it in place because this provision allowed the Chinese government to maintain biopolitical control over its citizenry, especially those who desired to cross the border between mainland and the SAR. By setting a small quota of 150 exit permits a day and by requiring all mainland Chinese applicants to first go through a vetting process through the Public Security Bureau, the

---

83. Shuning, "For Hong Kong's Smooth Transition, Stability and Prosperity"; Zhe, "How 'One Country, Two Systems' Ensures Hong Kong's Prosperity and Stability."

84. Article 158, Basic Law.

85. *Ng Ka Ling v. Director of Immigration*, FACV 14 (1998).

Chinese government was able to engineer the citizen compositions of mainland China and Hong Kong.[86] Thus, by making the exit permit unnecessary for mainland-born Hong Kong children, the court inadvertently—or perhaps purposefully—defied the authority mainland China held toward its nationals and enforced a legal distinction between mainland Chinese people and Hongkongers. When read politically, Li's decision to remove the provision not only asserted the autonomy of the judiciary system from the executive branch of the SAR government but also infringed upon the authority of the Chinese government. By overthrowing the court's judgment regarding the exit permit, Beijing made clear that it retained the ultimate political power in regulating the movements of Chinese nationals and in determining who got to become permanent residents of Hong Kong. This sudden turn of events also highlights the precariousness marginalized subjects face, even *after* they have obtained formal recognition through legal means. While these Hong Kong–mainland families were more recognizable in court than other familial configurations, they nevertheless were pawns in China's struggle for political power.

## CONFLICTING NATION-FAMILIES AND COMPETING INTERESTS

While the chief executive's decision to seek political help from Beijing enraged many Hongkongers, who saw this move as infringing upon the SAR's judiciary autonomy, it nevertheless received considerable support from the mainstream public as the Hong Kong government had successfully mobilized existing prejudice against mainland Chinese immigrants. By deploying intelligible tropes such as its responsibility to maintain the prosperity and stability of Hong Kong and to protect the interests of rightful local families, the Hong Kong government was able to justify its decision to seek intervention from Beijing, while appealing to the mainstream public's collective cultural identity as Hongkongers against the influx of inferior Chinese immigrants. While the chief executive's decision to hand the case over to Beijing violated the legal autonomy many Hongkongers valued deeply, it became palatable to the mainstream public once it was framed as a necessary act to maintain the integrity and future of the Hong Kong nation-family. In this section, I examine how immediately after the court's ruling the Hong Kong government deployed exclusionary familial tropes to generate panic and fear among mainstream

---

86. Hong Kong Special Administrative Region, "LCQ5."

Hongkongers so that they would support its decision to invite intervention from Beijing.

Three months after the ruling, Regina Ip, the secretary for security at the time, gave a speech in front of the Legislative Council that was later reprinted and broadcast citywide. In the speech, Ip presented numbers after numbers to highlight the grave potential outcome of the ruling. According to her calculation, 692,000 mainland children would become eligible for permanent residency in Hong Kong immediately, while 983,000 more would become eligible from the second generation.[87] To further highlight the gravity of the situation and to make these overwhelming numbers seem even more daunting, Ip stated that these numbers were likely an underestimation because they had not taken into account the ongoing fertility of the 100,000 mainland wives married to Hong Kong men, as these women would continue to produce children eligible for permanent residency in the SAR. Mainland women are depicted here not as people who have desires, intimate familial relationships, and affective ties that resemble those of mainstream Hongkongers; rather, in Ip's speech, they become machines devoid of personhood, whose only capacity is in producing babies that will one day overwhelm the SAR and take over the home of mainstream Hongkongers. Mainland Chinese women become a threat to the SAR because they are seen as the source and reproducer of contaminants. Because of the dangerous fertility of mainland women, while these split families in question included at least one Hong Kong permanent resident, for Ip, they are all considered outside of the boundary of the Hong Kong nation-family. Under Ip's characterization, the Hong Kong nation-family is defined less by biological kinship and familial affective ties than by the collective feeling of facing an imminent threat.

Ip's speech, together with the statistics and reports presented by other government bureaus, illustrate how the familial framework of citizenship is mobilized in conjunction with neoliberal ideologies to incite public fear and hatred of racialized bodies. After representing the children and wives of cross-border families as threats to the lifestyle and space of Hongkongers, Ip suggested that mainland immigrants were incompatible with the international knowledge economy and thus Hong Kong's economic growth. She mobilizes neoliberal values to highlight the economic burden Chinese immigrants would bring to the Hong Kong nation-family if they were ever incorporated in large amounts. Close to the end of her speech, Ip noted:

---

87. Hong Kong Special Administrative Region, "Speech by Secretary for Security."

We are now actively developing high technology and high value-added industries to seek economic revival, which, in the long run, can improve our living standard. In face of keen competition from our neighbours in Asia, the Government's fiscal restraints and the economic downturn, it is very difficult for us to absorb a large number of persons with right of abode.[88]

Implicit in Ip's statement is the message that mainland Chinese immigrants would hinder the development of Hong Kong's knowledge economy because they lack the skills to contribute as productive neoliberal subjects. As Charles T. Lee posits, citizenship is "a *cultural script* inscribed and utilized by liberal sovereignty to govern and regulate how citizen-subjects should conduct themselves in different realms of social life."[89] This cultural script demarcates "proper citizens" from "abject subjects" who disrupt the state's neoliberal governing template.[90] For Ip, despite their permanent residency status that at the time had been granted by the court, mainland immigrants were remaindered of the dominant script of citizenship: Namely, they were subjects who lacked the financial and cultural capital to contribute to the economic success of the SAR. As such, these immigrants were merely the abject that the Hong Kong government would have to, in Ip's word, "absorb."[91]

Ip's argument about the impending economic and social burden was substantiated by a report provided by the chief secretary for administration, which framed the influx of mainland-born children as an event that would harm the interests and well-being of rightful Hong Kong families and the nation-family as a whole. First, it states that Hong Kong "taxpayers would have to shoulder a capital expenditure of $710 billion in 10 years" in order for the government to provide all the necessary public services to the new immigrants.[92] The report also references the housing and urban planning problems these immigrants would cause, implying that should the court's ruling come into effect, Hongkongers would face an even more crowded living environment and encounter more competition with subsidized public housing. The report then cites government statistics to claim that in order to accommodate all the new residents, the Hong Kong government would have to make a series of compromises, such as giving up on the new initiative to enhance the quality

---

88. Ibid.
89. Charles T. Lee, *Ingenious Citizenship*, 26.
90. Ibid., 23.
91. Hong Kong Special Administrative Region, "Speech by Secretary for Security."
92. Legislative Council Panel on Security, "Issue of Right of Abode in the Hong Kong Special Administrative Region of Persons Born in the Mainland to Hong Kong Permanent Residents," LC Paper No. CB(2)2096/01–02(08).

of new teachers, increasing the wait time in public hospitals and clinics, and forgoing its plan to help all households acquire affordable housing.[93] To close, the report highlights that not only would the influx of immigrants cause a dramatic spike in Hong Kong's unemployment rate, it would also put immense pressure on the public transportation system and welfare services.

These claims not only heighten the outrage and panic among mainstream Hongkongers about the potential influx of Chinese immigrants, but they also render proponents of family reunification insensitive to the needs and interests of the existing citizenry. In addition, by suggesting that the interests of mainstream Hongkongers and Chinese immigrants are mutually exclusive, the report effectively dissuades Hongkongers from enacting empathy or sympathy toward the split families. As Ku points out, the statistics cited in the government's report assume that all the mainland-born children admitted in this case would grow up to be unemployed and dependent on public welfare.[94] When framed this way, the mainland immigrants become not only the remainder of citizenship but are also active threats that would undermine the well-being and comfort of Hong Kong families. As DeChaine argues, "by establishing a socially acceptable position for anti-migrant sentiment, one that places blame not on a person or an ethnic group but on an impersonal condition, the formal construction of alienization provides an inoculation against charges of racism and scapegoating."[95] By using questionable statistics to portray Chinese immigrants as an immense economic burden, the Hong Kong government pitted mainstream Hongkongers against the immigrants and also effectively justified its decision to seek political intervention from Beijing at the expense of the SAR's legal autonomy.

## THE AFFECTIVE ECONOMIES OF FEAR AND PANIC

The affective economies of fear and hatred of the Other, as Schaefer argues, often circulate in conjunction with the "economies of the dollar signs."[96] Under the neoliberal script of economy and citizenship, the fear and hatred of the Other is enhanced when the government makes clear that it will not help the existing citizenry maintain their standard of living should there be an influx of "inferior" immigrants. By pitting immigrants against local mainstream families, the Hong Kong government successfully mobilized and per-

---

93. Ibid.
94. Ku, "Hegemonic Construction, Negotiation and Displacement."
95. DeChaine, "Bordering the Civic Imaginary," 56.
96. Schaefer, *Religious Affects*, 122.

petuated the fear and contempt Hongkongers felt toward mainland Chinese immigrants; such feelings, in turn, justified Beijing's intervention and allowed both the Hong Kong and Chinese governments to protect their respective economic and political interests without appearing autocratic. As Schaefer pointedly puts it, "affective economies are the wobbling but durable infrastructure of power."[97]

The production and circulation of public fear and panic effectively limits the enactment of deliberative empathy, which calls for the subjects to modulate their rational, affective, and emotional responses. As researchers across disciplines have pointed out, emotion and affect are not opposed to reason; rather, as trauma psychiatrist Bessel van der Kolk argues, "emotions assign value to experiences and thus are the foundation of reason."[98] When subjects experience feelings that are viscerally overwhelming, such as panic, fear, and rage, their ability to reason and deliberate is impeded because the prefrontal cortex does not function as well under such conditions.[99] In addition to reasoning, the prefrontal cortex also enables the feeling of empathy—empathy, therefore, could easily be silenced by the affective intensities of anger, fear, and panic.[100] Neuroscientist Paul MacLean compares the relationship between the rational, deliberative part of the brain and the emotional part to that between a relatively competent rider and a somewhat unruly horse: As long as the path before them is clear, the rider is in control. However, unexpected sounds and signals of threats could trigger the horse to thrash and bolt, causing the rider to lose control.[101] Applying this analogy, the more fearful and angry Hongkongers were made to feel about mainlanders, the less capable they became in experiencing empathy and in engaging in deliberative processes.

Unfortunately, despite the vehement criticisms many public intellectuals had about the validity of the government's statistics, most mainstream Hong Kong media at the time aligned with the government's exclusionary rhetoric based on neoliberal logics; in fact, mainstream media actively helped perpetuate public panic and fear toward mainland immigrants.[102] After the government released the statistics on the potential socioeconomic outcome of incorporating all mainland-born Hong Kong children, the headlines from various popular local newspapers were as follows:

---

97. Ibid., 170.

98. Damasio, *Looking for Spinoza*; Marcus, *The Sentimental Citizen*; van der Kolk, *The Body Keeps the Score*, 64.

99. van der Kolk, *The Body Keeps the Score*.

100. Ibid.

101. MacLean, *The Triune Brain in Evolution*.

102. Ku, "Hegemonic Construction, Negotiation and Displacement."

Right of Abode Causing a Population Disaster; 1.67 Million Mainlanders.

Ruling Raises Squatter Fears.

1.67 Million New Immigrants Costing HK$710 Billion; The Economy Collapsing, Livelihood Deteriorating to a Dismal State, and the Hong Kong Government Surrendering Itself to It.

People Flooding into Hong Kong—An Unbearable Burden.[103]

These headlines echoed the rhetoric of resource scarcity that had surged in public discourse since the Asian financial crisis. As a result, they were readily intelligible and were effective in generating more fear among the mainstream Hong Kong audience. The fear, in particular, was attached to the bodies of mainland immigrants. As Sara Ahmed argues, fear "does not involve the defense of borders that already exist; rather, fear makes those borders, by establishing objects from which the subject, in fearing, can stand apart, objects that become 'the not' from which the subject appears to flee."[104] Fear allowed Hongkongers, who had historically treated mainland Chinese with disdain, to further demarcate the distinction between the two groups. By representing Chinese immigrants as an economic and social burden in numerical terms, these headlines invited the audience to dismiss the personhood of the claimants and see them merely as threats to the Hong Kong nation-family.

Public fear and panic, as Ahmed has cogently theorized, functions within an affective economy: The more the symbols of fear circulate, the more affective values these signs accumulate, and the harder it is to undo the association between the two.[105] As the figure of mainland immigrants circulated spatially, emotionally, and discursively in the SAR, it accumulated affective values and came to embody the anxiety Hongkongers felt toward the recent economic crisis and the uncertainty of newly becoming part of the Chinese sovereign state. Most of all, the bodies of the immigrants were imbued with the constant sense of insecurity that underwrote citizenship in a neoliberal context: the feeling that if one does not vehemently protect one's self-interests and the interests of one's immediate family—sometimes at the expense of others—one would be left with few resources to survive and thrive. This fear was particularly palpable among mainstream Hongkongers because the colonial and SAR government had always encouraged Hongkongers to be "enterprising individuals" who could shoulder the responsibility of maintaining the city's

---

103. Cited in ibid., 267.
104. Ahmed, "Affective Economies," 128.
105. Ahmed, *The Cultural Politics of Emotion*.

societal stability and economic prosperity.[106] This neoliberal expectation, as Newendorp points out, exacerbated the tension between Hongkongers and Chinese immigrants over the years because Hongkongers did not consider mainland Chinese people capable of meeting that expectation.[107] Under this amalgamation of fear and anxiety, mainland immigrants became the absolute, unredeemable Other in the local affective network in Hong Kong. Namely, they were "the one who cannot be interpolated into culture. He/she must be expelled, sent away, deported in order for the nation to define and imagine itself, its borders, and its citizenry."[108] As Sara McKinnon suggests, while the incorporation of a politically unthreatening Other (e.g., South Asians in post-colonial Hong Kong) could allow the nation-state to appear benevolent, the admission of an absolute Other would only undermine the foundation of the nation-state.[109]

Dominant circulating emotions such as fear and hatred not only inform the orientation the existing citizenry has toward others and the judgments they make about specific bodies but also help bolster the existing power hierarchy.[110] As Ku argues, "hegemonic construction presents a dominant account of social reality through a set of prevailing codes, symbols, discourses, and representations, which appeals to the common sense not only of the power-holders, but also of the wider public."[111] Bolstered by institutional power, the panic and fear generated and perpetuated by the Hong Kong government and mainstream news media came to form a dominant emotional pedagogy among mainstream Hongkongers, which informed the ways they understood their relationship to mainland Chinese immigrants. As sociologist Deborah Gould points out, an emotional pedagogy offers "ways to feel and to emote."[112] It dictates what feelings are socially permissible and what are rendered "infeel-able and inexpressible."[113] Once reproduced and stabilized through powerful institutions and repeated public enactments, the emotional pedagogy provides members of a social group a default disposition about how and what they ought to feel toward different circumstances and bodies.

Through the public debates surrounding the court case on the residency status of mainland-born children, the feelings mainstream Hongkongers had

---

106. Ku and Pun, *Remaking Citizenship in Hong Kong*, 1.
107. Newendorp, *Uneasy Reunions*.
108. Wingard, *Branded Bodies*, 5.
109. McKinnon, *Gendered Asylum*.
110. Ahmed, *The Cultural Politics of Emotion*; Nussbaum, *Political Emotions*.
111. Ku, "Hegemonic Construction, Negotiation and Displacement," 262.
112. Kinsman, "AIDS Activism and the Politics of Emotion."
113. Gould, "Political Despair,"103.

toward mainland Chinese people were cemented: Mainland bodies, particularly those who had crossed or were planning to cross the border into the SAR, were to be associated by default with fear, anger, and contempt. As I demonstrate in the following sections, as these viscerally negative emotions intensified, they prevented mainstream Hongkongers from engaging with alternative emotional responses that would prompt them to reconsider their relationships with mainland Chinese immigrants and the material interests they may share despite cultural and identity differences. The opportunity to enact deliberative empathy, in other words, was foreclosed by the established emotional pedagogy and the imminent sense of political threat.

## PUBLIC ANGER AND CHINESE MATERNAL TOURISM

The emotional pedagogy of anger directed toward mainland Chinese people strengthened during the early 2010s, when the number of Chinese maternal tourists in Hong Kong reached its peak. While Beijing's reinterpretation of the Basic Law in 1999 successfully prevented mainland-born children to Hong Kong parents from becoming permanent residents in the SAR, in an equally controversial court case two years later, the presiding judge granted all children born in Hong Kong to mainland parents the right of abode.[114] This ruling led to the practice of maternal tourism among mainland Chinese women who resided in cities with relatively easy access to Hong Kong. Many of these women chose to pay a substantial fee in transportation, health care, and accommodation to give birth in Hong Kong so that their children would enjoy the SAR's public health care and education systems and be able to obtain a Hong Kong passport that opens more doors to Euro-American countries.[115] Other women became maternal tourists in Hong Kong in order to circumvent China's One Child Policy, which remained active until late 2015.[116] In 2010, half of all babies born in Hong Kong were children of mainland couples.[117] Unlike the claimants in the 1998 court case, who had at least one Hong Kong parent, neither parent of these children was a permanent Hong Kong resident. These children were therefore derogatorily referred to by the Hong Kong public as the *neithers*.

---

114. Newendorp, *Uneasy Reunions.*

115. Lafraniere, "Mainland Chinese Flock to Hong Kong to Have Babies"; Simpson, "Chinese 'Birth Tourists' to Hong Kong Double."

116. "China to End One-Child Policy"; Lafraniere, "Mainland Chinese Flock to Hong Kong to Have Babies."

117. "HK to Limit Mainland China Maternity Services."

As a result of the influx of Chinese maternal tourists, the panic associated with mainland Chinese immigrants in the late 1990s translated into anger and contempt in early 2010s. The height of the conflict between mainland Chinese people and Hongkongers occurred between 2011 and 2014—a time when the city experienced a spike in the number of upper-middle-class mainland tourists and increased economic, political, and social encroachment from the Chinese government. In this case, the bodies of mainlanders, particularly Chinese maternal tourists and the *neithers,* not only represented a spatial transgression of the Hong Kong nation-family but also stood in as proxy for China's looming power over the SAR. Their presence, therefore, fueled mainstream Hongkongers' fear over the loss of their distinct cultural and political identity, together with their perceived superiority over mainland Chinese people, who had become much wealthier since China's exponential economic growth over the last decade. As the bodies of mainland Chinese people circulated within the local affective economy, they gathered more intensity that was powerful enough to motivate emotional representations and political actions driven not by deliberation, but by deep-seated cultural memories, collective identities, and the visceral feelings associated with protecting the Hong Kong nation-family and one's own kin.[118]

Framing the Hong Kong nation-family as being under siege and at the crux of a crisis, anti-China Hongkongers and media vehemently constructed exclusionary claims that deployed anger and disgust, directed specifically toward mainland Chinese families. A collective national-familial identity constructed during a moment of crisis is especially powerful because it is future oriented: As Ahmed points out, when a way of life is deemed under threat in the present, "that very thing becomes installed as that which we must fight for in the future, a fight which is retrospectively understood to be a matter of life and death."[119] Under the lens of futurity, Chinese maternal tourists and the *neithers* became even more threatening because they not only endangered the existing nation-family but would also contaminate the future generations of Hongkongers. As a figure, the mainland child was not treated as innocent and in need of protection. Rather, she embodied the threat that would harm both the Hong Kong nation-family and local family units by taking away valuable social resources. The mainland child therefore became the target of public anger. As ethnologist Patricia McConnell points out, fear and anger are often hard to discriminate because "anger is the emotion that allows an individual to move past fear and take action to save itself, to protect its young, or to save

118. Ahmed, *The Cultural Politics of Emotion*; Wingard, *Branded Bodies.*
119. Ahmed, *The Cultural Politics of Emotion,* 77.

its mate."[120] Unlike pure fear, which often paralyzes the subject, anger prompts protective and defensive actions, actions that allow one to maintain a sense of agency and control in a terrifying situation.

As a political emotion, anger provides a legitimate foundation to ground public actions, including the exclusion of certain groups, in the name of reason.[121] The representation of mainlanders as threatening alien figures that must be cast out intensified public anger and also allowed Hongkongers to strengthen their collective national identity. As Emily Winderman argues, at a time of perceived public crisis, anger functions as a "a collectivizing moral emotion [that] binds bodies together in relationship to other bodies and objects deemed harmful or unjust for the purpose of actionable redress."[122] For anger to be intelligible enough to perform a political function, Winderman reminds us, it must "generate affective intensity through the repetition of rhetorical figures."[123] Such rhetorical figures must be readily recognizable within the local affective network for them to circulate and gain sufficient emotional valence and political uptake. By blaming mainland parents for harming the well-being of local babies and children—figures associated with the future of Hong Kong—mainstream Hongkongers reinforced the racialized brands of mainlanders as damaging to the interests of Hong Kong families, and whose inclusion would lead to the demise of the Hong Kong nation-family. As Ahmed points out, "the fear of degeneration, decline, and disintegration as mechanisms for preserving 'what is,' becomes associated more with some bodies than others."[124] In order to, in Wingard's word, "brand" these bodies as contaminants unfit for inclusion, the mainstream citizenry must first dehumanize them so that they are seen only as threats to the survival of the nation-family.[125]

## DEHUMANIZING THE AGGREGATE

As immigration and rhetoric scholars have argued, alien subjects are often dehumanized as diseased or animal, and therefore unrecognizable as human beings; they are not represented as individuals whose circumstances deserve at least some degree of understanding and sympathy from the mainstream

---

120. McConnell, *The Education of Will*, 139.
121. Nussbaum, *Hiding from Humanity*.
122. Winderman, "S(anger) Goes Postal in the Woman Rebel," 386–87.
123. Ibid., 386.
124. Ahmed, *The Cultural Politics of Emotion*, 78.
125. Wingard, *Branded Bodies*, 9.

citizenry.[126] When compounded with the sense of impending doom and an established emotional pedagogy that promotes contempt and anger, systemic dehumanization prevents the mainstream citizenry from developing the affective openness to reexamine their relationships with and feelings toward the Other. As Gould points in *Moving Politics*, radical social change stems from the citizenry's ability to experience and express sensations that do not align with the existing emotional pedagogy. When alternative feelings are stifled and room for deliberation foreclosed, it is difficult for subjects to challenge the dominant feeling template. The process of alienization relies heavily on the emotional nature of dehumanizing tropes and narratives; in fact, it is exactly the emotional content of such discourse that motivates the existing citizenry to internalize dominant feelings of anger and disgust toward the Other, and to prohibit representations of the Other as a subject whose humanity deserves ethical consideration.

The dehumanization of mainlanders by the mainstream Hong Kong public was particularly salient during the early 2010s, when tension between mainstream Hongkongers and Chinese maternal tourists began to rise. Despite the fact that the mainland Chinese people in Hong Kong came from different social backgrounds and were in the city with different intentions, Hongkongers and anti-China news media often represented them as a conglomerate by referring to them all as "locusts." While this trope was used to describe all mainland Chinese perceived to be usurping the SAR's resources, it was most often deployed in relation to the *neithers* and their parents. This animalistic trope circulated in the local affective economy in a way that strengthened the identity of the Hong Kong nation-family and subsequently pushed out alternatives that would render mainland mothers deserving of empathy.

"Locust" became a popular trope among Hong Kong netizens in 2010, when the numbers of maternal tourists, wealthy Chinese travelers, and smugglers all increased significantly, thus challenging the way Hongkongers conceived of their home and their national identities.[127] Similar to visceral labels like "diseased," "animal," and "dirty" that have been ascribed to the alien subjects in the US, the trope of the locust functions as an othering signifier that both feeds off of and heightens public anxiety, further rendering these bodies unassimilable. As an anti-China grassroots organization explains on its website: "Locusts cannot be distinguished by ethnicity, age, identity, or educational background. A locust is not an individual, nor is it a type of people,

---

126. Ana, "'Like an Animal I Was Treated'"; Chavez, *The Latino Threat*; DeChaine, "Bordering the Civic Imaginary."

127. I use the term *netizens* to refer to internet users who participate in public deliberation—albeit not always constructively or ethically—that transcends their self-interests.

but it is a phenomenon: a desire to profit without contribution, to rob others of their success, and to occupy other people's resources and advantages."[128] By interpreting "locust" as related to types of behaviors instead of to a group of individuals, Hongkongers were able to evade criticisms of overt racism, while justifying their outrage toward mainlanders' supposedly unacceptable actions and attitudes. Evoking a sense of total and unstoppable consumption, the locust metaphor stemmed from and perpetuated the permeating affects of fear and anxiety. To counter the anxiety and fear, feelings that often immobilize rather than motivate, this animalistic trope allowed Hongkongers to use anger as an outlet and as a means to justify their alienization of mainland bodies.

While initially the trope was circulated only on particular online forums, it entered mainstream discourse in 2011 when netizens on Hong Kong Golden Forum—a wildly popular platform frequented by netizens who are part trolls and part social activists—raised US$12,900 in a week to print a full-page colored advertisement in two major local newspapers, vehemently reprimanding *neithers*. In bold fonts, the announcement, citing official statistics in the footnote, asks, "Are you willing to let Hong Kong spend HK$1,000,000 every 18 minutes feeding and caring for the *neithers*?" Right underneath the image of a disproportionately huge locust is another menacing headline—"Hongkongers, [We Have] Tolerated Enough!"—followed by the following passage:

> Because [we are] sympathetic that you have suffered from poisonous baby formula, [we] allow you to buy ours like a mob. / Because we pity your lack of freedom, [we] mercifully grant you the opportunity to travel independently to Hong Kong. / Because [we] understand that you have a backward education system, [we] share our educational resources with you. / Because you guys cannot understand traditional Chinese writing, [we] use the disabled Chinese fonts to say the following: /[129] "If you come to Hong Kong, please respect the local culture. Without Hong Kong, you guys will all be done by now."

The last line of the passage is a parodied response to a video clip that had gone viral earlier that year. The video shows an anonymous mainland tourist saying to a Hong Kong TV journalist on camera, "If the Chinese central government didn't take care of you, Hong Kong would have already been done!" This

---

128. The website had become defunct at the writing of this book. The quote cited here was gathered in 2014.

129. Hongkongers commonly refer to simplified Chinese characters as "disabled" fonts, contrasting them with the traditional—and therefore "normal"—characters used in the SAR and in Taiwan.

incident fueled the anger of mainstream Hongkongers as the tourist directly challenged the sense of superiority Hongkongers had over mainlanders, and bluntly pointed out the SAR's economic dependence on China. By appropriating this infamous tagline, the advertisement reasserts the dominance Hongkongers have over mainland Chinese people and uses it to justify the alienization of Chinese immigrants. While sarcastic in tone, this central passage of the announcement portrays Hongkongers as sympathetic, understanding, and well intentioned, while their mainland counterparts are shown as ungrateful aliens who do not deserve inclusion or sympathy because of their "poor attitude." This claim reinforces the Hongkongers' imaginary of mainland Chinese families as morally defective: Not only are they rude usurpers of Hong Kong's resources, but they are also unable to express gratitude.

The announcement ends with two forceful claims: "STRONGLY DEMAND the [Hong Kong] government to amend the Basic Law Article 24! / Stop mainland pregnant women from invading Hong Kong like refugees!" Despite such an overt expression of anger and resentment, this ad also communicates an underlying sense of anxiety. Featured in the background of the announcement is the Hong Kong landscape, shadowed and foregrounded by a gigantic photorealistic locust perching on top of Lion Rock—a major landmark and national symbol of the SAR. The locust, so huge that it occupies almost the entire rock, overlooks and surveils the city in a menacing and sinister manner. The city landscape—minuscule in comparison to the insect—appears defenseless against the overpowering predator. While the text conveys active resistance and justifiable outrage against mainlanders, the image suggests a permeating sense of anxiety and helplessness toward the impending threat. As Ulrich Beck argues, when the existing citizenry is in an affective state of fear, their solidarity is built based on insecurity and a sense of shared risk.[130] Compounded with loathing toward the intruding Other, fear motivates the existing citizenry to dehumanize the Other; if the Other is taken to be subhuman, the dominant citizenry, then, no longer has to consider its interests or needs.

After its initial publication in the two major local newspapers, this announcement was subsequently circulated by other mainstream Hong Kong, Chinese, and even American news media. It soon triggered heated duels between Hong Kong and mainland Chinese netizens. Within the Hong Kong affective network, the circulation of this announcement—particularly its interpretation and deployment of the locust trope—bonded the existing citizenry together through a shared sense of moral superiority against a collective enemy. For instance, the anti-mainland Chinese Facebook group referenced

---

130. Beck, *Risk Society.*

in the announcement gained over 100,000 "likes" within the first day of its publication. Quickly following the announcement, "locust" as a trope made its way into mainstream Hong Kong news media. Popular anti-Chinese tabloids such as *Apple Daily* and *Sharp Daily,* for example, frequently evoked the trope to describe the behaviors of mainlanders in the SAR. Such moral high ground in turn allowed Hongkongers to feel more empowered as they were able to make claims that were filled with immobilizing fear and anxiety, but a sense of justified righteousness. While Hongkongers' strong desire to concretize their national identity was initially triggered by their fear of China's overwhelming economic and political power, they were able to regain some sense of control by claiming moral legitimacy and superiority over their mainland Chinese counterparts through animalizing tropes.

The feelings of control and power were particularly important to Hongkongers regarding maternal tourism because unlike other mainland Chinese visitors, the *neithers* were recognized by the Chinese state and the SAR government as legal Hong Kong permanent residents. However, by referring to all mainlanders as locusts without distinguishing their residency status, Hongkongers effectively performed an alienizing process that detached legal citizenship status from membership and belonging to the nation-family. As Bhikhu Parekh has accurately pointed out, "citizenship is about status and rights; belonging is about acceptance, feeling welcome, a sense of identification. The two do not necessarily coincide."[131] In other words, gaining legal citizenship status does not always entail admission into the nation-family. By not distinguishing their residency status and representing the *neithers* also as locusts, Hongkongers were in effect ascribing a totalizing label that, as DeChaine argues, "performs an essentializing function that literally denies the possibility of a positive referent."[132] Mainstream Hongkongers made it clear that despite the legal recognition granted by the state to the *neithers,* they and their mainland mothers were first and foremost undeserving usurpers who would never be welcomed into the Hong Kong nation-family.

Calling mainland tourists and immigrants "locusts" and employing warlike tropes such as "invasion," "survival," and "defend" to describe the increased tension between maternal tourists and the Hong Kong public, Hongkongers and the mainstream mass media argued that these outsiders had unrightfully leached the city of all the resources necessary to support local families. In particular, Hongkongers claimed that public schools and hospital wards—particularly beds in the maternity ward—had been taken over by *neithers* and their

---

131. Parekh, "What Is Multiculturalism?"
132. DeChaine, "Bordering the Civic Imaginary," 51.

mainland Chinese mothers. Local news media and online communities at the time commonly represented Hongkongers as rightful taxpayers whose contributions to the SAR were now in vain. As David Bleeden, Caroline Gottschalk-Druschke, and Ralph Cintrón point out, "the topos of the burdened ordinary taxpayer represents a certain unassailable moral standing . . . [that] produce[s] a position impervious to counterargument."[133] By criticizing mainlanders as free riders undeserving of public goods, Hongkongers were able to represent themselves as the "authentic citizens" whose families deserved priorities over those of the alien Others.[134]

By linking the brand of the authentic citizen to the trope of the family, mainstream Hongkongers mobilized a rhetoric of home invasion and marked mainland Chinese immigrants and children as a threat they must defend against. Because the rhetoric of survival was mobilized, there was little room emotionally and politically for Hongkongers to experience deliberative empathy and to consider how their interests and concerns might overlap with those of the Chinese immigrants. The constant anxiety and insecurity Hongkongers experienced under a neoliberal governance, for example, were shared by the Chinese mothers who saw maternal tourism as a way to safeguard a more promising future for their children. However, for Hongkongers to admit that they had overlapping concerns with mainland mothers was to accept their commonalities and to recognize the humanity of mainland Chinese people. This acknowledgment would be politically dangerous because once mainlanders were no longer considered abject, Hongkongers would have difficulty demarcating their community from the mainland Chinese people and pushing back on the increased ideological and political encroachment from Beijing.

## DISGUST AS POLITICAL EMOTION

The dominant emotional pedagogy had been successful in suppressing any empathetic emotional response among the citizenry because in addition to inciting anger, it also encouraged Hongkongers to see all Chinese people as objects of disgust and revulsion. Mainstream news and social media often portrayed mainland Chinese as contaminants that must be condemned and expelled from the SAR. Specifically, public disgust and outrage were mobilized by anti-Chinese Hongkongers and media to construct mainlanders as morally deplorable and unfit to raise a proper family. These "moral defects,"

---

133. Bleeden, Gottschalk-Druschke, Cintrón, "Minutemen," 186.
134. Ibid.

in turn, helped explain why mainlanders, particularly as families, would pose harm to the Hong Kong nation-family and thus did not deserve empathy or any deliberative consideration. Unlike anger, disgust is particularly effective in alienizing the Others because it is by nature visceral and therefore does not call for any articulable, discursive pieces of persuasion.[135]

Disgust was deployed in order to circumvent criticisms surrounding the prejudice mainstream Hongkongers harbored against mainlanders. As mentioned earlier, popular media in Hong Kong have historically portrayed mainlanders as uneducated individuals from a lower-class background who speak with a country accent. Such class- and culture-based discourses, however, are often vehemently condemned by local human rights organizations and activists. While such formal criticisms have never gained enough rhetorical force to stall the discursive process of alienization, they nonetheless motivated the construction of a more affectively powerful narrative that demonstrated why it is both *legitimate* and *justifiable* for Hongkongers to exclude mainlanders from their national community. By doing so, disgust gave valence to the existing emotional pedagogy, further stabilizing the negative feelings Hongkongers had toward mainland Chinese people.

In April 2014, an altercation between two mainland tourists and a Hongkonger provided the Hong Kong public a key moment to heighten their alienizing discourse through disgust. The incident began when a mainland couple decided to let their toddler urinate and defecate in the middle of a busy sidewalk. The couple was quickly confronted by a local Hongkonger who began taking pictures with his cell phone while shaming the parents for allowing their child to behave in such a manner. A scuffle ensued, and images and videos of the incident soon flooded various social media platforms, triggering heated public debates between and among Hongkongers and Chinese netizens. While Chinese netizens condemned Hongkongers for not being more understanding of their cultural differences, many Hong Kong netizens used this example to demonstrate why mainland Chinese were unfit for citizenship and inclusion in the SAR: Namely, they and their offspring were offensive and disgusting objects that would contaminate the city.[136]

Jumping on the bandwagon of this incident, various Hong Kong news media, political commentators, and individual netizens soon began circulating reports, images, and videos of similar occurrences in the next few months, giving further valence to the narrative that mainland families were indefensibly unfit for inclusion because by enacting the disgusting acts of public uri-

---

135. Nussbaum, *Hiding from Humanity.*
136. Nelson, "Piss Gate Triggers Mainland Campaign."

nation and defecation, they had in turn become disgusting themselves.[137] As Ahmed points out, disgust is commonly associated with the lower half of the body, where waste is expelled. Lowness, then, also becomes associated with bodies that we deem disgusting, and thus inferior. For Ahmed, "disgust at 'that which is below' functions to maintain the power relations between above and below, *through which 'aboveness' and 'belowness' become properties of particular bodies, objects, and spaces.*"[138] By focusing on incidents of public urination and defecation committed by mainland families, the Hong Kong public was able to reestablish their sense of superiority over mainlanders and to justify their desire to cast out Chinese immigrants as warranted and natural.

Frequently accompanying these discursive responses are images of the parent and child caught in the act, further evoking the viscerality of disgust as it transcends the need for discursive persuasion. Also apparent in these responses is a sense of moral and cultural superiority, anchored by feelings of righteousness as Hong Kong netizens discursively connect mainland parents with bodily wastes and the act of public defecation. As Nussbaum points out, by linking primary objects of disgust to particular practices, and then further to those who enact those practices, the exclusion of those groups becomes almost instantly justifiable: "This act (or more often and usually insepara-bly, this person) is a contaminant; it (he or she) pollutes our community. We would be better off if this contamination were kept far away from us."[139] By linking mainland parents to bodily wastes—an almost uncontested primary object of disgust—Hongkongers who advanced such alienizing claims were able to avoid accusations of discrimination and, more importantly, to justify the expulsion of mainland families as prevention of public contamination.

While the acts of disgust were committed by mainland children, reports in Hong Kong placed the primary blame on the parents, who were constructed as recalcitrant animalistic subjects that could not be reformed. For instance, commentaries and reports on these incidents frequently highlighted the con-frontations between mainland parents and the local Hongkongers who called out their acts. Mainstream news media used sensational headlines such as "Mainland Couple Attacked Hong Kong Man Because of Piss" and "Photo-journalist Bravely Fought Mainland Parents." As such rhetorics circulated within the local affective economy, mainland adults were marked as belliger-ent, as unreasonable, and most of all, as unfit parents who defiled and allowed their offspring to contaminate Hong Kong.

137. Christy Lau, "Video of Young Girl Peeing on Hong Kong Metro Prompts Online Back-lash"; Christy Lau, "Family Allows Child to Defecate on Plane Aisle, Embarrassing Chinese Passengers."

138. Ahmed, *The Cultural Politics of Emotion,* 89.

139. Nussbaum, *Hiding from Humanity,* 123.

## THE LIMIT OF DELIBERATIVE EMPATHY

As the locust trope circulated and gained increasing cultural and political valence within the local affective economy in Hong Kong, it encouraged a binary emotional response toward mainlanders, particularly the *neithers,* whose permanent residency status made them an even more unsettling threat to the Hong Kong nation-family. Under this polarizing emotional landscape, Hongkongers who were loyal to their nation-family were expected by mainstream mass media and their peers to express a sense of righteous anger toward maternal tourists and their children, while those who engaged in empathetic responses were often immediately criticized as traitors of their own kin.

To counter the dominant representation of Chinese immigrants as locusts, both local TV stations and mainland mothers engaged in acts of storytelling in order to humanize mainland parents: These parents were shown to share similar concerns for their children as mainstream Hongkongers, and like most Hongkongers, they were trying their best to make do amid sociopolitical forces outside of their control. While these narratives had the potential to generate deliberative empathy among the Hong Kong audience, they received significant backlash from mainstream Hongkongers, which resulted in a deepening of alienizing discourses. Analyzing two of these attempts in generating deliberative empathy from the Hong Kong audience, I demonstrate how the existing emotional pedagogy actively disciplined and suppressed feelings that challenged the alienization and dehumanization of mainland women.

In addition to providing a stable framework that regulates public feelings, emotional pedagogy is also a key instrument in the production, regulation, and (re)articulation of citizenry relationships; it translates permeating and dominant affects into a terministic screen that prescribes what emotional representations of the Others are acceptable, what kinds of feelings a "proper" and "loyal" citizen should have toward members and nonmembers, and how and to whom these feelings should be directed. When dominant templates of public feelings and emotional representations are in place, they constitute a structure of feeling, which as Raymond Williams cogently describes, is "as firm and definite as 'structure' suggests, yet . . . operates in the most delicate and least tangible parts of our activity."[140] The power behind emotional pedagogy, in other words, is that it renders a highly discursive and ideological process embodied, definite, and seemingly natural—and as such, alternative articulations and emotional expressions are foreclosed. In a moment of national anxiety, the practice and process of alienization constituted a domi-

---

140. Williams, *Marxism and Literature,* 36.

nant emotional pedagogy among Hongkongers, sanctioning the negative emotions they harbored toward mainland Chinese people. As I demonstrate in this section, by actively suppressing emotions such as compassion, sympathy, and pity—which, despite being problematic in their respective ways, are nonetheless more humanizing than revulsion and disgust—the emotional pedagogy among mainstream Hongkongers deterred any narratives that rendered mainland Chinese families as subjects who shared overlapping concerns and interests with the mainstream citizenry.

Because the national identity of Hongkongers was constructed through a shared sense of anxiety—and subsequently anger, contempt, and disgust—toward mainlanders, any indicators of affective closeness toward them was immediately interpreted by other members of the nation-family as a sign of disloyalty. As Ahmed points out, "the turning away from the object of fear involves a turning towards home, as a 'fellow feeling.'"[141] By the same logic, any gestures that turn toward the feared Other entail a turning away from one's fellowship with other members in her nation-family and affective community. In the early 2010s, the affective economy in Hong Kong was so saturated with expressions of anger and utter disgust toward mainland Chinese people that alternative feelings and opinions were rendered impermissible. Commentators and organizations that called for an antidiscriminatory approach toward mainland immigrants were commonly criticized as "leftards" by the more vocal public. Wai-hung Wong, who identifies as a Hongkonger but lives in California, where he works as a philosophy professor, came under immense fire after publishing a blog post suggesting that the mass media in Hong Kong was perpetuating confirmation bias by representing mainlanders only in a negative light.[142] After the post was published, Wong received a slew of hate mail from Hong Kong netizens, calling his writing "garbage" and accusing him of being an academic leftard who "focuses too much on philosophical logics that cannot solve any real problems that Hongkongers face."[143] As Wong notes in response to such criticisms, many Hongkongers who previously were politically neutral or apathetic had turned vehemently against mainland China, promulgating the narrative that all mainland Chinese people are of "poor quality."[144] While Wong was unfazed by the criticisms he received because of his geographical distance and privilege as a professor in an American uni-

---

141. Ahmed, *The Cultural Politics of Emotion*, 74.
142. W. Wong, "Beginning at the Bad Behaviors of Mainland Tourists."
143. W. Wong, "魚之樂" [Fish and Happiness].
144. Ibid.

versity, it is not difficult to see why one may be deterred from making claims regarding mainlanders that do not follow the dominant emotional pedagogy.

The emotional pedagogy about the *neithers* and their mainland mothers was particularly salient among mainstream Hongkongers, which prompted significant backlash against any humanizing representations of mainland families. In July 2013, Radio Television Hong Kong, a mainstream media platform famous for maintaining political and editorial independence from the Chinese and Hong Kong governments, broadcast a twenty-minute documentary interviewing several *neither* women who shared their stories and intimate lived experiences with the Hong Kong audience. Challenging the dehumanizing representations of the *neithers,* the documentary was vehemently condemned by Hong Kong netizens who accused the producer and director of advancing a pro-China political agenda at the expense of local allegiances and interests.

Titled "Voices outside the Picture" (畫外的聲音), the documentary explores familial stories of mainland maternal tourists whose voices were never heard among mainstream discourse in Hong Kong. The documentary begins with the silhouette of a person with an undisclosed face. Using a first-person narrative, the young man identifies himself as one of the first generation of *neithers,* who by then numbered about 200,000. Juxtaposed with a montage of Hongkongers protesting against mainland maternity tourists and parents, the voice then quietly asks, "Despite all these [conflicts], how much of our story do you guys really know?" This opening scene challenges and problematizes dominant emotional responses of immediate anger as it represents the *neithers* not as an aggregate, but as a person who, despite being a Hong Kong permanent resident, encounters real struggles and limitations because of his outsider status. By asking the final question, this person, even with his face concealed, demands a form of affective recognition that Hongkongers have refused to provide thus far.

The emotional tone of the documentary, however, does not stem mainly from the opening scene, as the narrator is after all still only a disembodied voice that can easily be dismissed as an actor, rather than an actual person whose life is intertwined with the politics of maternal tourism and the alienizing sentiments directed toward mainland families in Hong Kong. The rest of the documentary focuses on three mainland mothers who have chosen to give birth in Hong Kong: Xiao Nan, Ah Fong, and Ah Yin. Xiao Nan, an upper-middle-class woman who received a university education in the UK, explains that she wants her daughter to become a Hong Kong permanent resident so that she does not have to be "brainwashed" by China's nationalist education curriculum. She also wishes her daughter to grow up in a "relatively free and open" place like Hong Kong, away from the rampant corruption in mainland

China.[145] Extremely vocal about what she sees as an injustice against the *neithers* and their parents, Xiao Nan had, prior to this documentary, published an article online explaining her decision to become a maternal tourist. In her personal narrative, she addresses Hongkongers' assumptions immediately by stating, "In fact, we are not here because we want to take advantage of Hong Kong's public welfare—we are a middle-upper-class family in the mainland, and will obviously not be eligible for any welfare programs in Hong Kong. What we really hope is for our daughter to lead a different life."[146] Xiao Nan then continues with the wishes she harbors for her daughter:

> I wish that when my daughter grows up and goes to school, she will not receive wrong education, will not have to learn in school the way adults cheat and hurt each other to get ahead; [I] wish that through her education, she will learn knowledge and good morals, but not memorization of "political lessons."

Xiao Nan's list continues as she describes the medical system and kinds of career development she hopes her daughter can enjoy through her permanent residency in Hong Kong. At the end of the article, she writes, "[I] sincerely hope that Hongkongers and mainlanders would stop hurling insults towards each other. . . . We are all humans after all—it's not worth angering yourself and lowering your own moral standing."[147]

Like the opening scene of the documentary, Xiao Nan's narrative demands Hongkongers to see *neithers* and maternal tourists as humans who share commonalities with the mainstream citizenry: Just like the Hong Kong parents who worry about the threats mainlanders would pose to the socioeconomic opportunities and well-being of their children, Xiao Nan too shares the same desires and well wishes for her daughter. Her narrative demands the Hong Kong audience to recognize and acknowledge the very human similarities they share. While Xiao Nan challenges the dominant alienizing discourse, she does so in a way that reinforces Hong Kong's superiority toward China and explicitly demonstrates her appreciation of that. In other words, Xiao Nan represents herself not as the stereotypical mainlander who undermines local values and culture, but as an ally who appreciates and respects the institutions and practices in Hong Kong. In addition to establishing shared goals and values, Xiao Nan also attempts to divert the public critique of the *neithers* to the

---

145. "Voices outside the Pictures," *Hong Kong Connection*, RTHK, July 22, 2013.
146. Xiao Nan, "A Letter to Both Places from a Neither Mother."
147. Ibid.

Chinese and Hong Kong governments, calling for Hongkongers to demand legal changes at the state level rather than ostracizing mainland mothers who are merely acting in the best interests of their children:

> Mainland tourists and mothers who obey the law to give birth should not be the target of Hongkongers' justice crusade. If we must speak in terms of justice, [Hongkongers] should appeal to the Hong Kong government, China's Liaison Office in the SAR, or even directly to Beijing (I am not encouraging anyone to do so—only making an example here), asking them to make revisions to the Basic Law or deny public medical service to the *neithers*. But before any legal changes are made, mainland mothers are innocent—please treat them fairly.[148]

Instead of outright denying the charges mounted by mainstream Hongkongers against mainland maternal tourists, Xiao Nan redirects the audience's attention to the state power that regulates both the movement of bodies and the resources such bodies receive. What Xian Nan suggests here is that rather than alienizing mainland mothers, whose love and concern for their children are no different from those of Hong Kong parents, Hongkongers should direct their energy toward appealing to governmental power. Xiao Nan's argument and the language she uses echo closely those of local Hongkongers, who at the time had also been demanding a legal revision from the Hong Kong government to limit the influx of maternal tourists. At the end of her essay, Xiao Nan writes,

> I sincerely hope that Hongkongers and mainlanders would stop hurling insults towards each other.... From others' point of view, this is just another internal conflict among Chinese people, [and] another round of nonsense comedy.[149]

While Xiao Nan made use of both emotional and political arguments to position herself as a mother, as a rational citizen, and as similar to Hongkongers, her narrative—and she herself as a person—were still mercilessly attacked by Hong Kong netizens with extremely dehumanizing language. After her article was published by *Ming Pao*, a mainstream and relatively politically impartial newspaper, Xiao Nan received many negative comments from local Hongkongers who were not sympathetic to her claims and vehemently

---

148. Ibid.
149. Ibid.

demanded that she returned to where she *really* belonged. Xiao Nan, together with the two women who were later interviewed in the documentary, were criticized even more brutally after the episode aired.

Unlike Xiao Nan, the other two women, Ah Fong and Ah Yin, are from a working-class background. Both women gave birth in Hong Kong because they could not afford to pay the hefty fines for violating China's one-child policy. Due to their restricted immigration status in Hong Kong as visitors, they were unable to find sustainable work and were not eligible for any social welfare either. Throughout the episode, Ah Fong and Ah Yin are shown to make do for the well-being of their children, given the discrimination and restrictions placed on maternal tourists and the *neithers*. The documentary portrays the intimate everyday life of the two mothers: the way they haggle in the market with fluent Cantonese, the way they gather with their children in a tiny bedroom that doubles as a dining room during meal time, and the moment when Ah Fong's young children teach her English using their school textbook. While the three women are from vastly different socioeconomic backgrounds, the documentary portrays them all as caring mothers who decided to become maternal tourists not only because of the poor sociopolitical conditions in China but also because of their appreciation of Hong Kong culture and the opportunities and infrastructure the SAR offers. The audience is implicitly asked to view maternal tourists as people who share their appreciation of the SAR, each attempting to provide for her family while struggling with material and political forces that are out of her control.

Despite such human portrayal, the documentary failed to change the negative emotional responses Hongkongers had toward mainland parents and the *neithers*. The viewers' negative reactions toward the documentary revealed how the dominant emotional pedagogy worked in a way that rendered humanizing representations of mainland families abhorrent. The night after it was aired, many Hong Kong netizens gathered on the Golden Forum and vehemently attacked the three women. Sprinkled with lewd slang, most of these comments suggest that the women deserve all their hardship, and that "if they are so pathetic here they should just go back to the mainland and be wealthy there; or they can just live like beggars in Hong Kong."[150] Many other netizens echoed the same sentiment, stating that these women should "go back to mainland and die there—they come [to Hong Kong] on their own accord, and now they are complaining about how pathetic they are."[151] Direct-

---

150. Wang Bun Jik Jau, "Re: Neithers in Hong Kong Seem so Pitiful in Hong Kong Connection's 'Voices outside the Picture,'" *HKGolden*, July 22, 2013.

151. Lam Jo Shun Ha Toi, "Re: Neithers in Hong Kong Seem so Pitiful in Hong Kong Connection's 'Voices outside the Picture,'" *HKGolden*, July 22, 2013.

ing their attacks to "locusts," "garbage," "Chinese pigs," and "shit-eating dogs," netizens on the Golden Forum almost immediately conflated the three women with animalistic and dehumanizing brands that had gained significant cultural valence in the local affective economy. Such outright disgust and outrage rendered alternative representations of mainland mothers nonsensical because no figures so debased and dehumanized should ever be considered permissible for inclusion.

The critiques made in response to the documentary echoed the dominant emotional claims Hongkongers were accustomed to for the past three years on other social media platforms. For instance, the popular Facebook group "Against Mainland Pregnant Women from Giving Birth in Hong Kong! 100,000 People 'Like' to Show the Government!" was filled with similar statements, arguing that mainland mothers and the *neithers* should not be given any sympathy or support because they deserved the hardship they encountered in Hong Kong. This sentiment was clearly expressed in an online column critiquing the documentary. The commentator writes that "the show has committed a simple logical flaw—'appeal to pity/empathy'—the production unit attempts to make use of the sympathy of Hongkongers to justify the way the state uses immigration policies on the *neithers* to colonize the Hong Kong people."[152] He continues that the situation here is akin to having your homeland ravished by robbers, while the government is demanding that "you listen to their voices, to understand these robbers, because they are victims just like you."[153] The commentator's argument suggests that by showing any emotions other than anger and disgust to mainlanders—particularly the *neithers*—one is essentially consenting to the invasion of Hong Kong.

At play here was a powerful emotional pedagogy constituted by the shared affective states among Hongkongers and their dominant political attitudes toward mainland China and its people. As Gould accurately points out, "our affective states are what temper and intensify our attentions, affiliations, investments, and attachments; they help to solidify some of our ideas and beliefs and attenuate others."[154] The deep sense of anxiety and unease Hongkongers experienced toward the increased encroachment of mainland China translated into hostile emotional responses toward mainland families—responses that foreclosed the enactment of deliberative empathy and critical reflections on sociopolitical and material commonalities Hongkongers share with the population they so despised.

152. Cheung, "The *Neithers* outside of the Picture," *PassionTimes*, July 27, 2013.
153. Ibid.
154. Gould, *Moving Politics*, 27.

The Hong Kong audience's responses toward the three mainland mothers demonstrated exactly that: Despite hearing intimate and humanizing details of the three women's lives, desires, and intentions, mainstream Hongkongers chose to see them not as people, each with a unique narratable self, but merely as representatives of the aggregate Other. Personal narratives and familial stories that seek to establish a more intimate affective tie despite cultural and political difference, in other words, were rendered ineffective in this case; in fact, they backfired and intensified the anger and contempt attached to the bodies of mainland women and children. These emotions were so persistent because they empowered Hongkongers politically and affectively and helped counter their fear of losing ground to mainland China.

Despite mainstream Hongkongers' vehement denial, they and Chinese maternal tourists did in fact share similar values and interests. For instance, while mainstream Hongkongers aligned maternal tourists with the mainland Chinese government and treated both of them with contempt and outrage, pregnant Chinese women were in the SAR exactly because they sought to defy the Chinese state's definition of the ideal citizen. Chinese maternal tourists and mainstream Hongkongers who were outraged by the perceived threats to their own family, in addition, shared similar love and concern for the well-being of their children. Socially and affectively, the two groups had more in common than the alienizing discourse allowed for. Such overlapping concerns, however, were not enough to overcome the revulsion, anxiety, and fear Hongkongers felt toward mainlanders and the political, ideological, and economic encroachment they represented.

## FORMAL EXCLUSION OF MATERNAL TOURISTS

As exclusionary claims toward the *neithers* continued to circulate and culminate through various popular media platforms at the expense of alternative articulations, anger and disgust saturated the local affective network. Such emotions in turn propelled and strongly influenced the political actions that Hongkongers took to combat who they saw as invaders of their nation-family. Arguing that the SAR government should privilege the interests of Hongkongers in their decision making, disgruntled Hongkongers—particularly mothers—staged multiple protests from 2011 to 2013. Most protesters claimed that the influx of the *neithers* and their mainland mother would overwhelm the local education and health care systems, thus harming the well-being of local Hongkongers. On January 1, 2013, the chief executive of the SAR, C. Y. Leung, implemented the "zero quota" policy. Under this new policy, mainland pregnant women who did not have prior booking with a local hospital would be banned from entering the SAR for delivery. As stated in the Immigration Department's annual review, "the Department has strengthened the complementary immigration measures including proactive interception at control points and analysis of the trends and methods used by [mainland pregnant women] on gate crashing, so as to arrange targeted interception and joint operations with other departments."[155] The department cited the number of mainland women who had been prosecuted and the sentence they received, which served to "prove the effectiveness of the measures."[156] While reports of mainland maternal tourists evading law enforcement or circumventing the "zero quota" policy continued to circulate, large-scale protests mostly subsided afterward.

In various press releases and policy statements, the SAR government commonly deployed exclusionary tropes and arguments that carried significant emotional valence among mainstream Hongkongers concerned about the interests of local family units. For instance, ten months after the "zero quota" policy was implemented, the secretary for food and health spoke in front of the Legislative Council, explaining that "in circumstances where resources are limited, the public healthcare service always seeks to privilege the needs of local Hongkongers. We carry out necessary measures to address the problem if we discover that providing healthcare service to non-local Hongkongers would negatively influence local residents."[157] Similarly, highlighting the "zero quota" policy, the chief executive of the SAR emphasized in his 2013 policy address that "the Government serves Hong Kong people and [its] objective is to safeguard their interests first and foremost. We must manage immigration properly to avoid negative impacts on our livelihood."[158] By mirroring popular discourse and tropes on the protection of local interests and resources, the Hong Kong government was able to temporarily appease the existing citizenry by signaling that it had heard and understood the public emotional demands to shun the Other.

Even though the Hong Kong government's haphazard "zero quota" policy did not address Hongkongers' core demand—namely, that the Basic Law needed to be revised—it nonetheless empowered them by legitimizing their

---

155. Hong Kong Immigration Department, "Immigration Department Review 2013 (with photos)."

156. Ibid.

157. "Legislative Council: Secretary for Food and Health's Concluding Speech for Motion 'Prioritizing Hongkongers' When Implementing Policies," 1.

158. Leung, "2013 Policy Address: Seek Change; Maintain Stability; Serve the People with Pragmatism."

concerns over the loss of a superior sociopolitical position and identity. The government's action also illustrates the way affects and emotional appeals materialize into a law that singlehandedly and drastically alters important life decisions. In the face of a perceived national crisis, the Hong Kong government had to either contain or dissipate the pervasive sense of anxiety and panic mainstream Hongkongers felt. As affective states, however, these feelings and intensities are overwhelming and unwieldy, and as Thompson and Hogget argue, "once they gather momentum, [they] become difficult forces to control," sometimes even eluding attempts made by political actors to redirect them productively.[159] Affective intensities generated by a perceived threat to the nation-family, in other words, not only produce specific emotional representations of the Other that have massive staying power but also materialize into political instruments that regulate and structure the lives of many.

Three years after the "zero quota" policy was implemented, there were still about 800 children each year born to mainland Chinese women in Hong Kong.[160] While under the policy, Hong Kong hospitals no longer accept advanced bookings from pregnant mainland women to deliver in Hong Kong, the hospitals nevertheless are obligated to assist in urgent deliveries. Continued to be motivated by the Hong Kong permanent residency status, numerous mainland women over the years have crossed the Hong Kong–China border right when they are at the brink of delivery. As a result, births under the "zero quota" policy have almost all been delivered in the emergency wards.[161]

Chinese maternal tourism does not take place only in Hong Kong. Since 2015, the number of Chinese women giving birth in the US has increased significantly, prompting local officials to crack down on maternity hotels in California.[162] The practice of maternal tourism, however, is not in itself illegal if the women arrive in the US through valid tourist visas—as most do.[163] Interviews with these women show that like their peers who have chosen to give birth in Hong Kong, they are embarking on this long and expensive journey because they want their children to enjoy the cultural capital, transnational mobility, and sociopolitical freedom that come with a more valued citizenship status.[164] However, perceived as inferior and as threats to the identity of the nation-family, the bodies of pregnant Chinese women are subjected to the cultural and political force of what Natalie Fixmer-Oraiz calls "homeland maternity":

---

159. Thompson and Hoggett, *Politics and the Emotions*, 3.
160. Tsang, "Mainland Women Gatecrashing Hong Kong's Maternity Wards."
161. Ibid.
162. Sheehan, "Born In The USA."
163. Chavez, *Anchor Babies*.
164. Ibid.; Shyong, "Why Birth Tourism from China Persists."

During times of perceived precarity, maternal bodies are intensely policed in order to secure the nation.[165] The maintenance of the dominant nation-family, in other words, is intimately connected to the regulation of women's reproductive and familial lives.

## CONCLUSION

The sociopolitical and national tension between local Hongkongers and mainland maternal tourists provides an opportunity for rhetorical scholars to consider how citizenship discourse is intimately connected to and negotiated through local affects and feelings, and how a locally dominant citizenry responds to a group of Others who rapidly acquire more political and economic capital at the national level. Given such a conflicting position, the existing citizenry must reinvent and deploy alienizing tropes not only to cast out the Other but also to help mitigate the permeating sense of fear and anxiety by recasting their own superiority and legitimacy. Indeed, the rhetorical tactics and emotional pedagogy that Hongkongers perform seek to fulfill both functions. By mobilizing emotions such as disgust and revulsion toward the bodies and families of mainland Chinese people, the mainstream Hong Kong public have been able to effectively defend the moral and social hierarchy that places local family units and their interests at the top.

Citizenship discourse and performance is not merely about branding and excluding the Other to reinforce the Self, nor is it only about concretizing and asserting a specific cultural or national identity. Rather, it serves significant affective functions that allow the existing citizenry to feel better about themselves, their home, and their conception of the nation-family during a time of perceived crisis. Citizenship rhetorics, therefore, must be considered as interactions across the affective, discursive, political, and material dimensions. The potent affective charge citizenship discourse and immigration statutes carry gives them staying power, and it renders alien bodies "sticky" and saturated with affects that justify their alienization.[166] As I have demonstrated in this chapter, when the mainstream citizenry is feeling under siege, as if the survival of their nation-family is at stake, rhetorical moves that attempt to alter established emotional patterns could in fact backfire to further marginalize the Others.

---

165. Fixmer-Oraiz, "Contemplating Homeland Maternity."
166. Ahmed, *The Cultural Politics of Emotion*, 11.

This chapter illustrates the conditions that prevented the enactment of deliberative empathy. Unlike the racialized subjects in the previous two chapters, Chinese maternal tourists circulated in the Hong Kong affective economy not as an unfamiliar and inferior Other, but as an abject and a threating presence that was all the more anxiety-inducing because of the family resemblances they shared with mainstream Hongkongers. To be empathetic toward mainlanders, in other words, is to accept that they in fact are not unlike the mainstream citizenry. Recognizing such commonality, however, is risky for Hongkongers as it reveals the fragility of the boundary they have created over time to separate themselves from both the mainland Chinese people and the Chinese government. Protecting this boundary and their sense of superiority over mainlanders is important because it gives Hongkongers the feeling of control amid the increased political and economic encroachment from mainland China that diminishes their cultural capital.

As the number of cross-border families increases over the years, it is already no longer possible for Hongkongers to clearly demarcate the boundaries of the Hong Kong nation-family from those of mainland China's, and subsequently to prevent China's further ideological encroachment. It is exactly this blurriness and close proximity that amplifies the anxiety and fear Hongkongers experience, to the extent that they are unwilling—or unable—to activate critical empathetic responses toward Chinese mothers despite their palpable humanity. Effective promotion of deliberative empathy in this situation, therefore, requires not only humanizing familial narratives but also an emotional and political reeducation that helps Hongkongers develop the ability to affectively discern mainland Chinese immigrants from the Beijing regime. That way, Hongkongers could continue to resist the Chinese government's encroachment while exploring different emotional responses and ways of relating to mainlanders without feeling like the survival of their nation-family depends entirely on their ongoing outrage, contempt, and disgust toward their mainland counterparts.

# CONCLUSION

# Deliberative Empathy, Habits, and Proximity

Solidarity does not assume that our struggles are the same struggles, or that our pain is the same pain, or that our hope is for the same future. Solidarity involves commitment, and work, as well as the recognition that even if we do not have the same feelings, or the same lives, or the same bodies, we do live on common ground.

—SARA AHMED, *THE CULTURAL POLITICS OF EMOTION*

IN THIS BOOK, I have examined how formal citizenship discourse and the dominant interpretive framework of the nation-family reify existing identity categories and power hierarchy, and how they fall short on recognizing marginalized subjects for their humanity alone. The primary limitation of citizenship discourse is that it fails to promote transformative deliberation between the mainstream citizenry and the marginalized Others outside of the nation-family. When subjects are demarcated as either members of the nation-family or as aliens who are inferior or threatening, there is little room for the dominant citizenry to consider how their lives and interests are intertwined with those of marginalized subjects. In a neoliberal economy that relies on the exploitation of racialized bodies, the state often pitches the mainstream citizenry—already in a constant state of fear, uncertainty, and anxiety—against marginalized subjects whose value is always contingent upon their labor. There is, therefore, little room and incentive for more privileged subjects to cross the threshold to reconsider their ethical relations with marginalized subjects, and through that process, to experience a shift in their own subjectivity and perceptions of the world.

Because transformative deliberation involves the crossing of an affective threshold—to simultaneously affect others and be affected—I have proposed *deliberative empathy* as a productive emotion to jump-start this process.[1] As

---

1. Massumi, *The Power at the End of the Economy.*

philosopher Shannon Sullivan argues, alienizing responses to racialized groups is a subconscious habit that has been institutionalized and enforced socially.[2] To effectively address the tendency to dehumanize the Other, therefore, we must take a simultaneously affective and deliberative approach, rather than relying only on either one of them. While deliberative empathy entails critical reflection on the shared material contexts and interests between mainstream audiences and marginalized subjects, it is also an affective response that opens the possibilities for bodies to affect and be affected by others in ways that are not predetermined. Different from affective empathy, which often promotes identification and misrecognition, deliberative empathy prompts the more dominant interlocutor to engage in two layers of deliberation as they experience empathy that draws them closer to the Other: First, they consider the structural and material causes that lead to the suffering of others, and second, they reflect on how they are implicated in the same structures that entrap others and engage in an internal deliberation on how their relations with others ought to shift. Deliberative empathy invites interlocutors across power difference to move toward each other affectively, while always keeping in the foreground the structural, political, and material factors that simultaneously bind them together and separate them.

As an emotional response, deliberative empathy prompts dominant subjects to critically examine their habituated response toward marginalized Others. As Sullivan explicates, "habit is a predisposition for transacting with the world in a particular way. Habits operate on subconscious and sometimes even unconscious levels: they are what we do 'without thinking.' . . . Habit is constitutive of the self."[3] Existing power hierarchies inform how one should transact in the world and interact with others not only through established institutions but also through the process of internalization, in which individuals come to see these modes of interactions as constitutive of their sense of self. By likening prejudice to habit, Sullivan points to the affective nature of othering: Rather than residing solely in the realm of signification, othering possesses an intensity that moves bodies toward and against each other without their conscious awareness. To effectively promote social change, therefore, we must attune simultaneously to the sociopolitical material contexts and to the affective stronghold the existing interpretive framework has on dominant subjects that prevents them from identifying their privilege and complicity in the oppression of others. The latter is particularly significant because if habits exert their influence at the subconscious or unconscious level, we cannot

---

2. Sullivan, *Revealing Whiteness*.
3. Sullivan, *Good White People*, 28.

assume that more dominant subjects could through persuasion alone elimi-nate their prejudice and negative emotional reactions toward the Other.[4] Since the affective nature of habits may render dominant subjects recalcitrant to change through conventional models of persuasion and deliberation, we must consider interlocutors as bodies with the capacities to be affected through other means. Rhetorical tactics that jolt the dominant interlocutors out of their existing subject position and worldview hold promise in creating a con-dition in which they realize how their lives are contingent upon the sociopo-litical and material network they inhabit and share with their less privileged counterparts. The concepts of transformative deliberation and deliberative empathy, therefore, are helpful in devising rhetorical acts that attend to the emotional tenet of social change.

If the overarching goal for transformative deliberation is to cultivate coali-tional moments in which interlocutors across power, racial, and cultural differ-ence engage in transformative deliberation with each other, then we must take seriously how proximity among interlocutors renders a rhetorical tactic effec-tive in fostering deliberative empathy in one situation, while making it coun-terproductive in another. For example, in chapter 2, while the South Asian community has been inhabiting the city alongside mainstream Hongkongers for at least three generations, a history of racism and de facto segregation has intensified the distance—both emotional and spatial—between the two popu-lations. As a result, mainstream Hongkongers do not see the interests of South Asians as relevant to them, nor do they readily consider South Asian subjects as members of the nation-family.

Chapters 3 and 4 demonstrate that domestic intimacy, spatial contiguity, and ethnic closeness are on their own insufficient in promoting deliberative empathy among dominant audiences. The proximity between the mainstream citizenry and racialized subjects is complicated in chapter 3 by government regulations that force migrant domestic workers to reside in the homes of their employers. The physical and emotional closeness local employers share with their migrant domestic workers are thus inevitably marred by the signifi-cant power difference between them, and by the diminished privacy in one's own home. Closeness and distance play out differently in chapter 4. Chinese immigrants and maternal tourists are ethnically the same as the mainstream citizenry in Hong Kong, and many of them already have strong familial and cultural ties to the city. Because of such close proximity, they pose a more

---

4. In his earlier work, W. E. B. Du Bois makes such an assumption, believing in the core goodness of white people and the power of education in undoing their racial prejudice. He was later disillusioned. See Du Bois, *The Souls of Black Folk*; Du Bois and Anderson, *The Philadel-phia Negro.*

menacing threat to Hongkongers than the other racialized populations; if mainstream Hongkongers are not careful in demarcating their identities and territories, they could be subsumed and replaced not only by mainland Chinese immigrants but by the Chinese state at large. The cultural, geographical, and ethnic closeness between the two groups, therefore, ironically intensifies the affective distance Hongkongers attempt to maintain.

The fear of being subsumed and replaced is particularly palpable in the case of Chinese immigrants and maternal tourists because those bodies stand in as a proxy of the Chinese state. In other words, while these immigrants may be marginalized in the local Hong Kong context, they symbolize a looming political power and state apparatus that has been actively encroaching upon the political values and cultural identity of mainstream Hongkongers. While Hongkongers are not completely misguided in their anxiety and fear for their political future, when the fear is superimposed onto the bodies of mainland immigrants, it forecloses room for them to build a coalition with mainlanders who also seek to resist the Chinese state regime. However, as chapter 4 highlights, the enactment of deliberative empathy is only possible when the mainstream audiences do not experience the fear that their survival is at stake.

This points to a limitation of deliberative empathy in promoting social change: How productive is this political and emotional response if it always hinges upon the experiences and feelings of the more dominant interlocutor? This is an important question because dominant members of the society could experience what feels to be "genuine" fear even when it cannot be justified by the existing material and sociopolitical contexts. Dominant subjects, as Sullivan points out, often experience "ontological expansiveness": the tendency to "act and think as if all spaces—whether geographical, psychical, linguistic, economic, spiritual, bodily, or otherwise—are or should be available for them to move in and out of as they wish."[5] This tendency could heighten the feeling that their survival is at stake whenever their privilege is hampered. While ungrounded in any sociopolitical evidence, this fear could feel so real that it crowds out the subject's capacity to experience and enact deliberative empathy.

I see this limitation as also a new opening. Ontological expansion, like the inability to discern one's rightful target of fear or anger, is a subconscious habit that is often left unexamined. I continue to uphold deliberative empathy as a productive feeling and process because it could disrupt the dominant audiences' habituated responses and could be mobilized in tandem with what Teresa Brennan calls "affective discernment"; as Brennan points out:

---

5. Sullivan, *Revealing Whiteness*, 10.

Discernment, in the affective world, functions best when it is able to be alert to the moment of fear or anxiety or grief or other sense of loss that permits the negative affect to gain a hold. Discernment then is allied to a position in which one receives and processes without the intervention of anxiety or other fixed obstacles in the way of the thinking process. [6]

By inviting the dominant audience to engage in the process of internal deliberation and temporarily decentering their feeling templates, deliberative empathy defamiliarizes one's everyday life and the way one transacts with the world so that the subject could understand that their perceptions of the world do not hold true for all, and that their emotional reactions toward marginalized others ought not to remain unchanged. Internal deliberation cannot be divorced from emotion because, as political theorist Jane Mansbridge points out, "understanding one's own needs requires gaining insight into why one fears, hates, loves, feels sorry for, and feels proud of aspects of oneself and other individuals and groups."[7] By reflecting critically on one's emotional reactions, one learns to discern, for instance, whether one's anger toward a racialized Other is due to their inherent flaw, or whether it is a symptom of transference.

While deliberative empathy does not promise to create coalitional moments overnight, its potential and power lie in its ability to promote self-reflexivity in a way that pays equal attention to the self and others, and the networks of material and power that bind them together. Without a critical understanding of one's self and where one stands in the interconnected network of sociopolitical, economic, and cultural forces, any empathy extended to the Other would be amiss as it would not produce a reciprocal relationship across difference. As Adams cogently puts it:

> The crucial difference here lies between denouncing a position and changing it. To accomplish the latter, it is necessary to fully occupy and take possession of the position as one's own. In this case, that means naming the interests that define self (legally, politically, economically), tether self (psychologically, affectively) and can be the means of better understanding and mobilizing self (collaboratively, progressively).[8]

While deliberative empathy is not a panacea to alienization and systematic oppression, it asks us to examine our habits, assumptions, and relations with

---

6. Brennan, *The Transmission of Affect*, 120.
7. Mansbridge, *Reconsidering the Democratic Public*, 99.
8. Adams, "At the Table with Arendt," 24.

others with a critical gaze, to acknowledge our material and affective interconnectedness with others, and through that process, to cultivate ethical relationships that are founded on shared interests and reciprocity that shift and are always open to change. As the epigraph from Ahmed suggests, it is through the open recognition of the simultaneous difference and commonality that bind them together that subjects arrive at a sustainable place of solidarity.

# BIBLIOGRAPHY

Abbas, M. Ackbar. *Hong Kong: Culture and the Politics of Disappearance.* Minneapolis: University of Minnesota Press, 1997.

Adams, Katherine. "At the Table with Arendt: Toward a Self-Interested Practice of Coalition Discourse." *Hypatia* 17, no. 1 (2002): 1–33.

Agamben, Giorgio. *Homo Sacer: Sovereign Power and Bare Life.* Translated by Daniel Heller-Roazen. Stanford, CA: Stanford University Press, 1998.

Ahmed, Sara. "Affective Economies." *Social Text* 22, no. 2 (2004): 117–39.

———. *The Cultural Politics of Emotion.* New York: Routledge, 2004.

———. "A Phenomenology of Whiteness." *Feminist Theory* 8, no. 2 (2007): 149–68.

———. *Strange Encounters: Embodied Others in Post-Coloniality.* London: Routledge, 2000.

Alexander, Michelle. *The New Jim Crow: Mass Incarceration in the Age of Colorblindness.* New York: The New Press, 2010.

Allen, Danielle S. *Talking to Strangers: Anxieties of Citizenship since Brown v. Board of Education.* Chicago: University of Chicago Press, 2006.

Amaya, Hector. *Citizenship Excess: Latino/as, Media, and the Nation.* New York: NYU Press, 2013.

Ana, Otto Santa. "'Like an Animal I Was Treated': Anti-Immigrant Metaphor in US Public Discourse." *Discourse & Society* 10, no. 2 (1999): 191–224.

Anzaldúa, Gloria, Norma Cantú, and Aída Hurtado. *Borderlands / La Frontera: The New Mestiza.* 4th ed. San Francisco: Aunt Lute Books, 2012.

Arendt, Hannah. *Men in Dark Times.* San Diego: Mariner Books, 1970.

Arendt, Hannah, and Margaret Canovan. *The Human Condition.* 2nd ed. Chicago: University of Chicago Press, 1998.

Arendt, Hannah, and Jonathan Schell. *On Revolution.* New York: Penguin Classics, 2006.

Asen, Robert. "Deliberation and Trust." *Argumentation and Advocacy* 50, no. 1 (2013): 2–17. https://doi.org/10.1080/00028533.2013.11821806.

———. "A Discourse Theory of Citizenship." *Quarterly Journal of Speech* 90, no. 2 (2004): 189–211.

———. "Neoliberalism, the Public Sphere, and a Public Good." *Quarterly Journal of Speech* 103, no. 4 (2017): 329–49.

"The Basic Law." Accessed January 28, 2019.https://www.basiclaw.gov.hk/en/basiclawtext/index .html.

Batson, C. Daniel. *The Altruism Question: Toward A Social-Psychological Answer*. Hillsdale, NJ: Psychology Press, 1991.

Batson, C. Daniel, Johee Chang, Ryan Orr, and Jennifer Rowland. "Empathy, Attitudes, and Action: Can Feeling for a Member of a Stigmatized Group Motivate One to Help the Group?" *Personality and Social Psychology Bulletin* 28, no. 12 (2002): 1656–66.

Beck, Ulrich. *Risk Society: Towards a New Modernity*. Newbury Park, CA: Sage, 1992.

Bell, Lee Anne. *Storytelling for Social Justice: Connecting Narrative and the Arts in Antiracist Teaching*. New York: Routledge, 2010.

Benach, Joan, Carles Muntaner, Carlos Delclos, María Menéndez, and Charlene Ronquillo. "Migration and 'Low-Skilled' Workers in Destination Countries." *PLOS Medicine* 8, no. 6 (2011): e1001043.

Benhabib, Seyla. *Situating the Self: Gender, Community, and Postmodernism in Contemporary Ethics*. New York: Routledge, 1992.

Benjamin, Jessica. *The Bonds of Love: Psychoanalysis, Feminism, and the Problem of Domination*. New York: Pantheon, 1988.

Berlant, Lauren, ed. *Compassion: The Culture and Politics of an Emotion*. New York: Routledge, 2004.

Berlant, Lauren. *Cruel Optimism*. Durham, NC: Duke University Press Books, 2011.

———. *The Queen of America Goes to Washington City: Essays on Sex and Citizenship*. Durham, NC: Duke University Press Books, 1997.

———. "The Theory of Infantile Citizenship." *Public Culture* 5, no. 3 (1993): 395–410.

Bloom, Paul. *Against Empathy: The Case for Rational Compassion*. New York: Ecco, 2016.

Bohman, James. "Realizing Deliberative Democracy as a Mode of Inquiry: Pragmatism, Social Facts, and Normative Theory." *The Journal of Speculative Philosophy* 18, no. 1 (2004): 23–43. https://www.jstor.org/stable/25670495.

Bosniak, Linda. *The Citizen and the Alien: Dilemmas of Contemporary Membership*. Princeton, NJ: Princeton University Press, 2008.

Bradsher, Keith. "Hong Kong Court Denies Foreign Domestic Helpers Right to Permanent Residency." *The New York Times*, March 25, 2013, Asia Pacific. https://www.nytimes.com/2013/ 03/26/world/asia/hong-kong-court-denies-foreign-domestic-helpers-right-to-permanent -residency.html.

———. "Once a Model City, Hong Kong Is in Trouble." *The New York Times*, June 29, 2017, Asia Pacific. https://www.nytimes.com/2017/06/29/world/asia/hong-kong-china-handover.html.

Brandzel, Amy L. *Against Citizenship: The Violence of the Normative*. Urbana: University of Illinois Press, 2016.

Brennan, Teresa. *The Transmission of Affect*. Ithaca, NY: Cornell University Press, 2004.

Bridges, Brian, Albert H. Y. Chen, Anne S. Y. Cheung, Fung Ho-lup, Kenneth Ka-loh Chan, Beatrice K. F. Leung, Anita Y. K. Poon, Ting Wai, and Timothy Ka-ying Wong. *One Country, Two Systems in Crisis: Hong Kong's Transformation since the Handover*. Edited by Wong Yiuchung. Lanham, MD: Lexington Books, 2008.

Brown, Wendy. *Undoing the Demos: Neoliberalism's Stealth Revolution*. Brooklyn, NY: Zone Books, 2017.

Buddle, Cluff. "The Right of Abode Cases That Shook Hong Kong." *South China Morning Post,* May 1, 2018. http://www.scmp.com/article/668742/right-abode-cases-shook-hong-kong.

Burke, Kenneth. *A Grammar of Motives.* Berkeley: University of California Press, 1969.

———. *A Rhetoric of Motives.* Berkeley: University of California Press, 1969.

Burns, John P. "Immigration from China and the Future of Hong Kong." *Asian Survey* 27, no. 6 (1987): 661–82.

Butler, Judith. "Is Kinship Always Already Heterosexual?" *Differences* 13, no. 1 (2002): 14–44.

Carroll, John M. *A Concise History of Hong Kong.* New York: Rowman & Littlefield, 2007.

Carsten, Janet. *After Kinship.* Cambridge: Cambridge University Press, 2003.

———. "The Substance of Kinship and the Heat of the Hearth: Feeding, Personhood, and Relatedness among Malays in Pulau Langkawi." *American Ethnologist* 22, no. 2 (1995): 223–41.

Cavarero, Adriana. *Relating Narratives: Storytelling and Selfhood.* London: Routledge, 2000.

Chan, Ming K., and Alvin Y. So, eds. *Crisis and Transformation in China's Hong Kong.* London: Routledge, 2002.

Chang, Grace. *Disposable Domestics: Immigrant Women Workers in the Global Economy.* Cambridge, MA: South End Press, 2000.

Chávez, Karma R. *Queer Migration Politics: Activist Rhetoric and Coalitional Possibilities.* Urbana: University of Illinois Press, 2013.

Chávez, Karma R, and Cindy Griffin, eds. *Standing in the Intersection: Feminist Voices, Feminist Practices in Communication Studies.* Albany: SUNY Press, 2012.

Chavez, Leo R. *Anchor Babies and the Challenge of Birthright Citizenship.* Stanford, CA: Stanford Briefs, 2017.

———. *The Latino Threat: Constructing Immigrants, Citizens, and the Nation.* Stanford, CA: Stanford University Press, 2008.

Chen, Te-ping. Interview with Mariko Sanchanta. "Hong Kong's Fear of Mainland Chinese Invasion." *Wall Street Journal,* August 29, 2012. https://www.wsj.com/video/hong-kong-fear-of-mainland-chinese-invasion/AF758B09-5CDA-4373-9340-7B868BD6178A.html.

Cheung, Simpson. "Hong Kong-Born Adoptee Wins Fight for Chinese Nationality." *South China Morning Post.* Last modified November 18, 2012, www.scmp.com/news/hong-kong/article/1084957/hong-kong-born-adoptee-wins-fight-chinese-nationality.

Childers, Jay P. "Rhetorical Citizenship and Public Deliberation." *Quarterly Journal of Speech* 100, no. 4 (2014): 495–98. https://doi.org/10.1080/00335630.2014.990178.

"China to End One-Child Policy." *BBC News,* October 29, 2015, China. http://www.bbc.com/news/world-asia-34665539.

Chiu, Joanna. "Indonesian Helper, 23, in Critical Condition after Alleged Beatings by Hong Kong Employers." *South China Morning Post,* January 13, 2014. http://www.scmp.com/news/hong-kong/article/1404697/indonesian-helper-23-critical-condition-after-alleged-beatings-hong.

Choi, Grace. "Integration Anxiety." *HK Magazine,* December 17, 2014. http://archive.fo/Mosn2.

Chowdhury, Elora, and Liz Philipose, eds. *Dissident Friendships: Feminism, Imperialism, and Transnational Solidarity.* Urbana: University of Illinois Press, 2016.

Chung, Adrienne H., and Michael D Slater. "Reducing Stigma and Out-Group Distinctions Through Perspective–Taking in Narratives." *Journal of Communication* 63, no. 5 (2013): 894–911.

Cisneros, Josue David. *The Border Crossed Us: Rhetorics of Borders, Citizenship, and Latina/o Identity.* Tuscaloosa: University of Alabama Press, 2014.

———. "(Re)Bordering the Civic Imaginary: Rhetoric, Hybridity, and Citizenship in La Gran Marcha." *Quarterly Journal of Speech* 97, no. 1 (2011): 26–49. https://doi.org/10.1080/00335630 .2010.536564.

———. "Rhetorics of Citizenship: Pitfalls and Possibilities." *Quarterly Journal of Speech* 100, no. 3 (2014): 375–88.

"CNBC Transcript: Allan Zeman, Founder & Chairman, Lan Kwai Fong Group." CNBC, April 28, 2017. http://www.cnbc.com/2017/04/28/cnbc-transcript-allan-zeman-founder-chairman -lan-kwai-fong-group.html.

Cleirmarie, "Love Begets Love." In *Wishing Well: Voices from Domestic Workers in Hong Kong and Beyond.* HelperChoice Ed. 31–33. 2016. https://issuu.com/helperchoice/docs/wishing_well _domestic_workers.

Code for America. *John Hagel: Moving from Story to Narrative.* YouTube. https://www.youtube .com/watch?v=v8oeAV6TTCI.

Constable, Nicole. *Born Out of Place: Migrant Mothers and the Politics of International Labor.* Berkeley: University of California Press, 2014.

———. *Maid to Order in Hong Kong: Stories of Migrant Workers.* 2nd ed. Ithaca, NY: Cornell University Press, 2007.

Damasio, Antonio. *Looking for Spinoza: Joy, Sorrow, and the Feeling Brain.* Orlando, FL: Harvest, 2003.

Davis, D. Diane. *Breaking up (at) Totality: A Rhetoric of Laughter.* Carbondale: Southern Illinois University Press, 2000.

Davis, Kimberly Chabot. *Beyond the White Negro: Empathy and Anti-Racist Reading.* Urbana: University of Illinois Press, 2014.

Deane, Daniela. "Hong Kong Minorities Fear Their Stateless Future." *Washington Post,* July 1, 1993. https://www.washingtonpost.com/archive/politics/1993/07/01/hong-kong-minorities -fear-their-stateless-future/0b415792-ba77-4cf0-b421-745004351fbc/.

DeChaine, D. Robert. "Bordering the Civic Imaginary: Alienization, Fence Logic, and the Minuteman Civil Defense Corps." *Quarterly Journal of Speech* 95, no. 1 (2009): 43–65. https://doi .org/10.1080/00335630802621078.

———. "Ethos in a Bottle: Corporate Social Responsibility and the Humanitarian Doxa." *The Megarhetorics of Global Development,* edited by Rebecca Ann Dingo, and J. Blake Scott, 75–100. Pittsburgh, PA: University of Pittsburgh Press, 2012.

Deigh, John. *The Sources of Moral Agency: Essays in Moral Psychology and Freudian Theory.* Cambridge: Cambridge University Press, 1996.

Delgado, Richard. *The Coming Race War: And Other Apocalyptic Tales of America after Affirmative Action and Welfare.* New York: NYU Press, 1996.

"Deng Xiaoping on 'One Country, Two Systems.'" *Bridging the Straits,* January 11, 2007. http:// english.cri.cn/4426/2007/01/11/167@184039.htm.

DeStigter, Todd. "Public Displays of Affection: Political Community through Critical Empathy." *Research in the Teaching of English* 33, no. 3 (1999): 235–44.

Dingo, Rebecca. *Networking Arguments: Rhetoric, Transnational Feminism, and Public Policy Writing.* Pittsburgh, PA: University of Pittsburgh Press, 2012.

Dow, Bonnie J. "Feminism, Difference(s), and Rhetorical Studies." *Communication Studies* 46, no. 1–2 (1995): 106–17.

Drew, Kevin. "Maids Test Residency Rules in Hong Kong." *The New York Times,* August 21, 2011, Asia Pacific. https://www.nytimes.com/2011/08/22/world/asia/22iht-maids22.html.

Du Bois, W. E. B. *The Souls of Black Folk.* CreateSpace Independent Publishing Platform, 2017.

Du Bois, W. E. B., and Elijah Anderson. *The Philadelphia Negro: A Social Study.* Philadelphia: University of Pennsylvania Press, 1995.

Edelman, Lee. *No Future: Queer Theory and the Death Drive.* Durham, NC: Duke University Press Books, 2004.

Ehrenreich, Barbara, and Arlie Russell Hochschild, eds. *Global Woman: Nannies, Maids, and Sex Workers in the New Economy.* New York,: Holt Paperbacks, 2004.

Enck-Wanzer, Darrel. "Barack Obama, the Tea Party, and the Threat of Race: On Racial Neoliberalism and Born Again Racism." *Communication, Culture & Critique* 4, no. 1 (2011): 23–30.

Engels, Jeremy. *The Politics of Resentment: A Genealogy.* University Park, PA: Penn State University Press, 2015.

Erni, John Nguyet, and Lisa Yuk-ming Leung. *Understanding South Asian Minorities in Hong Kong.* Hong Kong: Hong Kong University Press, 2014.

ExpatFocus. "Hong Kong—Citizenship." http://www.expatfocus.com/expatriate-hong-kong-citizenship.

Fanon, Frantz. *Black Skin, White Masks.* Translated by Richard Philcox. New York: Grove Press, 2008.

———. *The Wretched of the Earth.* 8th ed. New York: Black Cat, 1968.

Fei, Xiaotong. *From the Soil: The Foundations of Chinese Society.* Berkeley: University of California Press, 1992.

Felski, Rita. *Uses of Literature.* Malden, MA: Wiley-Blackwell, 2008.

Fisher, Walter R. "Narration as a Human Communication Paradigm: The Case of Public Moral Argument." *Communication Monographs* 51, no. 1 (1984): 1–22.

Fixmer-Oraiz, Natalie. "Contemplating Homeland Maternity." *Women's Studies in Communication* 38, no. 2 (2015): 129–34.

Foss, Sonja K., and Cindy L. Griffin. "Beyond Persuasion: A Proposal for an Invitational Rhetoric." *Communication Monographs* 62, no. 1 (1995): 2–18.

Fricker, Miranda. "Epistemic Oppression and Epistemic Privilege." *Canadian Journal of Philosophy* 29, no. S1 (1999): 191–210.

Fulkerson, Richard. "Transcending Our Conception of Argument in Light of Feminist Critiques." *Argumentation and Advocacy* 32, no. 4 (1996): 199–217.

Gandhi, Leela. *Affective Communities: Anticolonial Thought, Fin-de-Siècle Radicalism, and the Politics of Friendship.* Durham, NC: Duke University Press Books, 2006.

Goodman, Robin Truth. *Infertilities: Exploring Fictions of Barren Bodies.* Minneapolis: University of Minnesota Press, 2000.

Gottschall, Jonathan. *The Storytelling Animal: How Stories Make Us Human.* Boston: Mariner Books, 2013.

Gould, Deborah B. *Moving Politics: Emotion and ACT UP's Fight against AIDS.* Chicago: University of Chicago Press, 2009.

———. "Political Despair." *Politics and the Emotions: The Affective Turn in Contemporary Political Studies.* Paul Hoggett and Simon Thompsons, eds. 95–114. New York: Continuum, 2012.

GovHK. "Hiring Foreign Domestic Helpers." Last revision September 2018. https://www.gov.hk/en/residents/employment/recruitment/foreigndomestichelper.htm.

Greene, Joshua. *Moral Tribes: Emotion, Reason, and the Gap Between Us and Them.* New York: Penguin Books, 2014.

Grewal, Inderpal. *Transnational America: Feminisms, Diasporas, Neoliberalisms.* Durham, NC: Duke University Press Books, 2005.

Gross, Daniel M. *The Secret History of Emotion: From Aristotle's Rhetoric to Modern Brain Science.* Chicago: University of Chicago Press, 2007.

Grossberg, Lawrence. "Postmodernity and Affect: All Dressed up with No Place to Go." In *Emotions: A Cultural Studies Reader,* edited by Jennifer Harding and E. Deidre Pribram, 69–83. New York: Routledge, 2009.

Gruber, David R. "The (Digital) Majesty of All under Heaven: Affective Constitutive Rhetoric at the Hong Kong Museum of History's Multi-Media Exhibition of Terracotta Warriors." *Rhetoric Society Quarterly* 44, no. 2 (2014): 148–67.

Guinier, Lani. *Tyranny of the Majority: Fundamental Fairness in Representative Democracy.* New York: Free Press, 1995.

Haidt, Jonathan. *The Righteous Mind: Why Good People Are Divided by Politics and Religion.* New York: Vintage, 2013.

Halverson, J., S. Corman, and H. L. Goodall. *Master Narratives of Islamist Extremism.* New York: Palgrave Macmillan, 2011.

Hampshire, Angharad. "Forced Labour Common among Hong Kong's Domestic Helpers, Study Finds." *The Guardian,* March 14, 2016, Global Development. http://www.theguardian.com/global-development/2016/mar/14/forced-labour-common-among-hong-kongs-domestic-helpers-study-finds.

Hardt, Michael, and Antonio Negri. *Multitude: War and Democracy in the Age of Empire.* \New York: Penguin Books, 2005.

HelperChoice Ed. *Wishing Well: Voices from Domestic Workers in Hong Kong and Beyond.* 2016. https://issuu.com/helperchoice/docs/wishing_well_domestic_workers

Hesford, Wendy. *Spectacular Rhetorics: Human Rights Visions, Recognitions, Feminisms.* Durham, NC: Duke University Press Books, 2011.

"HK to Limit Mainland China Maternity Services." *BBC News,* April 25, 2012, sec. China. http://www.bbc.com/news/world-asia-china-17838280.

Hollingsworth, Julia. "Sleepless in Hong Kong . . . on Fridges and in Toilets: Worst Places City's Domestic Helpers Have Called a Bed." *South China Morning Post,* June 3, 2017. http://www.scmp.com/news/hong-kong/education-community/article/2096697/sleepless-hong-kong-fridges-and-toilets-worst.

Hochschild, Arlie Russell. *Strangers in Their Own Land: Anger and Mourning on the American Right.* New York: The New Press, 2016.

Hong Kong Commerce and Economic Development Bureau, Tourism Commission. "Tourism Performance in 2017." Last revised May 16, 2018. http://www.tourism.gov.hk/english/statistics/statistics_perform.html.

Hong Kong Immigration Department, "Immigration Department Review 2013 (with photos)," January 27, 2014.

———. "Meanings of Right of Abode and Other Terms." Last revised December 7, 2015. http://www.immd.gov.hk/eng/services/roa/term.html.

Hong Kong Special Administrative Region. "LCQ5: One-Way Permit Scheme" (press release). November 30, 2016. http://www.info.gov.hk/gia/general/201611/30/P2016113000657.htm.

———. "Speech by Secretary for Security in LegCo on Right of Abode" (press release). April 28, 1999. http://www.info.gov.hk/gia/general/199904/28/sfs0428.htm.

Honig, Bonnie, ed. *Feminist Interpretations of Hannah Arendt*. University Park, PA: Penn State University Press, 1995.

Honneth, Axel. *The Struggle for Recognition: The Moral Grammar of Social Conflicts*. Translated by Joel Anderson. Cambridge, MA: The MIT Press, 1996.

hooks, bell. *Black Looks: Race and Representation*. Boston: South End Press, 1992.

Human Library. "The Origin of the Human Library." http://humanlibrary.org/about-the-human -library/.

In, Nan-Hie. "Helper Abuse Still Widespread in Hong Kong, Says 'Erwiana: Justice for All' Film-maker." *Forbes,* June 25, 2016. https://www.forbes.com/sites/nanhiein/2016/06/25/filmmaker -of-erwiana-justice-for-all-says-maid-abuse-still-widespread-in-h-k/.

Ioanide, Paula. *The Emotional Politics of Racism: How Feelings Trump Facts in an Era of Color-blindness*. Stanford, CA: Stanford University Press, 2015.

Jackson, Michael. *The Politics of Storytelling: Variations on a Theme by Hannah Arendt*. Copenhagen: Museum Tusculanum Press, 2014.

Jing Jing. "Superstar." In *Wishing Well: Voices from Foreign Domestic Workers in Hong Kong and Beyond*. HelperChoice Ed. 25–26. 2016. https://issuu.com/helperchoice/docs/wishing_well _domestic_workers

Joanna. "Sadness to Smiles." In *Wishing Well: Voices from Foreign Domestic Workers in Hong Kong and Beyond*. HelperChoice Ed. 10–11. 2016. https://issuu.com/helperchoice/docs/ wishing_well_domestic_workers

Kammerer, Peter. "When Hong Kong Flats Are the Size of a Parking Space, Something Is Deeply Wrong." *South China Morning Post,* September 12, 2016. http://www.scmp.com/comment/ insight-opinion/article/2018561/when-hong-kong-flats-are-size-parking-space-something -deeply.

Kearns, Erin M., Allison Betus, and Anthony Lemieux. "Why Do Some Terrorist Attacks Receive More Media Attention Than Others?" *Justice Quarterly,* Jan 2019. https://papers.ssrn.com/ abstract=2928138.

Keen, Suzanne. *Empathy and the Novel*. Oxford: Oxford University Press, 2010.

Kinsman, Gary. "AIDS Activism and the Politics of Emotion: An Interview with Deboarh Gould." *Upping the Anti.* Accessed January 22, 2018. http://uppingtheanti.org/journal/article/08-aids -activism-and-the-politics-of-emotion/.

Kock, Christian, and Lisa S Villadsen. *Rhetorical Citizenship and Public Deliberation*. University Park: Pennsylvania State University Press, 2012.

Ku, Agnes S. "Immigration Policies, Discourses, and the Politics of Local Belonging in Hong Kong (1950–1980)." *Modern China* 30, no. 3 (2004): 326–60.

———. "Hegemonic Construction, Negotiation and Displacement: The Struggle over Right of Abode in Hong Kong." *International Journal of Cultural Studies* 4, no. 3 (2001): 259–78.

Ku, Agnes S., and Ngai Pun, eds. *Remaking Citizenship in Hong Kong: Community, Nation and the Global City*. London: Routledge, 2004.

Kuiken, Don, Leah Phillips, Michelle Gregus, David S. Miall, Mark Verbitsky, and Anna Tonkon-ogy. "Locating Self-Modifying Feelings within Literary Reading." *Discourse Processes* 38, no. 2 (2004): 267–86.

Kwok, Vivian Wai-yin, and Vivian Wai-yin Kwok. "Allan Zeman: Hong Kong's Mouse Killer." *Forbes,* February 13, 2007. https://www.forbes.com/2007/02/13/zeman-ocean-park-face-cx _vk_0213autofacescan01.html.

Lafraniere, Sharon. "Mainland Chinese Flock to Hong Kong to Have Babies." *New York Times,* February 22, 2012, World / Asia Pacific. http://www.nytimes.com/2012/02/23/world/asia/ mainland-chinese-flock-to-hong-kong-to-have-babies.html.

Lagman, Eileen. "Moving Labor: Transnational Migrant Workers and Affective Literacies of Care." *Literacy in Composition Studies* 3, no. 3 (2015): 1–24. https://doi.org/10.21623/1.3.3.2.

Lai, Yuen-shan. *Colours of Justice: Fermi Wong and the Road to Justice for Ethnic Minorities.* Hong Kong: Joint Publishing, 2017.

Lakoff, George, and Mark Johnson. *Metaphors We Live By.* Chicago: University of Chicago Press, 2003.

Lan, Pei-Chia. *Global Cinderellas: Migrant Domestics and Newly Rich Employers in Taiwan.* Durham, NC: Duke University Press Books, 2006.

Langellier, Kristin M. "Personal Narratives: Perspectives on Theory and Research." *Text and Performance Quarterly* 9, no. 4 (1989): 243–76. https://doi.org/10.1080/10462938909365938.

Lau, Christy. "Family Allows Child to Defecate on Plane Aisle, Embarrassing Chinese Passengers." *Shanghaiist,* May 5, 2018. http://shanghaiist.com/2014/07/26/family-allows-child-to -defecate-on-plane-aisle.php.

———. "Video of Young Girl Peeing on Hong Kong Metro Prompts Online Backlash." *Shanghaiist,* May 5, 2018. http://shanghaiist.com/2014/07/25/mainland_girl_peeing_on_hk_metro_ar .php.

Lau, Ka-kuen, and Dan Bland. "The Cost of a Family in Hong Kong." *South China Morning Post,* July 25, 2016. http://www.scmp.com/infographics/article/1994399/cost-family-hong-kong.

Lau, Siu-kai. *Society and Politics in Hong Kong.* Hong Kong: The Chinese University Press, 1983.

Lee, Charles T. *Ingenious Citizenship: Recrafting Democracy for Social Change.* Durham, NC: Duke University Press Books, 2016.

Lee, Don. "Hong Kong Was Supposed to Be a World Financial Capital in a Communist System. Contradiction?" *Los Angeles Times,* June 30, 2017. http://www.latimes.com/la-fg-hong-kong -financial-capital-20170630-story.html.

Leib, Ethan J. *Deliberative Democracy in America: A Proposal for a Popular Branch of Government.* University Park: Pennsylvania State University Press, 2004.

Levinas, Emmanuel. *Otherwise Than Being or Beyond Essence.* Translated by Alphonso Lingis. Pittsburgh, PA: Duquesne, 1998.

Leung, Hon-Chu. "Politics of Incorporation and Exclusion: Immigration and Citizenship Issues." In *Remaking Citizenship in Hong Kong: Community, Nation, and the Global City,* Agnes S. Ku and Ngai Pun, eds. 97–114. New York: Routledge, 2004.

Liljas, Per. "Beaten and Exploited, Indonesian Maids Are Hong Kong's 'Modern-Day Slaves.'" *Time,* January 15, 2014. http://world.time.com/2014/01/15/beaten-and-exploited-indonesian -maids-are-hong-kongs-modern-day-slaves/.

Linfield, Susie. *The Cruel Radiance: Photography and Political Violence.* Chicago: University of Chicago Press, 2012.

Liu, JeeLoo. *An Introduction to Chinese Philosophy: From Ancient Philosophy to Chinese Buddhism.* Malden, MA: Wiley-Blackwell, 2006.

Lozano-Reich, Nina M., and Dana L. Cloud. "The Uncivil Tongue: Invitational Rhetoric and the Problem of Inequality." *Western Journal of Communication* 73, no. 2 (2009): 220–26.

Lu, Shen, and Katie Hunt. "As Hostility Grows, Some Chinese Say So Long Hong Kong." CNN, June 30, 2015. https://www.cnn.com/2015/06/30/asia/china-mainlanders-in-hongkong/index.html.

Luibhéid, Eithne. *Pregnant on Arrival: Making the Illegal Immigrant.* Minneapolis: University of Minnesota Press, 2013.

Lynch, Dennis A. "Rhetorics of Proximity: Empathy in Temple Grandin and Cornel West." *Rhetoric Society Quarterly* 28, no. 1 (1998): 5–23.

Lyon, Arabella. *Deliberative Acts: Democracy, Rhetoric, and Rights.* University Park, PA: Penn State University Press, 2013.

———. *Intentions: Negotiated, Contested, and Ignored.* University Park, PA: Penn State University Press, 2004.

Ma, Eric Kit-wai. *Culture, Politics and Television in Hong Kong.* London: Routledge, 1999.

MacLean, P. D. *The Triune Brain in Evolution: Role in Paleocerebral Functions.* New York: Springer, 1990.

Madianou, Mirca, and Daniel Miller. *Migration and New Media: Transnational Families and Polymedia.* Abingdon, Oxon: Routledge, 2012.

Man, Joyce. "In Hong Kong, a Setback for Domestic-Worker Rights." *Time,* March 29, 2012. http://world.time.com/2012/03/29/in-hong-kong-a-setback-for-domestic-worker-rights-2/.

Mansbridge, Jane. *Reconsidering the Democratic Public.* Edited by Russell Hanson and George E. Marcus. University Park, PA: Penn State University Press, 1993.

Marcus, George E. *The Sentimental Citizen: Emotion in Democratic Politics.* University Park, PA: Pennsylvania State University Press, 2002.

Martinez, Aja Y. "A Plea for Critical Race Theory Counterstory: Stock Story versus Counterstory Dialogues Concerning Alejandra's 'Fit' in the Academy." *Composition Studies* 42, no. 2 (2014): 33–55.

Massumi, Brian. *Parables for the Virtual: Movement, Affect, Sensation.* Durham, NC: Duke University Press Books, 2002.

———. *The Power at the End of the Economy.* Durham, NC: Duke University Press Books, 2014.

Mathews, Gordon. *Ghetto at the Center of the World: Chungking Mansions, Hong Kong.* Chicago: University of Chicago Press, 2011.

Mathews, Gordon, and Tai Lok Lui, eds. *Consuming Hong Kong.* Hong Kong: Hong Kong University Press, 2001.

Mathews, Gordon, Eric Ma, and Tai-Lok Lui. *Hong Kong, China: Learning to Belong to a Nation.* London: Routledge, 2007.

McConnell, Patricia B. *The Education of Will: A Mutual Memoir of a Woman and Her Dog.* New York: Atria Books, 2017.

McCoy, Mary E. "Purifying Islam in Post-Authoritarian Indonesia: Corporatist Metaphors and the Rise of Religious Intolerance." *Rhetoric and Public Affairs* 16, no. 2 (2013): 275–316.

McKinnon, Sara L. *Gendered Asylum: Race and Violence in U. S. Law and Politics.* Urbana: University of Illinois Press, 2016.

"Meet HelperChoice.com, the LinkedIn for Domestic Helpers." *Bloomberg,* June 15, 2015. https://www.bloomberg.com/news/videos/2015-06-16/meet-helperchoice-com-the-linkedin-for-domestic-helpers.

Micciche, Laura R. *Doing Emotion: Rhetoric, Writing, Teaching.* Portsmouth, NH: Boynton/Cook Publishers, 2007.

Mohanty, Chandra Talpade. *Feminism without Borders: Decolonizing Theory, Practicing Solidarity.* 5th ed. Durham, NC: Duke University Press Books, 2003.

Narayan, Uma. "Working Together across Difference: Some Considerations on Emotions and Political Practice." *Hypatia* 3, no. 2 (1988): 31–47.

Nelson, Katie. "Piss Gate Triggers Mainland Campaign Calling for Children to Pee in Hong Kong's Streets." *Shanghaiist,* May 5, 2018. http://shanghaiist.com/2014/04/25/piss-gate-triggers-mainland-campaign.php.

Newendorp, Nicole DeJong. *Uneasy Reunions: Immigration, Citizenship, and Family Life in Post-1997 Hong Kong.* Stanford, CA: Stanford University Press, 2008.

Ng, Naomi, and Chan, Wilfred. "Hong Kong to Chinese Shoppers: 'Go Home.'" CNN, March 3, 2015. http://www.cnn.com/2015/03/03/china/hong-kong-china-conflict/index.html.

Ng, Ngoi-yee Margaret. "Maggie's Story." *Yahoo! News Hong Kong.* Last modified November 27, 2012, hk.news.yahoo.com/blogs/margaretng/%E7%BE%8E%E5%A7%AC%E7%9A%84%E6%95%85%E4%BA%8B-161037010.html.

Ng, Phoebe. "Domestic Helper Loses 'Live-In' Court Challenge." *The Standard,* February 15, 2018. http://www.thestandard.com.hk/section-news.php?id=192895&sid=46198215.

Ngai, Mae. "The Dark History of Defining 'Family.'" *New York Times,* July 19, 2017, Opinion. https://www.nytimes.com/2017/07/19/opinion/travel-ban-upheld-supreme-court.html.

———. *Impossible Subjects: Illegal Aliens and the Making of Modern America.* Princeton, NJ: Princeton University Press, 2014.

Ngo, Jennifer. "July 1 Protest Is Hong Kong's Taste of Democracy." *South China Morning Post,* June 30, 2013. http://www.scmp.com/news/hong-kong/article/1272052/july-1-protest-hong-kongs-taste-democracy.

Ngo, Wing-see. *She Says: Photographing Ethnic Minority Women of Hong Kong.* Hong Kong: Hong Kong Unison, 2017.

"'Nothing Has Changed' Says Abused Hong Kong Maid Erwiana." *Hong Kong Free Press* (blog), March 28, 2016. https://www.hongkongfp.com/2016/03/28/nothing-has-changed-says-abused-hong-kong-maid-erwiana/.

Nussbaum, Martha C. *Hiding from Humanity: Disgust, Shame, and the Law.* Princeton, NJ: Princeton University Press, 2006.

———. *Political Emotions: Why Love Matters for Justice.* Cambridge, MA: Belknap Press, 2015.

———. *Upheavals of Thought: The Intelligence of Emotions.* Cambridge: Cambridge University Press, 2003.

Ochs, Elinor, and Lisa Capps. *Living Narrative: Creating Lives in Everyday Storytelling.* Cambridge, MA: Harvard University Press, 2002.

Oliver, Kelly. *Witnessing: Beyond Recognition.* Minneapolis: University of Minnesota Press, 2001.

Oliver, Mary Beth, James Price Dillard, Keunmin Bae, and Daniel J. Tamul. "The Effect of Narrative News Format on Empathy for Stigmatized Groups." *Journalism & Mass Communication Quarterly* 89, no. 2 (2012): 205–24.

Ong, Aihwa. *Buddha Is Hiding: Refugees, Citizenship, the New America*. Berkeley: University of California Press, 2003.

———. *Flexible Citizenship: The Cultural Logics of Transnationality*. Durham, NC: Duke University Press, 1999.

———. *Neoliberalism as Exception: Mutations in Citizenship and Sovereignty*. Durham, NC: Duke University Press Books, 2006.

Pallares, Amalia, and Nilda Flores-Gonzalez, eds. *Marcha: Latino Chicago and the Immigrant Rights Movement*. Urbana: University of Illinois Press, 2010.

Pan, Zhongdang, Chin-Chuan Lee, Joseph Man Chan, and Clement K. Y. So. "Orchestrating the Family-Nation Chorus: Chinese Media and Nationalism in the Hong Kong Handover." *Mass Communication and Society* 4, no. 3 (2001): 331–47. https://doi.org/10.1207/S15327825MCS0403_05.

Parekh, Bhikhu. "What Is Multiculturalism?" *Multiculturalism* #484, December 1999. http://www.india-seminar.com/1999/484/484%20parekh.htm.

Park, Bernadette, and Myron Rothbart. "Perception of Out-Group Homogeneity and Levels of Social Categorization: Memory for the Subordinate Attributes of In-Group and Out-Group Members." *Journal of Personality* 42, no. 6 (1982): 1051–68.

Parreñas, Rhacel Salazar. *The Force of Domesticity*. New York: NYU Press, 2008.

———. "The Reproductive Labour of Migrant Workers." *Global Networks* 12, no. 2 (2012): 269–75. https://doi.org/10.1111/j.1471-0374.2012.00351.x.

———. *Servants of Globalization: Migration and Domestic Work*. 2nd ed. Stanford, CA: Stanford University Press, 2015.

Parreñas, Rhacel Salazar, and Rachel Silvey. "Domestic Workers Refusing Neo-Slavery in the UAE." *Contexts* 15, no. 3 (2016): 36–41. https://doi.org/10.1177/1536504216662235.

Parry, Simon. "Beaten, Hit with an Iron, Doused in Bleach: The Hong Kong Domestic Helpers Facing Systemic Abuse and How the City Could Protect Them." *South China Morning Post*, February 12, 2017. http://www.scmp.com/lifestyle/families/article/2069843/beaten-hit-iron-doused-bleach-hong-kong-domestic-helpers-facing.

Phelan, James. *Narrative as Rhetoric: Technique, Audiences, Ethics, Ideology*. Columbus: Ohio State University Press, 1996.

Plascencia, Luis F. B. *Disenchanting Citizenship: Mexican Migrants and the Boundaries of Belonging*. New Brunswick, NJ: Rutgers University Press, 2012.

Plüss, Caroline. "Constructing Globalized Ethnicity: Migrants from India in Hong Kong." *International Sociology* 20, no. 2 (2005): 201–24. https://doi.org/10.1177/0268580905052369.

Pollock, Mark A., Lee Artz, Lawrence R. Frey, W. Barnett Pearce, and Bren A. O. Murphy. "Navigating between Scylla and Charybdis: Continuing the Dialogue on Communication and Social Justice." *Communication Studies* 47, no. 1–2 (1996): 142–51. https://doi.org/10.1080/10510979609368470.

Puar, Jasbir K. *Terrorist Assemblages: Homonationalism in Queer Times*. Durham, NC: Duke University Press, 2007.

Ratcliffe, Krista. *Rhetorical Listening: Identification, Gender, Whiteness*. Carbondale: Southern Illinois University Press, 2006.

Reddy, Chandan. *Freedom with Violence: Race, Sexuality, and the US State*. Durham, NC: Duke University Press Books, 2011.

Reuters. "Beijing to Limit Hong Kong Visits by Mainland Chinese." *The Guardian,* April 12, 2015, World News. http://www.theguardian.com/world/2015/apr/12/beijing-to-limit-hong-kong -visits-by-mainland-chinese.

Rice, Jenny. *Distant Publics: Development Rhetoric and the Subject of Crisis.* Pittsburgh, PA: University of Pittsburgh Press, 2012.

Ricoeur, Paul. *The Course of Recognition.* Translated by David Pellauer. Cambridge, MA: Harvard University Press, 2007.

Rogin, Michæl. *Blackface, White Noise: Jewish Immigrants in the Hollywood Melting Pot.* Berkeley: University of California Press, 1998.

Romero, Mary. *Maid in the USA: 10th Anniversary Edition.* New York: Routledge, 2002.

Rothfelder, Katy, and Davi Johnson Thornton. "Man Interrupted: Mental Illness Narrative as a Rhetoric of Proximity." *Rhetoric Society Quarterly* 47, no. 4 (2017): 359–82.

Rowe, Aimee Carrillo. *Power Lines: On the Subject of Feminist Alliances.* Durham, NC: Duke University Press Books, 2008.

Rushkoff, Douglas. "No, You Can't Have It All." CNN, October 20, 2015. https://www.cnn.com/ 2015/10/19/opinions/rushkoff-slaughter-having-it-all/index.html.

Saleem, Muniba, Grace S. Yang, and Srividya Ramasubramanian. "Reliance on Direct and Mediated Contact and Public Policies Supporting Outgroup Harm." *Journal of Communication* 66, no. 4 (2016): 604–24.

Sartre, Jean-Paul, and Fredric Jameson. *Critique of Dialectical Reason.* Vol. 1. Edited by Jonathan Ree. Translated by Alan Sheridan-Smith. London: Verso, 2004.

Schaefer, Donovan O. *Religious Affects: Animality, Evolution, and Power.* Durham, NC: Duke University Press Books, 2015.

Schenk, Catherine R. "Economic History of Hong Kong." EH.net. https://eh.net/encyclopedia/ economic-history-of-hong-kong/.

Schmitt, Carl, and Tracy B. Strong. *Political Theology: Four Chapters on the Concept of Sovereignty.* Translated by George Schwab. Chicago: University of Chicago Press, 2006.

Scudder, Mary F. "Beyond Empathy: Strategies and Ideals of Democratic Deliberation." *Polity* 48, no. 4 (2016): 524–50.

Sheehan, Matt. "Born in the USA: Why Chinese 'Birth Tourism' Is Booming in California." *Huffington Post,* May 1, 2015. Updated December 6, 2017. https://www.huffingtonpost.com/2015/ 05/01/china-us-birth-tourism_n_7187180.html.

Shuman, Amy. *Other People's Stories: Entitlement Claims and the Critique of Empathy.* Urbana: University of Illinois Press, 2010.

Shuning, Yu. "For Hong Kong's Smooth Transition, Stability and Prosperity." *University of Pennsylvania Journal of International Law* 18, no. 1 (1997): 25.

Shyong, Frank. "Why Birth Tourism from China Persists Even as U. S. Officials Crack Down." *Los Angeles Times,* December 30, 2016. http://www.latimes.com/local/lanow/la-me-ln-birth -tourism-persists-20161220-story.html.

Silverman, Kaja. *The Threshold of the Visible World.* New York: Routledge, 1995.

Simpson, Peter. "Chinese 'Birth Tourists' to Hong Kong Double." *Telegraph,* February 9, 2012, World. http://www.telegraph.co.uk/news/worldnews/asia/hongkong/9072457/Chinese-birth -tourists-to-Hong-Kong-double.html.

Siu, Phila. "Hong Kong Will Need 600,000 Domestic Helpers in Next 30 Years amid Demand for Elderly Care, Labour Chief Says." *South China Morning Post,* November 5, 2017. http://www.scmp.com/news/hong-kong/community/article/2118462/hong-kong-will-need-600000-domestic-helpers-next-30-years.

———. "New Employee Abuse Victims Emerge as Thousands March for Justice for Erwiana." *South China Morning Post,* January 19, 2014. http://www.scmp.com/news/hong-kong/article/1408970/new-victims-emerge-maids-rally-justice-erwiana-sulistyaningsih.

Skultans, Vieda. "Culture and Dialogue in Medical Psychiatric Narratives." *Anthropology & Medicine* 10, no. 2 (2003): 155–65.

Slaughter, Anne-Marie. "Why Women Still Can't Have It All." *The Atlantic,* August 2012. https://www.theatlantic.com/magazine/archive/2012/07/why-women-still-cant-have-it-all/309020/.

So, Mei-Chee. *Migrant Domestic Workers: Strangers at Home.* Hong Kong: Joint Publishing, 2015.

Spelman, Elizabeth V. *Fruits of Sorrow: Framing Our Attention to Suffering.* Boston: Beacon Press, 1998.

Spiegel, Alix. "Inspired by "American Idol," Somali TV Show Aimed to Change the World." *Invisibilia* (podcast), NPR. March 16, 2018. https://www.npr.org/sections/goatsandsoda/2018/03/16/593593501/invisibilia-inspired-by-american-idol-somali-tv-show-aimed-to-change-the-world.

Stone-Mediatore, S. *Reading across Borders: Storytelling and Knowledges of Resistance.* New York: Palgrave Macmillan, 2003.

Sullivan, Shannon. *Good White People: The Problem with Middle-Class White Anti-Racism.* Albany: State University of New York Press, 2014.

———. *Revealing Whiteness: The Unconscious Habits of Racial Privilege.* Bloomington: Indiana University Press, 2006.

Szeto, Mirana May. "Identity Politics and Its Discontents." *Interventions* 8, no. 2 (2006): 253–75. https://doi.org/10.1080/13698010600782006.

Thompson, Simon, and Paul Hoggett. *Politics and the Emotions: The Affective Turn in Contemporary Political Studies.* New York: Bloomsbury Academic, 2012.

Torpey, John. "States and the Regulation of Migration in the Twentieth in the North Atlantic World." In The Wall Around the West: State Borders and Immigration Controls in North America and Europe. Andreas, Peter, and Timothy Snyder, eds. 31–54. Lanham: Rowman & Littlefield, 2000.

Tsang, Emily. "Mainland Women Gatecrashing Hong Kong's Maternity Wards, 3 Years after CY Leung's 'Zero-Quota' Policy." *South China Morning Post,* April 24, 2016. http://www.scmp.com/news/hong-kong/health-environment/article/1938268/mainland-women-gatecrashing-hong-kongs-maternity.

Tumbaga, Maricris C. "Is it Worth it?" In *Wishing Well: Voices from Domestic Workers in Hong Kong and Beyond.* HelperChoice ed. 34–35. 2016. https://issuu.com/helperchoice/docs/wishing_well_domestic_workers

Tung, Chee-Wah. "Report on Seeking Assistance from the Central People's Government in Solving Problems Encountered in the Implementation of the Basic Law of the Hong Kong Special Administrative Region of the People's Republic of China." *Chief Executive's Report to State Council,* May 20, 1999. https://www.info.gov.hk/gia/general/199906/10/0610094.htm

"Unclear Identity." *Hong Kong Connections.* Radio Television Hong Kong, October 15, 2012.

Van der Kolk, Bessel. *The Body Keeps the Score: Brain, Mind, and Body in the Healing of Trauma.* New York: Penguin Books, 2015.

Vickers, Edward. *In Search of an Identity: The Politics of History as a School Subject in Hong Kong, 1960s–2005.* Hong Kong: Comparative Education Research Centre, Hong Kong University, 2007.

Vieira, Kate Elizabeth. "'American by Paper': Assimilation and Documentation in a Biliterate, Bi-Ethnic Immigrant Community." *College English* 73, no. 1 (2010): 50–72.

Visweswaran, Kamala. *Un/common Cultures: Racism and the Rearticulation of Cultural Difference.* Durham, NC: Duke University Press Books, 2010.

Walzer, Michael. *Spheres of Justice: A Defense of Pluralism and Equality.* New York: Basic Books, 1984.

Wan, Amy. *Producing Good Citizens: Literacy Training in Anxious Times.* Pittsbirgh, PA: University of Pittsburgh Press, 2014.

Weiss, Anita M. "South Asian Muslims in Hong Kong: Creation of a 'Local Boy' Identity." *Modern Asian Studies* 25, no. 3 (1991): 417–53.

Whiteman, Hilary. "Indonesia Maid Ban Won't Work in Mideast, Migrant Groups Say." CNN, May 6, 2015. http://www.cnn.com/2015/05/06/asia/indonesia-migrant-worker-ban/index .html.

Wiegman, Robyn. *American Anatomies: Theorizing Race and Gender.* Durham, NC: Duke University Press Books, 1995.

Williams, Raymond. *Marxism and Literature.* Oxford: Oxford University Press, 1978.

Winderman, Emily. "S(anger) Goes Postal in the Woman Rebel: Angry Rhetoric as a Collectivizing Moral Emotion." *Rhetoric and Public Affairs* 17, no. 3 (2014): 381–420.

Wingard, Jennifer. *Branded Bodies, Rhetoric, and the Neoliberal Nation-State.* Lanham, MD: Lexington Books, 2015.

Wong, Maggie Hiufu. "Lan Kwai Fong: The Hottest Place to Party in the World?" CNN, January 3, 2016. http://www.cnn.com/2016/01/03/travel/lan-kwai-fong-allan-zeman-interview/index .html.

Wong, W. "魚之樂: 替「強國人」說好話？." ["Apologizing for people from the 'Strong Nation'?"] 魚之樂 [Fish and Happiness] (blog), September 16, 2013. http://fishandhappiness .blogspot.com/2013/09/blog-post_16.html.

———. "魚之樂: 由陸客的劣行說起." ["Beginning at the Bad Behaviors of Mainland Tourists"] 魚之樂 [Fish and Happiness] (blog), September 15, 2013. http://fishandhappiness.blogspot .com/2013/09/blog-post_15.html.

Xiao Nan, "A Letter to Both Places from a Neither Mother." Last modified March 3, 2012, http:// blog.sina.com.cn/s/blog_4c7cb5d10100x622.html.

Xu, Bin. *The Politics of Compassion: The Sichuan Earthquake and Civic Engagement in China.* Stanford, CA: Stanford University Press, 2017.

Yam, Shui-yin Sharon. "Affective Economies and Alienizing Discourse: Citizenship and Maternity Tourism in Hong Kong." *Rhetoric Society Quarterly* 46, no. 5 (2016): 410–33.

———. "Education and Transnational Nationalism: The Rhetoric of Integration in Chinese National and Moral Education in Hong Kong." *Howard Journal of Communications* 27, no. 1 (2016): 38–52.

———. "Grassroots Tactics and the Appropriation of State Nationalist Rhetoric: Protest, Mockery, and Performance in Hong Kong." *Present Tense* 4, no. 2 (2015). http://www

.presenttensejournal.org/volume-4/grassroots-tactics-and-the-appropriation-of-state
-nationalist-rhetoric-protest-mockery-and-performance-in-hong-kong/.

Yeung, Tuk-ming. "Pakistani Girl with a Hongkonger's Heart: Repeated Failures with Citizenship
Application." *Sina News Hong Kong.* Last modified November 18, 2011, www.life.mingpao
.com/cfm/dailynews3b.cfm?File=20121118/nalgg/gga1.txt.

Ying-kit, Lai, and Li Jing. "2 in 3 Hongkongers Want Curb on Mainland Chinese Visitors." *South
China Morning Post,* March 5, 2015. http://www.scmp.com/news/hong-kong/article/1729515/2
-3-hongkongers-wantcurb-mainland-visitors?page=all.

Young, Iris Marion. *Justice and the Politics of Difference.* Princeton, NJ: Princeton University
Press, 2011.

Zak, Paul J. *The Moral Molecule: The Source of Love and Prosperity.* New York: Dutton, 2012.

Zhe, Song. "How 'One Country, Two Systems' Ensures Hong Kong's Prosperity and Stability."
*South China Morning Post,* July 16, 2014. http://www.scmp.com/comment/article/1555365/
how-one-country-two-systems-ensures-hong-kongs-prosperity-and-stability.

# INDEX

Abeer, 74–75; narratives of, 75–76, 78–79

abuse, 14, 89, 90–91, 95–96, 117

Adams, Katherine, 25, 26, 27, 28, 64, 136

affective empathy, 43, 68, 69, 72, 96, 116, 118, 119n97, 133, 134, 191; cognitive empathy and, 35, 36; critical empathy and, 35

affective networks, 133, 168, 171, 174, 186

affective ties, 20, 57, 64, 85, 97, 110, 122, 126, 127, 133, 136, 154; developing, 92; self and, 23; tropes of, 49, 59–60

Agamben, Giorgio, 111

Agdeppa, Jhun, 131–32

agency, 41, 77, 171; constructing, 73–82

Ah Fong, 181, 184

Ah Yin, 181, 184

Ahmed, Sara, 23, 54, 170, 178, 180, 196; citizenship and, 58; on degeneration, 171; on fear, 167; on solidarity, 191

alienization, 13, 65, 171, 173, 177, 186, 189, 195–96; exclusion and, 17; process of, 172, 179–80

Andrews, Jeffrey, 63

Andrews, Jenny, 61, 63

anger, 156, 169–71

anxiety, 151, 172, 175, 176, 185, 186, 188, 189, 190, 191, 194; fear and, 173; national, 113, 179; sense of, 174; social, 150

Anzaldúa, Gloria, 28

*Apple Daily,* 175

Aquino, Benigo Junior, 133

Arendt, Hannah, 72, 85, 88, 118–19, 138; compassion and, 119; human relationships and, 40; inter-est and, 26, 27, 40; inter-space and, 27, 84

Asian Domestic Worker Union, 130

Asian financial crisis, 161, 167

Asian Migrant Credit Union, 136

assimilation, 6, 43, 69

autonomy, 122, 155, 162, 165

Basic Law, 93, 109, 110–11, 139, 151, 155, 156, 158, 160, 161, 169, 174, 183, 187

Baston, C. Daniel, 31n66, 32

Beck, Ulrich, 174

belonging, 23, 87; communities of, 85; differential, 140; sense of, 3, 18–19, 75, 84, 156

Benhabib, Seyla, 40n103, 42, 138

Berlant, Lauren, 19, 23, 37, 52, 100

biopolitical control, 3, 46, 94, 100, 103, 110, 161

Bleeden, David, 176

Bloom, Paul, 34

Borlongan, Remy, 130, 131, 133–135

Brandzel, Amy L., 3, 22

Brennan, Teresa, 194–95

British Nationality Act (1981), 147

Brown, Wendy, 12

Bushra, 80; narratives of, 76–77, 79

213

# INTERSECTIONAL RHETORICS

## KARMA R. CHÁVEZ, SERIES EDITOR

This new series takes as its starting point the position that intersectionality offers important insights to the field of rhetoric—including that to enhance what we understand as rhetorical practice, we must diversify the types of rhetors, arguments, frameworks, and forms under analysis. Intersection works on two levels for the series: (1) reflecting the series' privileging of intersectional perspectives and analytical frames while also (2) emphasizing rhetoric's intersection with related fields, disciplines, and research areas.

*Inconvenient Strangers: Transnational Subjects and the Politics of Citizenship*
SHUI-YIN SHARON YAM

*Culturally Speaking: The Rhetoric of Voice and Identity in a Mediated Culture*
AMANDA NELL EDGAR

CPSIA information can be obtained
at www.ICGtesting.com
Printed in the USA
JSHW031224250720
6895JS00001B/1